Financial Planning

For The Older Client

4th edition

by Dana Shilling, J.D.

NATIONAL UNDERWRITER®
The Last Word For Over 100 Years

The National Underwriter Co. • P.O. Box 14367 • Cincinnati, OH 45250-0367
www.nuco.com

This publication is designed to provide accurate and authoritative information in regard to the subject matter covered. It is sold with the understanding that the publisher is not engaged in rendering legal, accounting or other professional service. If legal advice or other expert assistance is required, the services of a competent professional should be sought. — **From a Declaration of Principles jointly adopted by a Committee of the American Bar Association and a Committee of Publishers and Associations.**

ISBN: 0-87218-253-3

4th Edition

Printed in U. S. A.

ABOUT THE AUTHOR

Dana Shilling, a member of the Harvard Law School class of 1975, has spent more than a decade researching and writing about issues of personal finance and law. Recently, she has concentrated on the study of elder law, and is co-author of a major legal treatise on this subject (and is co-author of almost two dozen other books on legal and financial planning topics). She has also produced a two-videocassette series on basic elder law concepts for professionals.

TABLE OF CONTENTS

INTRODUCTION

After awhile, it was time for a change. The Second and Third Editions of this book were prepared by revising the First Edition. But in the intervening years, the laws have changed; caregiving has changed; and my own perspectives on elderplanning have changed. The Internet has become a greater factor in planning and furnishing financial services, in elderplanning as in other sectors. So I started all over again, from scratch, to create a Fourth Edition that takes a fresh look at the problems you may encounter in planning for older clients and carrying out those plans.

The Fourth Edition reflects changes in federal taxation and NAIC regulation of long-term care insurance, accelerated death benefits, and viatical settlements. Information on these topics can be found in Chapter Two and Four.

Many of the most striking changes in elderplanning come from the Taxpayer Relief Act of 1997 (TRA '97), whose impact is still being phased in. Eventually, estates of up to $1 million will be free of federal estate taxation. See Chapter Thirteen for a discussion of planning estates during the transitional period. The non-deductible, back-loaded Roth IRA will revolutionize both saving for retirement and estate planning — see Chapter Ten.

Thanks to 1996, 1997, and 1998 legislation, the tax and financial issues of retirement planning have changed-developments reflected in Chapter Eight. Social Security, annuities, and housing and care alternatives now get their own chapters, to reflect the deeper consideration and additional detail provided in this edition.

A really complete elderplan confronts the needs of senior citizens for a comfortable lifestyle; an appropriate living situation; the right mix of acute medical and custodial health care; and copes with the risk of incapacity. The planner needs to understand the cash-flow, tax, and estate planning implications of the choices. Many plans require wise use of public benefits: Medicare (see Chapter Five, including a discussion of the new "Medicare + Choice" managed care program, and Chapter Three for a discussion of Medigap insurance), Social Security (Chapter Nine) and Medicaid (Chapter Six). Even individuals who never expect to apply for Medicaid benefits should nevertheless consider the impact of Medicaid on all their financial transactions.

One thing that hasn't changed: I still believe that elderplanning offers both the greatest challenges (in terms of complexity, variety of issues, speed of change) and the greatest rewards (in terms of making a real difference to the lives of the elderly and their families) that a financial planner or insurance professional can encounter in his or her professional life.

Chapter 1

THE ELDER CARE PERSPECTIVE

Money isn't everything. That may seem like a strange way to kick off a financial planning book, but the fact is that although money is an important element in elder care planning, it cannot solve all the problems single-handed. A quality elder care plan will, in fact, be concerned with quality; the quality of life for the older client's remaining lifespan, which could be a few months or even three decades.

One task of the family members and professional advisors involved in the planning team is to make sure that the pension and other post-retirement funds are chosen and deployed wisely. But that is not the end of the story. People over 65 vary greatly in their physical and mental capacities and needs. Some need a few more nice days to perfect their golf swing, while others need constant hands-on care to perform even the most basic tasks of survival.

Health care is fairly peripheral to most financial plans, but it is crucial and central to elder care plans. With luck, very little medical care will be required and whatever care is necessary will be fully covered by Medicare (Chapter 5) and Medigap insurance (Chapter 3). Yet, for many senior citizens, Alzheimer's Disease or some other type of dementia will cause a gradual, but eventually severe, loss of cognitive power and ability for self-care. Or a chronic illness or a combination of several illnesses and conditions will call for home care assistance, a move to specialized housing, or a move to a nursing home.

Therefore, sound planning for the post-retirement years requires (1) a health care plan to ensure that quality care will be available when it is needed, and (2) a way to pay for the care. Care mechanisms could include treatment by physicians, hospitalization, skilled or custodial nursing homes, care at home, or a move from the community to specialized housing. Payment sources might include the retiree's own funds, contributions by family members, an employer's health plan,

Medicare, Medigap insurance, long term care insurance, or Medicaid. More to the point, the plan will probably evolve over time as the older person's needs change.

DEPLOYING THE PLANNING TOOLS

In many ways, sound planning remains the same no matter the age or medical condition of the client. Certainly, the planner will want to make sure that the client can achieve lifestyle objectives: having the appropriate income level, taking reasonable planning steps to minimize the tax burden, and drafting any documents needed for transactions or transfers (including trust documents and a valid will).

In many instances, financial planners work with married couples, or are consulted by a married man who takes the lead in planning for the family. One type of typical client is a mid-life male executive or professional. But elder planning also involves many clients who are widowed or who never married. The typical client might be the elderly widow. Many planning devices are tailored for married couples: for instance, the gift and estate tax marital deduction (see Chapter 13) and Medicaid protection for the community spouse (see Chapter 6). Of course, if the client is widowed or never married these devices are inapplicable.

Good planning requires an unprejudiced mind. It is most common that in a married couple the husband will be older, earn more, have more assets, become sick first, and die first, leading to a prolonged period of widowhood for his spouse. But this assumption does not necessarily pan out in a particular case. The younger spouse may die first, leaving a spouse suffering one or more serious physical or cognitive problems. This spouse may nevertheless survive for many years, requiring a large and ever-increasing amount of care in each year.

Not every senior citizen suffers from mental incapacity, and some will never suffer diminished capacity. Do not forget that senior citizens, just like their younger counterparts, are entitled to express generosity and romantic feelings. They are allowed to make mistakes about relationships or investments, as long as they are not the victims of illness, fraud, duress, undue influence, or financial elder abuse.

UNDERSTANDING THE ELDER COHORTS

In statistics, a "cohort" means a group of people born at about the same time. Perhaps the most famous cohort is the "Baby Boom" generation: an unprecedented large group that has dramatically affected the U.S. economy. However, it is not very accurate or helpful to think of senior citizens as a monolithic group. They vary greatly in their economic status, physical health, and needs for care. That is why many analysts think of senior citizens as two or three groups: the "young-old" and the "old-old," with perhaps a middle group in between.

After the 2000 census is completed and processed, we will have a complete picture of the U.S. population. In the meantime, 1997 is the last year for which we have complete figures. At that time, there were 18.5 million people in the 65-74 age bracket. That was about 7 percent of the total population. In that year, about 10 million people were aged 75-84 (4.4 percent of population) and 3 million were 85 or over. Because of women's longer life expectancy, there were more women than men in each of these sub-categories, increasing dramatically over time. In the 65-74 group, for instance, there were about ten women for every eight men, while there were almost three times as many women as men in the 85 or over category.[1] Federal government figures estimate that by 2030, 20 percent of the population will be aged 65 or over. The Bureau of the Census notes that the elderly population of the U.S. tripled between 1940 and the mid-1990s, and predicts that it will double again by 2050. Over this same period, the number of people aged 85 and over is expected to increase fivefold.[2]

In 1990, the life expectancy at birth for all U.S. citizens was 75.8 years. There were significant differences in life expectancy for different demographic groups. Black males had the shortest life expectancy at 65.2 years, versus 73.9 years for black females, 73.4 for white males, and 79.6 for white females. Not only is life expectancy at birth significant, so is life expectancy at age 65, the traditional date for entrance into the senior citizen stage of life. But, in a sense, a person must be fairly sturdy to survive to age 65, and perhaps can be expected to survive for many more years. In 1990, the average 65-year-old had a life expectancy of 17.4 years, and a person of 85 was deemed to have a life expectancy of 6 years.[3]

In other words, if everybody retired at age 65 (and many people retire earlier),[4] the statistically average retirement would last for over 15 years. There would be nothing exceptional about a 25-year retirement, and even three decades of retirement would not be surprising.

The aging of the population has profound implications in many ways. Presently, a healthy person of 65 is really middle-aged, not old. However, an 85-year-old almost certainly suffers from at least one serious health problem. The odds are that the 65-year-old will have years of independent living in front of him, while the odds are that the 85-year-old will require assistance with at least some basic daily activities. This means that the demand for home care agencies, specialized housing, and nursing home beds will increase. Unless trends can be reversed, and costs brought under control, the economy will face a double whammy from elder health care needs: an expanding demand for care as well as constantly rising prices.

The Social Security system can be predicted to have problems simply because the Baby Boom group is so large, with many of this group earning enough to receive maximum Social Security benefits. There are other, subtler effects that can be expected. As the population ages, there are fewer workers paying contributions into the Social Security system, while a larger retiree group draws benefits. This condition is known as being "upside down," referring to a large volume of retirees being supported by a small number of workers, rather than vice versa.

THE ECONOMIC IMPACT OF ALZHEIMER'S DISEASE

In January, 1998, the GAO estimated[5] that in 1995, at least 1.9 million, and probably closer to 2.1 million American senior citizens suffered from Alzheimer's Disease at some level of severity. The prevalence increased greatly with age for those between 65 and 85, doubling every five years until leveling off at age 85.

The Alzheimer's Association estimates that the economic impact of this tragic disease is at least $33 billion a year. That is just the cost to business, as distinct from the Medicaid costs and out-of-pocket costs of caring for people with dementia.[6] The Association's estimate is higher than GAO's. The Association believes that there are about four million Alzheimer's sufferers in the United States, that at least 19 million people have a family member with Alzheimer's, and that 90 percent of Alzheimer's patients have a family member who provides caregiving assistance.[7]

Although some caregivers are forced to quit their jobs or shift to a part-time schedule to meet their caregiving obligations, about four-fifths of employed caregivers work full-time. About $26 billion of the cost to business comes from lost productivity among caregivers absent from work to cope with family needs. Replacing caregivers who are forced to quit their jobs costs over $3.5 billion. An estimated $1.3 billion is allocated to keeping up health insurance for caregiver-employees who take leave under the Family and Medical Leave Act, to heavy usage of Employee Assistance Programs by caregivers, and to fees for temporary agencies. Industry also spends an estimated $7.14 billion on health insurance and taxes that are allocated to senior citizens' health care and federal Alzheimer's Disease research.

It should be noted that Alzheimer's is not the only source of mental confusion among the aging. Problems can be caused by depression (which often responds well to medication), hardening of the cerebral arteries, strokes, or adverse reactions or over-concentration of medications. There is an increasing number of programs for Alzheimer's patients, including day care centers and specialized housing and nursing units, that provide stimulation and calm agitation. These programs make it possible for Alzheimer's patients to use energy safely without wandering and getting lost.

CARE NEEDS

As it stands now, Baby Boomers are doing the bulk of the caregiving, but eventually they will be senior citizens and in need of care themselves. In 1995, long term care for the elderly cost over $90 billion.[8] Medicare and Medicaid paid 60 percent of those costs, while most of the rest came out of the pockets of the elderly and their families. In 1995, long term care insurance paid less than one percent of the total bill for long term care. As the size of the senior population increases, and as health care continues to become more expensive, the overall bill for long term care can only increase (as well as the productivity impact of younger relatives providing unpaid care). In 1998, close to one-quarter of the elderly population (at that time, more than 7 million people fell into this category) needed assistance with daily activities. The aging of the Baby Boomers could double or even quadruple the eventual number of disabled elderly people who need care.

It is hard to estimate exactly who will need nursing home care, and when they will need such care. In fact, it is hard even to find comprehensive data about actual nursing home utilization. However, once a decade, the federal Department of Health and Human Services performs a comprehensive nationwide survey. The latest survey was done in 1995, and it took until 1997 to compile and analyze the results.[9]

In the decade between 1985 and 1995, the number of nursing homes actually declined due to the shift toward larger nursing homes (many of them owned by health-care chains). Between 1985 and 1995, the number of nursing home beds increased nine percent, but the number of nursing homes decreased 13 percent. In 1995, there were about 1.8 million beds in 16,700 nursing homes with 1.5 million beds occupied. Thus, nursing homes were full but not over-full (87 percent of capacity).

Close to 90 percent of nursing home residents were at least 65 years old with younger residents victims of accidents or disease preventing their living independently. More than a third of nursing home residents were aged 85 or older. Close to three-quarters (72 percent) of residents were female. About one-sixth of residents were married. To look at it another way, Medicaid's provisions for the financial protection of the healthy spouses of nursing home residents (see Chapter 6) are actually applicable to only about one-sixth of nursing home residents. Of the rest, 66 percent are widowed, 5.5 percent are divorced or separated, and 11.1 percent never married.

Nursing home residents are typically very ill and quite dependent. Of the approximately 1.5 million nursing home residents, 1,385,400 needed help with basic daily activities. Nearly all needed help with bathing; 86.6 percent with dressing, and 57.8 percent with using the toilet. However, less than half (45.1 percent) needed help to feed themselves. Those having continence problems with both bowels and bladder constituted 43.6 percent of residents while 1.4 percent had bowel problems only, and 12.3 percent had bladder problems only.

In a December, 1998 speech, financial planner Norma Severns estimated that about 72 percent of Americans who reach age 65 will need long term care at home. About half of them (48 percent) would trigger care needs after age 85, but 17 percent would require care at ages 65-74 and 20 percent at ages 75-85. Single people, especially single women, are more likely to need formal paid care than married people (especially married men) because of the availability of a spouse as informal caregiver. Informal networks of families and friends are more available in small towns than in big cities. Ms. Severns' estimate of the cost of intensive home care in the Washington D.C. area was $140-$240 a day, which is comparable to the cost of nursing home care.

CAREGIVER ISSUES

The term "caregiver" is usually used to describe a family member or friend who provides informal, unpaid care. Caregivers differ in the amount of care they provide. Some live in the same home as the person receiving the care, and are responsible for significant amounts of hands-on care. Others, especially those who live far away, have a role that may include emotional and financial participation but not hands-on care.

The typical caregiver is a middle-aged woman caring for her aged mother. Caregivers are sometimes described as part of the Sandwich Generation because they are caught between the needs of their parents, their spouses, and their children. Caregiving is emotionally stressful and often physically difficult. It limits the caregiver's productivity at work if the caregiver is employed. It may require the caregiver to quit a job or to cut back hours. For these reasons it imperils the caregiver's own financial security and ability to save for retirement.

PLANNING TIP: Caregivers should be aware that a federal statute, the Family and Medical Leave Act (FMLA), 29 USC section 2612, requires employers to grant up to 12 weeks unpaid leave per year (including full and partial days off) so that caregivers can deal with a parent's serious medical condition. It should be noted that the federal FMLA does not require employers to grant leave to care for a parent-in-law, although many caregivers are responsible for a mother-in-law or father-in-law. Many of the states have their own family leave acts, which may be more generous toward "caregivers-in-law."

In many cases, the caregiver will also serve as agent under a Durable Power of Attorney, as trustee, or will be appointed as guardian for a mentally incapacitated senior citizen. The caregiver may also be named on the older person's joint accounts. Documents should set out exactly what powers the caregiver will have over the older person's finances, especially with regard to gifts. In some cases, "self-gifts" (gifts made by a caregiver to himself, or to his spouse or children) are appropriate when they carry out the wishes of the older person and satisfy legitimate planning objectives, such as reducing the taxable estate. But in other instances they may be inappropriate, unfair to other family members, or possibly illegal as a violation of fiduciary responsibility.

The U.S. Department of Labor's Women's Bureau has released an excellent report on Work and Elder Care: Facts for Caregivers and Their Employers, available on-line at www.dol.gov/dol/wb/public/wb_pubs/elderc.htm.[10] This report is rich in statistics; to quote only a few, it describes the average caregiver as a 46-year-old woman who spends an average of 18 hours a week to care for her 77-year-old, chronically ill mother, and also holds a paid job. According to this report, the average duration of caregiving is 4.5 years.

In early 1999, the Clinton Administration proposed a tax credit for caregivers. This was significant not because of immediate passage (when this book went to press, the proposal's fate was still unresolved) but because of its response to the strength of caregivers as a political group.

END OF LIFE ISSUES

It can confidently be predicted that all clients will die, sooner or later, as a result of one cause or another. Although nothing can alter this basic fact of existence, good planning can do a great deal to enhance the quality of life in the client's later years, including the time when the client is terminally ill or otherwise incapacitated.

The basic premise of our medical and legal systems is that health care is rendered based on a contract between the health care provider and the consenting patient. This model often breaks down at the end of life, because the patient is unconscious, suffers from Alzheimer's Disease or another illness that impairs cognition, or is otherwise unable to make care choices or give informed consent to care.

The legal system has responded in several ways, principally by making provisions for Advance Directives. That is, an adult who has mental capacity signs a document expressing his treatment wishes under various circumstances. The document can then be consulted if and when the patient is unable to express wishes directly. There are two main kinds of Advance Directives: the Living Will, and the Durable Power of Attorney for Health Care. The Durable Power of Attorney for Health Care is also known as a health care proxy.

The Living Will is a written expression of the person's desire that treatment be either terminated or continued in the event the person ever becomes terminally ill and unconscious, or otherwise unable to express treatment preferences. States differ in the extent to which Living Wills can be used to refuse care or direct that nutrition and hydration be provided if the person is also unable to eat. Most states do allow Living Wills to be used for this purpose, as long as the person's wishes are clearly and unequivocally expressed. Also, an advance directive can be used to express a preference for maximum as well as minimum treatment.

The proxy works differently. It designates a person, such as a spouse, adult child, or family friend, to make treatment decisions if the patient cannot make the decisions personally. This is broader than the

Living Will, because it can come into play when the person who granted the proxy is mentally incapacitated but not terminally ill. Once again, it is probably possible to give the proxy decision-making power over nutrition and hydration decisions, but this is a matter of state law.

Certain health care providers that participate in Medicare, including hospitals and nursing homes, have an obligation under federal law to raise the subject of advance directives with their patients. The facility is not allowed to force patients to sign an advance directive. If a patient does sign an advance directive, the facility is required to make it a part of a patient's medical record. If a patient signs an advance directive, the health care provider is not required to provide care that conflicts with the advance directive. The health care provider is not required to implement an advance directive if, as a matter of conscience, the provider cannot implement an advance directive and state law allows any health care provider or any agent of such provider to conscientiously object.

An increasing number of states have laws dealing with Do Not Resuscitate (DNR) orders. DNRs make it possible for an individual to say that he does not want CPR to be performed if he suffers a heart attack or respiratory arrest. Even in states that do not have specific statutes, it is worthwhile to discuss with the attending physician whether or not a "No Code" order should be placed in the medical record. If state law permits "out of hospital" DNR orders, and this is the client's wish, then local ambulance and EMS services should be notified and given a copy of the order so they will not perform an unwanted resuscitation.

Another trend in state law is the creation of "surrogate decision making" laws. These laws set out a hierarchy of people (usually, the spouse first, then if there is no spouse, an adult child, and so forth) who have a legal right to make medical decisions for an incapacitated patient who has not created an advance directive. Since the vast majority of people do not create advance directives, these statutes solve many problems. Without such a statute, the health care facility must obtain a court order appointing a guardian, and then approach the guardian for permission to carry out non-emergency health procedures, which is a cumbersome drain on both medical and legal resources.

PRACTICE TIP: You can find the language of your state's advance directive statutes from a law school library (be sure to check the pocket part in the back of the book to make sure you have the latest version). You can also contact the not-for-profit organization Choice in Dying, from which you can order state-specific documents for $5 a set by calling (800) 989-9455, or download the documents from www.choices.org. If the client wishes to become an organ donor, it is important to sign the necessary forms ahead of time, to carry organ donor identification, and, most importantly, to let close family members know of this intention. Otherwise, it is unlikely that the donation will take place, because the intention to donate will not be discovered in time.

THE PLANNING PROCESS AND THE PLANNING TEAM

The optimum elderplan reflects the wishes of the senior citizen and family (to the extent that these wishes can realistically be carried out). It provides for quality care in the optimum setting. It can also provide for different settings as needs change, since needs typically increase rather than decrease. The plan balances strictly financial issues such as investment and tax planning against medical, social, and psychological needs. It deploys financial products and services, as well as health care products and services, to meet these objectives.

You would not expect the average senior citizen to have access to a single person who combines the skills and perspectives of half-a-dozen professionals. The obvious solution is to create a planning team, each of whose members brings a set of skills and a professional perspective to the project of creating and monitoring the elderplan.

Depending on the facts of the situation, the preferences of the elder and family, and the size and complexity of the plan, the team might include:

- An attorney, preferably an attorney with current information about elder law. Certain states have a program that allows an attorney to become a Certified Elder Law Attorney (CELA). Becoming a CELA is evidence of commitment to elder law, and of having achieved status within the field, although there are fine elder law attorneys who are not CELAs;

- A Geriatric Care Manager (GCM), usually trained in nursing or social work, with practical expertise not only with services available to the elderly, how to coordinate a service plan, and how to apply for public benefits, but also day-to-day knowledge of, and contacts with, local service providers;

- An accountant to deal with tax and financial matters (e.g., valuation of a closely held business when the founder retires);

- A financial planner, whether fee- or product-based;

- An insurance professional; and

- A broker or investment advisor or both (the number and qualifications of people involved depending on the size and complexity of the portfolio).

Forming the Team

Professional ethical standards mandate that not only must a professional avoid practicing professions for which he is not licensed, but he should suggest the involvement of other professionals whenever the professional encounters a situation that he is not trained or equipped to deal with.

It should be made clear to the client that he can assemble the team personally, but that the professional initially consulted is willing and able to make referral suggestions. (Consult the various codes of ethics for the extent to which fees can be shared, or if referral fees are appropriate.) In many instances, the client will not be aware of the full scope of services available, or of the division of labor among professionals. (For example, few people outside the elderplanning community even know that GCMs exist, and of those who are aware of GCMs, even less know how to work with them effectively.)

The planner will want to develop a network of other elderplanning professionals to work together on complex projects and to make referrals for simple tasks that fall into only one professional domain. An excellent way to do this is by attending multi-disciplinary continuing education programs. Not only will this hone the planner's skills, the planner will be able to observe local members of other professions.

In fact, it makes sense for a planner to offer his services as a speaker at single-profession or multi-disciplinary seminars, or to offer his own seminars (e.g., to employee groups, at senior centers, or to a congregation), because individuals who have seen the planner offering useful professional advice are more likely to want to retain his services or purchase financial products from him.[11]

Standards for making referrals, or adding a person to the team the planner recommends, include:

- Where and when did the person obtain basic education about elderplanning?
- How does he stay current on elderplanning issues? (e.g., from continuing education programs, committee activities, reading journals and newsletters, consulting Web sites that deal with planning issues)
- If professional specialty or certification programs are available, has the person obtained certification?
- Is elderplanning central to the person's professional practice, or is it an afterthought?
- Is he aware of the functions of other professions in the team, and does he know when to refer the case or bring in another team member?
- Is he aware of potential legal pitfalls (so he will not give dubious advice) and sensitive to Medicaid and tax consequences of transactions?
- How much time will the person have to devote to this case?
- Will the person handle the case personally or delegate it to assistants? If it is delegated, how knowledgeable and skillful are the assistants?
- Does the person belong to important professional associations? Some professional associations are about as intellectually fruitful as a fraternity party, but others offer a year-round program of services, publications, and continuing education. On the other hand, some people just are not joiners, or they need to spend money that would otherwise go to dues on building a library or automating their practice; and
- Is the person easy to work with, and comfortable with older people and their families? How is his equivalent of a doctor's "bedside manner?"

CONTINUING EDUCATION AND CERTIFICATION IN ELDERPLANNING

Late 1998 and early 1999 were marked by the development of several programs to train and certify elderplanners. These programs merit investigation. One or more may offer a planner insights, planning tools, and enhanced credibility in the market. The Institute of Elder Planning Studies offers the Certified Elder Planning Specialists (CEPS) designation, covering many of the planning issues discussed in this book. The SRM (Senior Risk Manager) designation covers financial planning for individuals aged 60 to 85, but focuses on psychological factors rather than technical Medicare, Medicaid, and long term care insurance issues. The Certified in Long Term Care Program (CLTC) deals with aging issues, Medicaid, long term care insurance, and ethical issues, among others. An American Association of Long Term Care Insurance and National Forum on Long Term Care have both been formed, and may provide their own certifications.[12]

ETHICAL ISSUES

In practical terms, when a planner takes on an elderplanning case he is working for the whole family. The plan that is created may have implications that carry on for generations. The classic ethical issue for elderplanners is "who is the client?" In the ideal case, everyone is "on the same page" and agrees what should be done. In the real world, it is far more likely that there will be disagreements and hard choices will need to be made. For example, it may cost more for a frail senior citizen to be cared for at home (with three shifts of attendants, plus professional care) than in a nursing home. If home care continues for years, and little or none of the cost is reimbursed by Medicare or insurance, there probably will be less for the senior citizen's heirs to inherit. Similarly, the decision of whether to discontinue life support may be colored by financial as well as religious and compassion-related motives.

Sometimes the older-generation member gets greater tax benefits from a lifetime gift, but the potential donee prefers an inheritance. Sometimes the potential recipient wants a gift now, but the potential donor wants to hang on to the money. If a son or daughter is named as agent under a Durable Power of Attorney (see Chapter 13 for a discussion of a Durable Power of Attorney), the question becomes whether the agent is allowed to make gifts of the senior citizen's money to himself or to his family, and how this will affect the rest of the family.

As can be seen, there can be many interests and many opinions involved in creating a plan. The planner must decide who is the client and whose interests he must protect in case of conflict. Sometimes it is necessary for individuals with seriously conflicting interests to have separate representatives, or at least to sign a waiver indicating that they are aware of the potential conflict but choose to have the same attorney, accountant, or other adviser. It also matters who writes the check to pay the fee (if the planner is a fee-based planner). That person may technically be the client, even if the planner was hired to make a plan for someone else.

No matter who is technically the client, make sure that the planner receives the honest, unbiased, and uninfluenced opinion of the senior citizen who is the subject of the plan. It is often necessary to remove the children and in-laws from the room, and perhaps repeat the inquiries several times to find out what the senior citizen wants and not just what he thinks the children or in-laws want, or what an ideally unselfish parent would want.

PRACTICE TIP: Check with an experienced elder law attorney, or the local government agency that protects the elderly, for clues for how to spot physical or financial elder abuse and the scope of the legal duty to report suspected abuse. Most state laws provide that professionals have a legal duty to report suspected abuse that they observe as part of their professional practice. These laws provide that there is no penalty for making a good-faith report that turns out to be unfounded.

Another important ethical issue is how to handle a client who definitely would benefit by a particular transaction but perhaps lacks legal capacity to engage in the transaction. It is possible to reassure yourself, by taking extra time and trouble, that the older person finally understands the transaction and gives informed consent to engaging in it. See if the family or attending physician can suggest times when the older person is especially alert. But if capacity is permanently lacking, then it may be necessary to have a guardian appointed, to use a Durable Power of Attorney already in existence, or to have a guardian appointed for the specific and limited purpose of carrying out the necessary transaction.

Psychological Issues

The families the planner meets in his elderplanning efforts will certainly be facing up to hard facts. Many of them will be going through a crisis. That means that sometimes the planner sees people at far from their best. Elderplanning puts us in touch with some very frightening realities: chronic illness, debilitation, loss of physical and mental capacity, loss of independence, confrontation with death, and the loneliness and anguish of survivors.

To be an effective elderplanner, a planner will have to understand how this work will affect him psychologically. On the good side, he may be "adopted" as a surrogate child by a really nice family who is grateful for the help he can give them. The flip side? He may become caught in a swirling maelstrom of emotions in a family who is still angry and resentful about decades-old, half-forgotten events. He may be blamed for things that are not his fault and that he is not able to change: that he cannot bring back a lonely widow's beloved husband, that he cannot reverse a lifetime of bad financial choices by drafting a few documents, or that he cannot cure an inoperable cancer or restore capacities eroded by Alzheimer's Disease.

The planner must be able to separate his professional skills from feelings about clients. He will also have to be able to sort out feelings about his own family from feelings about his clients and their families. If this professional work inspires the planner to be a more thoughtful, sensitive, and effective son, daughter, or parent, then that is all to the good.

COMPUTERS AND ON-LINE ISSUES IN ELDERPLANNING

For the professional involved in elder care planning, desktop and laptop computers, and especially World Wide Web (Web) access, have an important part to play in creating and communicating the care plan. In many instances, carrying a laptop computer is key to the sales process, especially for complex products such as long term care insurance and equity indexed annuities.

Using a laptop computer, the planning professional can provide current information about the entire category of products, as well as extremely detailed information about specific products that the client might purchase. Not only can the professional retrieve text, but he can retrieve or create graphics or use multi-media such as sounds, music, and video. Furthermore, complex calculations involving the client's own financial situation can be performed almost instantly. So instead of having an unwieldy pile of brochures, the client sees an easy-to-understand presentation that is perfectly tailored to his needs.

For the planning professional, the Web is a wonderful source of current information on almost any topic. However, some of this easily accessible information should be taken with a grain of salt. It is just as easy to post outdated, incomplete, inaccurate, or even completely fraudulent information as it is to provide a real service.

"E-commerce" (electronic commerce) is still developing. It is easy to use the Web to deliver information to clients who have computer access, or to obtain information and communicate it to the client verbally or in writing. Consumers can gather information on-line, then "sign on the dotted line" with an agent, or they can both find information and make credit card purchases on-line. However, it is not yet possible to carry out an entire insurance sales transaction on-line, because there is still no standard for legally enforceable on-line "signatures."[13]

The Internet makes it just as easy to send information 10,000 miles as to send it across the street. Insurance products, though, are still regulated by states that decide who is licensed to sell them. The National Association of Insurance Commissioners (NAIC) is working on a simple, uniform license application for agents outside a particular state who want to sell within the state. The NAIC is also working on a Producer Information Network to centralize the process of applying for multiple licenses.[14]

A Web Tour for the Planning Professional

Some important sites for the insurance professional, financial planner, attorney, broker, accountant, or other member of the elder planning team:

- AARP: www.aarp.org
- Administration on Aging (federal): www.aoa.dhhs.gov
- Alzheimer's Association: www.alz.org/
- American Bar Association Commission on Legal Problems of the Elderly: www.abanet.org/elderly/home.html
- Bet Tzedek Legal Services (a non-profit public interest law firm in Los Angeles; the name is Hebrew for "The House of Justice"): www.comquest.com/bet-tzedek
- Elder Law at Georgetown University Law School: www.ll.georgetown.edu/lr/rs/elder.html

- Elder Law Section of the New York State Bar Association: www.nysba.org/sections/elder/elderlinks.html
- Elder Web (site of CPA Karen Stevenson Brown): www.elderweb.com
- Kansas Elder Law Network (KELN): www.ink.org/public/keln
- Medicare and Medicaid information: www.hcfa.gov and www.medicare.gov (See especially www.medicare.gov/nursing/home.asp for information about local nursing homes.)
- National Academy of Elder Law Attorneys: www.naela.com (includes a directory so other professionals and consumers can locate member attorneys in their geographic area)
- National Senior Citizens Law Center: www.nsclc.org
- Senior Law (from the elder law firm of Goldfarb & Abrandt): www.seniorlaw.com
- Social Security Administration: www.ssa.gov
- United States Senate Special Committee on Aging: www.senate.gov/aging/

This is by no means a complete listing of on-line elder law resources, and no implication is intended that sites that do not appear here are inferior. If a site is not included it just means that the author did not know about them in time to include them in this listing. For a more extensive list, many of the sites listed above include a section of links to other elder law and related sites.

Seniors on Line

Senior citizens tend to fall into two categories when it comes to using computers and especially going on line. There is a small group of enthusiasts, and a much larger group of people who are afraid of the technology and feel incapable of learning how to use it. There do not seem to be too many older people in between, who feel that they can use computers and on-line tools, but are emotionally indifferent to them.

Getting comfortable with computers is an important step for people who want to remain intellectually active and maintain family and friendship relationships (or create new ones), but who have budget or mobility limitations. Even a modest modem-equipped computer, and free or low-cost Internet access, will permit the older person to do health and financial research, shop and compare prices for almost any kind of goods, play games, and “talk” to one person at a time or participate in a broad and free-ranging chat environment. Hobbyists can get in touch with people all over the world who share an interest that might have made them feel isolated if nobody in their social circle shared it.

Older people who cannot afford or do not want to maintain their own computers can find access to computers in public places, such as libraries. The federal Department of Health and Human Services also has a project to place computers in senior centers so older people can access government sites of interest to the elderly. See www.hcfa.gov/news/pr1997/n970925.htm for information about this program and locations of the participating senior centers.

INCOME TAX ISSUES

Under our current system, where there are few tax brackets and the brackets are fairly close together, there is not much significance to the fact that many people drop into a lower tax bracket after retirement. For most purposes, senior citizens face the same income tax planning issues as any other taxpayer. See the various substantive chapters for income tax issues of, for instance, Social Security benefits, annuities, and retirement planning.

Persons over 65 are entitled to have approximately $1,000 more income than non-senior citizens before the need to file an income tax return at all is triggered. A senior citizen is entitled to a larger standard deduction than a non-senior citizen; an additional enhancement to the standard deduction is available to those who are legally blind. (These additional standard deductions are reduced if the senior citizen can be claimed as someone else’s dependent.)

PRACTICE TIP: IRS Publication 1614 is a large-print version of Form 1040, while Publication 1615 is a large-print 1040A. The forms can be ordered from the IRS toll-free number, (800) 829-3676. The large-type version is purely for the convenience of the senior citizen or visually impaired taxpayer. Filing is required on ordinary tax forms.

Low-income persons over 65 (and persons who have retired because of a permanent and total disability) may also qualify for a tax credit under Internal Revenue Code Section 22. The maximum amount of the credit is $1,125. The maximum credit may be reduced by non-taxable pension and Social Security benefits, and is phased out at higher income levels. For a married couple filing jointly, where both spouses qualify for the credit, the phase-out level starts at an Adjusted Gross Income (AGI) of $10,000 and completely phases out at an AGI of $25,000. See IRS Publication 524 for details. (A credit reduces the actual amount of tax due, while a deduction reduces the amount of taxable income that is used to calculate tax liability.)

PRACTICE TIP: Note that the Credit for the Elderly can be claimed on either Form 1040 or 1040A, but not Form 1040EZ.

In some instances, the senior citizen is considered, for tax purposes, as a dependent of a caregiver child, or of several children who have combined to provide a "multiple support agreement" covering the senior citizen. Five tests are used to determine whether a deduction may be taken:

- Whether the elderly person lives in the taxpayer's home for the entire year, or is a relative of the taxpayer;
- The elderly person is either a U.S. citizen or a legal resident of the U.S. or a country contiguous to the U.S.;
- The senior citizen's gross income does not exceed $2,750 (in 1999 — this amount is indexed for inflation); non-taxable Social Security benefits are not counted in gross income;
- The senior citizen does not file a joint return;
- The taxpayer provides at least half of the senior citizen's support (or at least half of the senior citizen's support is provided under a multiple support agreement).

If there is a multiple support agreement, it should be drafted to specify which contributor will take advantage of deductions arising out of the senior citizen's dependent status. The taxpayer claiming the deductions must personally provide at least 10 percent of the senior citizen's support.

An unmarried caregiver whose dependent parent lives in his household can pay taxes at head-of-household rates, which are lower than rates for single persons. Head-of-household status may also be claimed by an unmarried person who pays more than one-half the cost of maintaining a separate household in which the parent lives. The child is deemed to maintain the household even during the parent's health-related absences (e.g., while hospitalized).

A caregiver child can claim a medical-expense deduction for expenses actually paid on behalf of a dependent parent. Even if the child is not able to take a dependency deduction (because the parent's income is too high, or because the parent files a joint return), the child can claim a medical expense deduction for amounts paid toward the parent's medical expenses. If there is a multiple support agreement, only the child who is entitled to claim the dependency deduction is allowed to deduct the parents' medical expenses. Other contributors to the multiple support agreement cannot, even if they actually paid the expenses.

Of course, the parents' medical expenses can be deducted only if they were not reimbursed by insurance or otherwise, if they are legitimate medical expense deductions, and only to the extent that, in conjunction with all other medical expense deductions, they exceed 7.5 percent of the taxpayer's adjusted gross income.

Not all health-related expenses are deductible. Unreimbursed costs of prescription drugs and insulin are deductible, but costs of over-the-counter medications are not. If an individual enters a nursing home primarily in order to receive medical care, all of the costs (including those that substitute for ordinary living expenses) are deductible. But if the primary motive is the convenience of the resident and the resident's family, then only the portion of the bill that can be allocated to medical and nursing care is deductible; the portion allocable to room and board is not.

Under appropriate circumstances, long term care insurance premiums may give rise to a tax deduction (see Chapter 4). Long term care insurance benefits can be received tax-free, within statutory limits. The same limits apply to accelerated death benefits or viatical settlements that are received by a chronically (but not terminally) ill person who applies the benefits to the costs of health care. Tax advantages are not available to a healthy elderly person who chooses to enter into a viatical settlement for purely financial reasons.

CHAPTER FOOTNOTES

1. These figures come from the Statistical Abstract of the United States, 118th Edition (October, 1998), Table No. 14.

2. This prediction is made in GAO/HEHS-97-81, "Retirement Income: Implication of Demographic Trends for Social Security and Pension Reform" (July 11, 1997).

3. There were ethnic differences here, too. Life expectancy at 65 was 13.6 years for black males, 17.1 years for black females, 15.7 years for white males, and 19.1 years for white females; life expectancy at 85 was 5.1 years, 6.2 years, 5.2 years, and 6.3 years respectively. See 1998 Statistical Abstract of the United States, Table No. 130.

4. In 1997, only about 17% of males over 65 were still in the work force; only about 9% of female senior citizens were still in the work force. 1998 Statistical Abstract, Table No. 645.

5. "Alzheimer's Disease: Estimates of Prevalence in the United States," GAO/HEHS-98-16 (January 28, 1998).

6. See Mary Jane Fisher, "Alzheimer's Costs Business Billions Annually," *National Underwriter*, Life and Health/Financial Services Edition, October 5, 1998, p. 33.

7. It should be noted that the GAO estimates a significantly lower prevalence of Alzheimer's Disease: GAO/HEHS-98-16, "Alzheimer's Disease: Estimates of Prevalence in the United States," (January 28, 1998) estimates that in 1995, between 1.9 and 2 million senior citizens suffered from mild, moderate, or severe Alzheimer's Disease, or Alzheimer's Disease complicated by other dementia. The incidence of Alzheimer's Disease doubles about every five years between 65 and 85, but levels off around 85. Using Census Bureau figures, the GAO estimates that the Alzheimer's population will reach 2.9 million in 2015, and more than 1.7 million of these sufferers will need personal care assistance.

8. See GAO/T-HEHS-98-107, "Long Term Care: Baby Boom Generation Presents Financing Challenges" (March 9, 1998).

9. See www.cdc.gov/hchswww/data/ad280.pdf for details.

10. This publication refers to a major study on caregiving, "Family Caregiving in the U.S., Findings From a National Survey," performed by the National Alliance for Caregiving on behalf of the AARP. The survey was performed in 1996 and published in 1997. Also see Sue Shellenbarger, "More Children Start Making Plans Early to Care for Elders," *Wall Street Journal,* July 8, 1998, p. B1, noting that people in their 20s may have important caregiver responsibilities, not just for their Baby Boomer parents, but for their grandparents.

11. For seminars as a marketing tool in the elder planning market, see Linda Koco, "LTC Specialists Offer LTC Sales Tips," *National Underwriter*, Life and Health/ Financial Services Edition, December 7, 1998, p. 23.

12. See Linda Koco's *National Underwriter*, Life and Health/Financial Services Edition, articles, "LTC Designation Program Unveiled at Conference," November 23, 1998, p. 1 and "What is the National Forum on LTC?" November 30, 1998, p. 19; Carole Ann King, "New 'Senior Risk Manager' Designation," *National Under-*

writer, Life and Health/Financial Services Edition, November 9, 1998, p. 31; "National Association Established for Long-Term Care Industry," *Best's Review,* Life/Health edition, December 1998, p. 80; "Association Promotes LTC Insurance," *Best's Review* Life/Health edition, January 1999, p. 70.

13. The *National Underwriter*, Life and Health/Financial Services Edition, issue of January 25, 1999 includes several articles about the Internet in insurance marketing, including Hal Stucker, "Term Life Sales on the Internet are Seeing Rapid Growth" (p. 7); Steven Aldridge, "Web Challenges Service Cos" (also p. 7); Trevor Thomas, "Study: Women Buying More Insurance Online," p. 8; Darrell Ticehurst and Kevin Keegan, "Planning, Branding Are Keys to Online Sales" p. 10, and Dennis M. Groner, "Agents, How Compliant Is Your Web Site?" p. 18. Also see Sam Friedman, "Web-Savvy Agents Get Competitive Edge," *National Underwriter*, Life and Health/Financial Services Edition, November 9, 1998, p. 28. However, poor design and operation of insurance sites may create customer dissatisfaction; see Alex Maurice, "Insurance Frustrates Online Shoppers," *National Underwriter*, Life and Health/Financial Services Edition, December 7, 1998, p. 40.

14. Joel V. Volker, "Selling on the Internet May Not Be as Different as It Seems," *Best's Review,* Life/Health edition, October 1998, p. 97.

Chapter 2

LIFE INSURANCE IN THE ELDER CARE PLAN

INTRODUCTION

Odds are that, if you're reading this, you are aware of the central role that life insurance plays in financial planning. In the early stages of an individual's, couple's, or family's planning cycle, life insurance creates an "instant estate" at a time when there may be few other resources available for the family if a breadwinner dies. It's typical for older clients to have completed the accumulation phase of the plan and to look for tax-wise ways to transmit assets to a surviving spouse or other heirs. Once again, life insurance plays a valuable role. Congress considers life insurance a worthwhile purchase, so it qualifies for favorable tax treatment.

In a small-to-medium size estate, where the surviving spouse is incapable of personal management of large sums of money, a life insurance policy paid out under a settlement option is an efficient, low-cost, low-maintenance way to provide additional income without subjecting the survivor to unwanted investment management tasks. In a large estate, life insurance, particularly second-to-die insurance, is often used to provide funds to pay estate taxes, thus preserving the entire estate for transmission to the heirs. In any size estate, life insurance furnishes liquidity: cash that can be used for daily expenses pending the settlement of the estate. (It's sensible to add other liquidity features to the plan: each spouse should have a separate account containing enough funds to pay living expenses for several months since joint accounts are typically frozen when one joint owner dies.)

No matter how valuable life insurance is to the elder care plan, it must be viewed in context. Sometimes life insurance represents too large a percentage of the overall insurance program, or the plan as a whole. In some circumstances, a healthy senior citizen with an ample, diversified portfolio, and a spouse with significant personal assets such as investments or pension rights may have too much life insurance. In this instance, it may make sense to reduce the life insurance coverage (or borrow against its cash value) and use the premium dollars that are freed up to purchase long-term care insurance. As illustrated throughout this book, the high cost of long-term care is a major peril to the financial security of older individuals. Once the survivor's needs are taken care of, it often makes sense to add long-term care insurance to the insurance portfolio or even increase the coverage, if possible.

Older insured individuals run a greater risk than other insured persons of losing insurance coverage simply because they are more likely to forget to pay the premiums. Several states have passed laws requiring additional protection against involuntary lapse (such as an additional grace period for senior citizens), and allowing the insured to designate someone else (typically, a son, daughter, or family friend) to receive notice of potential lapse and make sure that the payment is made. This valuable feature, which is offered voluntarily by some insurers, could be the deciding factor in choosing a policy. A "tickler" in the client files of older clients to check with them to make sure the payments are kept up is a good idea.

TYPES OF LIFE INSURANCE PRODUCTS

The balance of this chapter discusses life insurance issues specific to the elder insured beginning with a summary of general life insurance principles in this section.

A life insurance policy can be pure insurance with a limited duration (term insurance) or permanent insurance that accrues cash value (whole life insurance). Some products are limited to providing insurance coverage; others (universal life; variable life; variable universal life) combine insurance and investment aspects. The various types of life insurance are discussed in greater detail later in this chapter.

If the policy is "participating" rather than "non-participating," the insurer issues policy dividends out of its surplus earnings, and these dividends reduce the effective net cost of life insurance. (However, a number of "mutual" companies that pay dividends have "de-mutualized" and reorganized as "stock" companies that do not pay dividends to policyholders.)

The actual ownership of the policy is also significant. A group policy, typically purchased by an employer or organization, has only one master policy which belongs to the purchaser. The individuals covered under the policy are known as "certificate holders," and receive certificates evidencing their coverage rights. An individual policy is purchased by an individual (often, but not always, the insured), who can choose the policy terms, options, and riders. To purchase a policy on the life of someone else, the purchaser must have an "insurable interest" in that person's life, e.g., a family or business relationship.

A policy can be purchased by one individual, then ownership can be transferred to another individual, or to a trust or other entity. This might be done to keep the policy proceeds out of the estate of the original owner/insured, as part of a charitable giving program, or for other practical or tax reasons.

Term Insurance

Term insurance is pure insurance, with no investment element. It extends either for a term of years or until the insured reaches a particular age (typically, age 65). The death benefit under a term policy can be level, increasing, or decreasing, depending on the purchaser's needs and financial condition. For instance, decreasing term is often used to secure the payment of a mortgage or other financial obligation. As continuing payments are made, the balance declines, and so does the need for coverage. Increasing term insurance goes up either by a specified amount or based on an economic index. It might be selected by someone who feels that inflation will increase the financial needs of beneficiaries.

Term insurance is not always suitable in an elder care plan, because any term insurance obtainable on a senior citizen is likely to be quite costly. Middle-aged and healthy "young-old" clients might prefer convertible term insurance, which can be converted to whole life insurance at the point where term insurance becomes hard to get or prohibitively expensive.

A renewable term policy permits the insured to renew the policy at the end of the term. The renewal is usually made on the same or less favorable terms, rather than for a longer term and/or greater amount of coverage. However, proof of continued insurability is not required before renewing.

A re-entry term policy lets the insured submit proof of insurability in exchange for a lower premium rate. Typically, term policies either set an age (such as 65) after which further renewals will not be permitted, or limit renewals to a certain number (e.g., only three renewals). At renewal, the premium can be adjusted based on the insured's attained age at the renewal date, but not based on medical condition. Term premiums are usually level throughout the term, so the renewal premium is often significantly higher than the premium for the previous term.

A conversion privilege allows a switch from term to permanent coverage without proof of insurability. The permanent life insurance premium is usually set based on the insured's age at the time of conversion. A few policies permit "original age conversion" where the premium for the post-conversion whole life policy is calculated based on the insured's age when the original term policy was purchased. Common provisions limit conversion either in time (e.g., not after 55; not after 65; not after the first five years of a ten-year term) or amount (e.g., only 50 percent of the face amount of the original term policy).

If the policy does not include renewal or conversion provisions, it will simply expire at the end of its term and there will be no further insurance coverage. The renewal and conversion privileges offer flexibility and greater access to insurance, so they add to the cost of the policy.

For Medicaid purposes, insurance cash value in excess of $1,500 is considered an available asset. A term policy, of course, has no cash value and thus is not included in the calculation. As a general rule, the purchase of term insurance is not a transfer, because there is no gratuitous element: it is an ordinary arm's length commercial transaction. However, at least one state has taken the position that the purchase of term insurance during the "look-back" period can be a transfer if the death benefit adds up to less than twice the sum of the premiums. See Chapters 5 and 6.

The purchase of a pre-need funeral policy is not considered a transfer, but if the policy provides benefits greater than the actual cost of the funeral, the state Medicaid agency is entitled to recover the excess.

Whole Life Insurance

Term insurance provides nothing but insurance coverage for a limited time. In contrast, whole life insurance combines pure insurance with a savings element. This type of policy generates cash value, which can be borrowed against, although any loan amounts outstanding at the insured's death will reduce the benefits paid to the beneficiary.

As described below, in some circumstances whole life benefits can be used during the insured's lifetime, especially to pay expenses of a terminal illness. Since 1996, such benefits are treated more or less like long-term care insurance for tax purposes.

The basic whole life policy's premium is level, based on the age of the insured person at the time of purchase. The premium on a whole life insurance policy is due each year for the remainder of the insured person's life. This mode of payment is known as "straight life" or "continuous premium." However, whole life insurance is also available as a "single premium" coverage or via payments over a shorter duration (e.g., "20 pay" or "30 pay" or payments until a certain age) that result in a paid-up policy.

Investment-Oriented Insurance

Some clients want to combine life insurance with an investment product that offers potential for gain. Naturally, along with the potential for gain comes the risk of loss of value. Under current conditions (early 1999), given low interest rates paid on bonds and other yield-oriented investments, these products are probably not suitable for clients who have enough money to separate their insurance needs from their investment portfolios. However, a client who does not have much money to invest, or who is financially impulsive and might benefit from a forced saving element, might find these products useful.

A "universal life" policy is more flexible than a conventional whole life policy in that the cash value, the premium, and the face amount can be altered at the insured's option. The insurer sets limits, but within these limits the insured decides how much premium he or she will pay. The larger the premium, the higher the cash value, given a steady death benefit. (The Internal Revenue Code limits the ratio between the cash value and face value of the universal life policy in order to preserve its nature as an insurance contract rather than a pure investment.)

As each universal life premium is paid, the insurer deducts charges for administrative expenses and predicted mortality costs. Because mortality risks are higher for older insureds, the deductions will also be greater. The rest of the premium is credited to the cash value of the policy. Interest is accrued at a market rate; the insurer guarantees a minimum interest rate (e.g., 4 percent). Universal life insurance works best when interest rates are high and thus cash value grows quickly.

If the insured wishes to increase the face amount, the insurer will probably demand proof of continued insurability. To decrease the face amount, it may be necessary to withdraw part of the cash value to stay within IRS criteria for insurance contracts. Universal life is not a suitable product for older clients who are unable or unwilling to monitor the policy and decide when changes should be made in the policy parameters.

Variable life insurance is the insurance counterpart of the variable annuity (see Chapter 12). It can be purchased either with a single premium or with a continuing premium stream. The insurer provides life insurance whose face amount and cash value are both dependent on the investment results of one or more mutual-fund-like funds offered by the insurer and reflecting differing investment philosophies. The policy determines when and how often the insured will be able to move funds between the accounts.

The original face value of the policy, or other amount defined by the policy, operates as a floor beneath which the face amount will not fall. Therefore, the insured always has at least a defined minimum of life insurance protection, but the policy's cash value is not guaranteed and can fluctuate or even disappear. Variable life insurance is considered a security, so only individuals with a securities license can sell it.[1]

Combination policies known as variable universal life or flexible premium variable life are also available, permitting the insured to control the investment of the premium funds, as well as the amount of the premium and the face amount of the policy. Once again, these products are only suitable for older individuals who have the capacity and desire to monitor market conditions on a regular basis and make decisions about the policies.[2]

Second-to-Die Insurance

If a married couple's assets are greater than the amount that can be sheltered from estate tax by the unified credit (see Chapter 13), then clearly there is some risk of federal estate taxation. What usually happens is that the marital deduction, perhaps in conjunction with a qualified terminable interest property (QTIP) trust and/or credit shelter trust, reduces the first estate below the taxable level. However, the estate of the surviving spouse is then large enough to encounter an estate tax bill. Funds provided by second-to-die life insurance become especially important if the estate is illiquid (e.g., contains a high proportion of stock in a close corporation), because there will be few other available sources of ready cash and assets will otherwise have to be sold on unfavorable terms to pay the taxes.

Second-to-die life insurance, also called survivorship insurance, covers a couple, but does not pay benefits until both of the spouses have died. At this point, if the second estate is taxable, the second-to-die policy will provide cash that can be used to pay the estate taxes without depleting the provision intended to be made for children and other beneficiaries. In effect, the premiums are used to add a new asset to the estate, earmarked for tax payments. Some plans are written with a "double death benefit" to cope with the unusual case of spouses both of whom die during the first four years a policy is in force, requiring two expensive and cumbersome estate administrations.[3]

It is often worthwhile to place the second-to-die policy in an irrevocable life insurance trust (ILIT, discussed below), so that the proceeds will be kept out of the estate of the second spouse to die. However, this trust must be separate from the ordinary ILIT which benefits the surviving spouse, for the simple reason that there will be no second-to-die benefits until both spouses have died. It makes sense to draft the second-to-die ILIT so that it is allowed to (but not forced to) purchase assets from the estate, or lend money to the estate, thus creating flexibility to assist the estate without making the policy proceeds part of the taxable estate.

Employment-Related Life Insurance

For some older individuals who are still employed, life insurance is offered by their employer. The most common form of employer-related life insurance is group term life insurance. Basically, the premium for the coverage is paid by the employer and the death benefits are paid, in the event of the employee's death, to a beneficiary named by the employee.

The cost of up to $50,000 of group term life insurance coverage is not taxed to the employee. However, the cost of coverage in excess of $50,000 is taxable. The cost of the excess coverage is measured using a set of rates generally referred to as the "Table I" rates. Found in regulations issued by the Treasury Department to accompany Section 79 of the Internal Revenue Code, these rates have recently been lowered.[4]

Incidental Insurance

In addition to plans whose purpose is limited to providing life or health insurance coverage, employers can adopt plans that have another purpose, but also offer "incidental" life insurance or retiree health benefits. In order for the underlying plan to retain its status as a qualified retirement plan for tax purposes, life insurance must satisfy one of two tests.

The first test is that the face amount of the insurance does not exceed 100 times the monthly pension benefit under the plan. The second test is that the life insurance premium paid by the employer is not more than 25 percent (for term insurance) or 50 percent (for whole life insurance) of the annual cost of the entire benefit plan.

A qualified retirement plan is authorized, under Internal Revenue Code section 401(h), to provide benefits for the sickness, hospitalization, or medical costs of retirees and their spouses, as long as the retiree health benefits are "subordinate" to the plan's retirement benefits. The requirement is that the aggregate cost of both incidental life insurance and retiree health benefits must not exceed 25 percent of the employer's total actual contributions to the retirement plan. Unlike most tax calculations, this is not performed on an annual basis; the test is the total amount involved over the entire period for which the plan provided retiree health benefits.

Split Dollar Arrangements

Business owners[5], or major executives in corporations, are often able to take advantage of "split dollar" arrangements, under which the business or employer pays part of the insurance premium, and the insured person, or the insured person's irrevocable life insurance trust (ILIT; see Chapter 13) pays the balance. The insured person or the ILIT pays the PS-58 cost (i.e., the cost of term insurance, calculated under the official table promulgated by the IRS), while the employer corporation pays the part of the premium that represents the increasing cash value. While the arrangement continues during the insured's life, the employer's premium payments are not considered taxable compensation or a gift to the employee.

At the insured person's death, most of the policy death benefit goes to the ILIT or designated beneficiaries while a lesser amount of the death benefit, generally equal to the employer's cumulative premiums, goes to the employer as reimbursement for the premium advances made.

The most popular method of structuring split dollar is the collateral assignment method under which the insured or ILIT owns the policy, but assigns an interest in the policy to the employer. In contrast, another popular approach, the endorsement method, has the employer own the policy, endorsing a large portion of the death benefit to the insured's ILIT or other beneficiary.

Split dollar arrangements[6], as well as reverse split dollar arrangements, can be useful in charitable planning, although the reverse arrangements particularly have come under criticism recently.[7]

BASIC TAX RULES FOR LIFE INSURANCE

Internal Revenue Code section 101 favors life insurance. Life insurance death benefits are not taxable income for any beneficiary whether or not the beneficiary paid any of the policy premiums. Thus, the entire amount of the proceeds can be used to support the beneficiary and his or her family.

There are several exceptions to this basic rule. The Code section 101(a)(2) "transfer for value" rule provides that the proceeds of a policy that is sold or otherwise transferred for value (i.e., is not the subject of a gift) escapes income taxation only to the extent of the consideration paid by the individual purchasing the policy plus premiums paid by this individual after the transfer. All other proceeds are taxed to the purchasing individual. This rule is not applied if the policy is transferred to the insured, a partner of the insured, a partnership in which the insured is a partner, or to a corporation in which the insured is an officer or stockholder.[8]

Life insurance death benefit proceeds paid under settlement options are also not completely free of income taxation. The portion of the proceeds representing the death benefit is received tax-free, but the portion that represents appreciation during the time the funds are under the insurance company's administration is taxable. Generally, unless the amount paid out is defined so that it cannot exceed the amount payable at the death of the insured, each payment to the beneficiary must be prorated into a tax-exempt and a taxable portion.

The Medicaid implications of settlement options must also be considered. In a "medically needy" state, the income paid out under the option will affect the amount that has to be spent down, but will not preclude Medicaid eligibility; but in a "cap" state, the consequences of additional income are more serious. See Chapter 5.

Internal Revenue Code section 1035 allows the tax-free exchange of a life insurance contract for another life insurance contract, an endowment contract, or an annuity contract. One endowment contract can be exchanged for another endowment contract that begins payments no later than the first one or for an annuity contract. Annuity contracts, however, can only be exchanged tax-free for other annuity contracts, not life insurance policies or endowment contracts. See Chapter 12 for more about annuities.

The tax rules discussed in this section apply to amounts paid under a "life insurance contract." Clearly, a conventional whole life policy will qualify, but certain investment-oriented policies (as discussed earlier in this chapter) may fail to satisfy the requirements of Internal Revenue Code section 7702. This section sets forth the requirements that a policy must meet in order to be considered a life insurance policy for tax purposes. Variable life policies based on a segregated asset account must meet further requirements, including a diversification requirement. A portion of the death benefits of a policy that fails to meet the Section 7702 requirements will be taxable income.

ILITs: IRREVOCABLE LIFE INSURANCE TRUSTS

The general rule is that life insurance is not included in the estate of the person on whose life the benefits are payable, provided that the insurance is not payable to the estate of the deceased insured. However, insurance will not be included in the estate, no matter who it is payable to, if the insured never had incidents of ownership in the policy (e.g., the right to designate the beneficiary) or if the insured once had incidents of ownership but transferred the policy more than three years before death.

Spouses have an insurable interest in one another, so the immediate problem can be solved by having each spouse purchase insurance on the life of the other (so that neither ever has incidents of ownership in the policy on his or her own life). But this can create a second estate problem, if the surviving spouse doesn't spend the proceeds of the policy on the life of the first spouse to die, thus enhancing his or her own taxable estate. If the older client's children are financially responsible, it might make sense to transfer ownership of the policies to the children, again to prevent estate inclusion. However, once they own the policies the children gain access to incidents of ownership. For instance, the children can take loans against the policy cash value and use the funds for their own purposes rather than for the benefit of the insured parent.

A clear alternative is to have an irrevocable trust purchase the policy, or accept transfer of a policy, in the hope that the three-year rule can be avoided. If the trust were revocable, the grantor's power to modify or revoke the trust would operate as an incident of ownership, throwing the proceeds right back into his or her estate. The downside of irrevocability is that the grantor may later have second thoughts about having placed a valuable policy into trust. For instance, if the spouses divorce and the grantor is no longer pressingly interested in the financial well-being of the ex-spouse.

But when an irrevocable trust is used, the insurance stays out of the estate, and the surviving spouse gets income from the trust, and perhaps invasions of principal, if necessary.

If the surviving spouse is given the power to invade the trust principal, it probably makes sense to limit this power to "five or five," i.e., no more than five percent of the principal or $5,000 a year, whichever is greater. "Five or five" powers are frequently used because they avoid unfavorable tax consequences.

Usually, ILITs are drafted so that the trustee is both the owner of the insurance on the life of the insured person and the beneficiary of the policies. The trust should provide that the trust cannot give the proceeds to the insured's estate (because this would result in estate inclusion), but it should be permissible for the trustee of the ILIT to lend money to the estate or buy assets from the estate (if it needs immediate cash). Many ILITs are unfunded, i.e., they are drafted but do not contain any assets (a life insurance policy will be deposited later) or do not contain any assets except the policy. If a paid-up policy is deposited, there is no need to make further premium payments. Otherwise, there will have to be some arrangement for the payment or a funded trust (containing income-producing assets that throw off enough income to pay the premiums) will have to be used instead. It is permissible for the insured person to lend money to the trust for payment of the premiums. This is not considered an incident of ownership.[9]

If practical, it is usually better for the trust to purchase the insurance policy. But it is not always practical. The insured is probably elderly and may be in poor health, making the policy unaffordable. The insured may also have life insurance policies that will not really be needed for the immediate financial support of the surviving spouse and could better be transferred to the ILIT.

In the Medicaid context, life insurance cash value is an asset, but term policies are not. So transferring term insurance into an ILIT is not a "transfer" for Medicaid purposes and does not generate a penalty period (see Chapter 5). But a Medicaid applicant who continues to own a cash value policy with more than nominal cash value will have an excess asset that may limit eligibility. So it could make sense to place the cash value policy into the ILIT and hope that the penalty period generated by the transfer will run before it is necessary to apply for Medicaid.

It pays to remember that making contributions to a life insurance trust or paying premiums on the policy is considered a gift to the trust. However, the gift does not qualify for the gift tax annual exclusion because it is not a gift of a present interest. Therefore, the person who makes such contributions will be using up part of his or her unified credit. (See Chapter 12.) A way around this problem is to include a "Crummey" power (named after the tax case that authorizes the strategy) in the ILIT. By giving beneficiaries of the trust the right to make a "five or five" withdrawal once a year for a short period (usually 30 to 45 days) gifts to the trust become present interest gifts that qualify for the gift tax annual exclusion. This is true even if nobody ever does make a withdrawal. In fact, Crummey powers are almost never exercised.

Prosperous senior citizens who would otherwise keep their Roth IRA accounts intact, or would make only minimum withdrawals from a conventional IRA, might wish to make slightly larger withdrawals to pay insurance premiums or to purchase second-to-die insurance that will pay estate taxes.

ARRANGING THE LIFE INSURANCE POLICY

Designating the Beneficiary

The simplest situation is that of the person who buys a policy on his or her life, makes all the premium payments, always has access to any cash value the policy possesses, and always controls any investment decisions that can be made about the policy. This insured names a beneficiary and contingent beneficiary (who will receive benefits only if the initial beneficiary dies before the insured) and never changes the beneficiary. The designated beneficiary might be an individual, a corporation, a charitable organization, or an estate.

Even this simplest case can give rise to some problems. For instance, naming "my wife" or "my children" as beneficiaries creates problems if there has been a divorce and remarriage or if children are born after the purchase. Therefore, it's better to name beneficiaries as well as identifying them by title. Part of the divorce process should be checking state law to see how it affects beneficiary designations and making any necessary modifications. (However, it is a fairly common separation agreement provision to require maintenance of life insurance to protect the children of the marriage, and sometimes to ensure that the ex-spouse will receive at least the amount of property and income provided under the agreement.)

If a beneficiary or contingent beneficiary is a minor at the time he or she becomes entitled to insurance proceeds, ownership of funds is likely to be subject to legal limitations. To avoid the need for appointment of a guardian, the better strategy is to name an adult to be the beneficiary in the capacity of guardian or custodian for the minor or to direct payment of the funds to a trust benefiting the minor.

In many cases, however, the spouse will be designated as beneficiary. In this situation, selection of contingent beneficiaries becomes vital because it is not unlikely that the beneficiary-spouse will die before the insured-spouse or will have impaired mental capacity. Furthermore, if the surviving spouse is already a Medicaid beneficiary, or is likely to become so in the near future, receiving insurance proceeds will be detrimental. In this situation, it is better to name a child, grandchild, or charity as policy beneficiary. At the other end of the financial continuum, the survivor may not need the insurance funds, if his or her personal funds and other inheritance from the deceased spouse are ample. If the life insurance proceeds are not needed, then terminating the policy, borrowing against its cash value, or shifting some premium dollars to long-term care insurance may make sense.

Changing the Beneficiary

The beneficiary designation under most life insurance policies is revocable. That is, the owner of the policy can change the beneficiary at will. The person originally named as beneficiary has no right to protest a change in beneficiary or the policy owner's borrowing against the cash value even if it reduces the amount actually paid to the beneficiary.

However, changing the beneficiary of the policy is a business transaction that requires contractual capacity. A person who is unconscious, mentally ill, or suffers from Alzheimer's disease or other similar illness will not be able to change the beneficiary designation. Thus, the appropriateness of current beneficiary designations should be carefully considered given the fact that it may be impossible to change them in the future.

Another possibility is an irrevocable beneficiary designation which, in effect, makes the beneficiary a co-owner of the policy whose consent is required before exercising incidents of ownership including changing the beneficiary designation.

Policy Ownership

The insured is not the only possible owner of the policy. Indeed, it is often better for the policy to be owned by someone other than the insured for estate tax purposes. Anyone with an insurable (i.e., a legitimate financial) interest in someone else's life can purchase a policy on that person's life.

Because a life insurance policy is an item of property it can be sold, assigned, or given away by its owner. Annual exclusion gifts (i.e., gifts of present interests of up to $10,000 per year as adjusted for inflation, or $20,000 a year as adjusted if the donor's spouse joins in the gift) can be made to children to permit them to purchase insurance on the donor's life. Or insurance gifts can be used to benefit a favorite charity.

For Medicaid purposes, life insurance cash value in excess of $1,500 is an available resource. Transfer of a policy to the spouse will not give rise to a penalty (no interspousal transfer is penalized), but the cash value will become part of the "snapshot" that determines the amount of resources that the couple owns.

Application of Policy Death Benefit Proceeds

A 1998 survey conducted by an insurance industry association[10], found that household income declined by 26 percent when men lost their wives but declined much more, by 38 percent, when women lost their husbands. About 400 life insurance beneficiaries participated in this study, with death benefit proceeds ranging from $20,000 to $250,000.

Death benefits paid to widows, on the average, were more than double those received by widowers. This was because couples tended to have much more insurance on the husband than on the wife. On average, men were insured for $162,000, women for $73,100. The average group policy provided $75,700 to widows, $35,300 to widowers. The corresponding figures for individual policies were $109,300 and $52,500.

From these figures, it seems that widows would be financially more secure than widowers. However, just the opposite was true due in large part to the fact that life insurance represented over 90 percent of non-pension assets for widows as compared to only 70 percent for widowers. Typically, men usually have access to larger pensions and greater Social Security benefits.

The survey found that close to 60 percent of life insurance beneficiaries used the proceeds to pay every day bills and loans (14 percent paid their mortgages). About 20 percent used proceeds to keep or renovate a home, improve or maintain their lifestyle, or invest for future financial security.

DEATH BENEFITS PAID BEFORE DEATH

Accelerated Death Benefits

A common life insurance benefit, either drafted as part of the original policy or offered as a rider at no additional cost, is the ability to accelerate the death benefit. Accelerated death benefits (ADB) may be made available on the basis of a diagnosis of terminal illness or for either terminal illness or chronic illness requiring long-term care. In a sense, this is an extremely logical development. Cash value life insurance always gives its owners the potential to tap the cash value by policy loan, so why not let them have access to the value during life?

If an older person can afford $50,000 or so, a single-premium life insurance policy with a death benefit that can be accelerated by a chronically ill person can be used as an estate planning hedge. A 65-year-old female non-smoker might be able to purchase a single-premium policy with a $110,000 death benefit in exchange for a one-time deposit of $50,000. The death benefit can be accelerated up to

$150 a day for nursing home or home care, or $75 a day for adult day care. After the death benefit is used up, the insured has access to a long-term benefit fund of $220,000. However, if the insured dies without using any accelerated benefits, the policy operates like a conventional life insurance policy and pays the death benefit to the designated beneficiary.[11]

Viatical Settlements

Instead of turning to the insurer to provide liquidity, another possibility is a viatical settlement. A viatical settlement is a contract with a third party. The third party collects funds from investors. The investors then, in effect, purchase life insurance contracts at a discount. (The viatical settlement company takes over premium payments subsequent to the purchase.) The longer the life expectancy of the insured person, the greater the discount. The financial risk for the investor and viatical settlement provider is that a person diagnosed as terminally ill will, in fact, live longer than anticipated.

In general, viatical settlement payments are made in a lump sum, which the viator can use to settle debts, pay for medical treatment, etc. It is permissible for the viatical settlement provider to buy an annuity for the viator instead of paying a lump sum. Generally, no one involved on the business side of viatical settlements is allowed to offer or pay a commission or finder's fee to doctors, lawyers, or financial advisers of potential viators.

The National Association of Insurance Commissioners (NAIC) has a working group which has promulgated a model act and regulations applicable to viatical settlements. Under the NAIC rules, viatication is available to people who are either terminally ill (life expectancy under 24 months) or chronically ill (unable to perform at least two activities of daily living (ADLs), or cognitively impaired).

In its materials, the NAIC provides two options for determining the reasonableness of the return on a viatical settlement. The first requires payment of at least a certain percentage of the policy net face value while the second leaves the question of reasonableness up to the state's insurance commissioner who would look to such factors as the rating of the underlying insurer, the insured's life expectancy, and market factors in the state or the entire viatical settlement market.

Generally speaking, licensed viatical settlement providers are subject to reporting requirements under which they must disclose, to state regulators, facts about all of their settlements and death benefits collected after viators' death. They must also furnish a uniform disclosure document to potential viators.

Taxation of Accelerated Death Benefits and Viatical Benefits

The Health Insurance Portability and Accessibility Act of 1996 (HIPAA) addressed the taxation of accelerated death benefits and viatication at the same time that it clarified the tax treatment of long-term care insurance (see Chapter 4). Many of the same rules and concepts apply. Any funds that a terminally ill person (one with a life expectancy under 24 months) receives through an accelerated death benefit payment or a viatical settlement will be free of income tax. But if the recipient fits the definition of "chronically ill" but is not "terminally ill," then only amounts that represent the actual cost of care or do not exceed $190 per day (as indexed for 1999) can be received tax-free.[12] Furthermore, funds from a viatical settlement are tax-free only if the investor in the contract meets NAIC standards or has a state license.

Planning Strategies for Viatication

One theme that emerges is consideration of estate tax consequences. For instance, a person who is seriously ill and is at risk of dying with a large insurance policy in his or her estate (and unlikely to live for three years, so even an immediate transfer would run afoul of the three-year rule) has a good estate planning reason to viaticate even if cash is not needed for last-illness expenses. (Viatication is considered a sale for value, not a donative transfer, and thus does not trigger the three-year rule.)[13]

Viatication can also be done by a third-party owner, such as the trustee of an ILIT. The seriously ill owner of a closely held business might be at risk of heavy taxation on his or her estate. If the ILIT includes life insurance on the business owner's life, it might make sense for the trustee to viaticate the policy and use the funds to buy a minority interest in the business from its owner. A significant discount would probably be available, because the closely held business interest is a minority interest with little marketability. And, of course, the interest purchased by the trust is removed from the business owner's estate as is any appreciation between the date of sale and the owner's eventual death.

Some insurance policies can be viaticated based on the insured having reached age 70 or 75. A healthy but aged business owner might want to use viatication in a similar way. This is especially true since he or she might survive for five or even ten more years, allowing a significant amount of appreciation to be kept out of the estate.

Viatication can also be done in conjunction with charitable gift planning. From the estate planning perspective, the best charitable gift is a highly appreciated asset because the income tax deduction is based on the fair market value, not the donor's (typically much lower) basis. However, highly appreciated assets usually throw off income that can be useful to the potential donor. One planning option is to give the highly appreciated assets to charity, then viaticate and either use the settlement proceeds to replace the income from the donated assets or give away the income as well, powerfully reducing the potentially taxable estate.

Selling an insurance policy can also be a good strategy for the "borderline" estate, one that is not much greater than the current breaking point for estate taxation. If the life insurance policy is the most expendable asset getting it out of the estate could tip the balance away from taxation.

As noted above, viatical settlement companies are increasing their willingness to purchase large (e.g., $500,000) policies purely on the basis of age (for men over 70, women over 75). One industry leader predicted that, in 1998, it would purchase between $250-$300 million in insurance face value of which 80 percent would derive from the healthy aged policy owners. Another company did 90 percent of its 1997 business from policy sales by the terminally or chronically ill, but forecast a 50-50 split between the ill and the healthy elderly for 1998. Senior citizens who feel they no longer need the coverage, or who are unable or unwilling to continue premium payments, may derive more financial benefit from viatication than from lapse.[14]

However, it should be noted that favorable tax treatment of viatical settlements is applicable only to the terminally or chronically ill, not the aged who fit neither category. If a viatical settlement is involved, favorable tax treatment is denied if the settlement provider lacks a state license. Furthermore, although proceeds of viatication for a person with a limited life expectancy are likely to range between 50 and 80 percent of policy face value, settlements of between 5 and 25 percent are more typical in the healthy senior market, given the greater life expectancies.

CHAPTER FOOTNOTES

1. For recent sales statistics, see Murtagh, Geraldine, "3rd Qtr VL Sales Increased 27% Over Last Year," *National Underwriter*, Life and Health/Financial Services edition, January 11, 1999, p. 4.

2. See Koco, Linda, "New Approaches Needed for VUL Sales Success," *National Underwriter*, Life and Health/Financial Services edition, November 9, 1998, p. 1.

3. See Kite, Chris, "The Ins and Outs of Second-to-Die Life Insurance," *Trusts & Estates*, February, 1998, p. 63.

4. To compute the cost of group term life insurance coverage provided after June 30, 1999, the rates set forth in Regulation §1.79-3(d)(2) should be used.

5. Note that, if the insured person owns 50 percent or more of the shares in the corporation, the split dollar arrangement may give incidents of ownership to the corporation, which are then attributed to the majority stockholder, throwing the proceeds back into the stockholder's estate.

6. See Ritter, Robert B. Jr., "Charitable Split Dollar: New Kid on Block," *National Underwriter*, Life and Health/Financial Services edition, July 6, 1998, p. 12.

7. Scroggin, John J., "Does Charitable Reverse Split Dollar Work?", *National Underwriter*, Life and Health/Financial Services edition, July 6, 1998, p.13; Langley, Monica, "A Popular Tax Shelter for 'Angry Affluent' Prompts Ire of Others," *Wall Street Journal*, January 22, 1999, p. A1; and Langley, Monica, "Archer Introduces Legislation to Curb Split-Dollar Plans," *Wall Street Journal*, February 10, 1999, p. B10.

8. Code section 264(a)(4) disallows interest deductions for indebtedness that relates to life insurance. However, for life insurance contracts issued after June 8, 1997, interest that would be disallowed under Section 264(a)(4) can be added to the exempt amount.

9. Let. Rul. 9809032.

10. Reported in a news item, "Widows Fare Worse Than Widowers," *Best's Review*, Life/Health, January, 1999, p. 62.

11. This strategy is suggested by Jeffrey Baskies and Neal Slafsky, "A Deposit-Based Approach to Long-Term Care Insurance Planning," *Trusts & Estates*, June, 1997, p. 41.

12. See IRC Sections 101(g), 7702B.

13. The *Trusts & Estates* web site has published a valuable white paper on the planning options that viatical settlements offer to high net worth individuals. See http://www.trustsandestates.com/edit/viatical.html. Fifteen prominent estate planning attorneys contributed their ideas and strategies.

14. See Murray, M. Christian, "Viatical Companies Pitch Healthy Seniors," *National Underwriter*, Life and Health/Financial Services edition, September 7, 1998, p. 7 and "Group Aids Healthy Seniors With Viaticals," *National Underwriter,* Life and

Health/Financial Services edition, February 1, 1999, p. 33; Connolly, Jim, "Healthy Viators Rattle Insurers," *National Underwriter*, Life and Health/Financial Services edition, December 14, 1998, p. 3 and "Viatical Questions Mount," *National Underwriter*, Life and Health/Financial Services edition, January 25, 1999, p. 1; Stucker, Hal, "Viatical Settlement: What's a Good Fit?" *National Underwriter*, Life and Health/Financial Services edition, February 1, 1999, p. 8.

Chapter 3

MEDIGAP INSURANCE

The Medicare system includes a variety of deductibles and coinsurance requirements. Medicare Supplementary insurance (Medigap) helps the elderly with these payments. The Medicare system also excludes various services and medically-related items. With one prominent exception, coverage of prescription drugs, Medigap insurance does not cover items that are excluded by the basic structure of Medicare. Therefore, Medigap insurance does not provide custodial nursing home or home care, although long-term care insurance does (see Chapter Four).

Medigap insurance is essentially a commodity product, like flour or sugar. Insurers are only allowed to offer 10 basic plans of Medigap insurance, known as Plans A-J.[1] (Plans F and J can be adapted for coordination with Medical Savings Accounts (MSAs; see Chapter 5).)

Medigap policies have certain coverages that are shared by all plans. Plan A provides certain basic benefits, with the other plans adding further benefits. In particular, all the other plans cover the Part A deductible. (Only a few cover the Part B deductible, but that is a comparatively minor $100 per year.) Plans C-J include coverage of coinsurance for Days 21-100 of a stay in a Skilled Nursing Facility covered by Medicare.

Although generally Medigap insurance is standardized nationwide, there are some state-to-state variations. The standard Medigap policies are available in 47 states. Massachusetts, Minnesota, and Wisconsin have their own standards for supplementary policies.

Insurers that want to sell Medigap insurance within a state must offer Plan A, the basic package. In most states, they decide which of the other plans they will offer. However, certain states do not allow all the plans to be sold in that particular state.[2]

As a general rule, people who are enrolled in a Medicare managed care plan do not need Medigap insurance, because they are not liable for copayments and have coverage broader than fee-for-service Medicare. In fact, in certain circumstances, it is illegal to sell a Medigap policy to someone who the seller knows to be enrolled in Medicare managed care. However, in 1998, many HMOs signalled their intention not to renew their Medicare contracts for 1999. Participants in those plans might or might not have access to another Medicare managed care plan or Medicare+Choice plan, and even if they had access, they might choose to return to fee-for-service Medicare. However, these participants might find it difficult to find affordable Medigap coverage because of their increased age (and possible premium increases occurring while they were covered by managed care). See below for transition provisions governing issuance of Medigap policies to former HMO enrollees.

It should be noted that most Medicare Part B claims are assigned, meaning that the service provider has agreed not only to bill HCFA directly for 80 percent of the schedule amount (with the patient paying the 20 percent coinsurance), but has agreed to accept the schedule amount in full payment. Even for non-assigned claims, in most instances it is illegal for the provider to charge more than 115 percent of the schedule amount. (Sometimes even tougher limitations on such "balance billing" apply.) Therefore, the role of Medigap in reimbursing Medicare beneficiaries for their Part B copayments has lessened, because the possible amount of the copayment obligation has been reduced.

PLANNING TIP: The National Bipartisan Commission on the Future of Medicare was directed to report to Congress by March 1, 1999 about the effect of Medigap insurance on the Medicare budget. Ironically, HCFA spent more on the care of people who had Medigap insurance than those who did not: $4,000 per beneficiary for those without supplemental insurance versus $5,400 for Medigap owners.[3]

THE MEDIGAP MARKETPLACE

As of 1988, the market for Medigap insurance was about $7 billion. By 1995, it had risen to more than $12 billion, with most of the market growth occurring between 1988 and 1992. Earned premiums went up over 50 percent during the high-growth 1988-1992 period, but stagnated from 1992-1995.

Although, in 1995, 352 companies were involved in Medigap sales, the market was quite concentrated. There were 33 companies earning premiums of over $100 million each. These companies garnered over 75 percent of the overall premium dollars. A single company dominated the market, with close to one-quarter of the total market. This one company was the underwriter of AARP's Medigap policies. Until January 1, 1998, Prudential undertook this role, when it was replaced by United HealthCare Corporation.[4]

Growth in the Medigap market leveled off as Medicare managed care became more popular.[5] This was because Medicare managed care provides services that might otherwise be paid for by Medigap policies. But, as mentioned above, in late 1998 many Medicare beneficiaries who received their care through managed care were notified that their managed care organizations were not renewing their contracts with HCFA. Out of this group of beneficiaries, some had access to other Medicare HMOs and chose to sign up with them. Others did not live in an area covered by any other HMOs. Still others were displeased by their earlier experience with managed care and wanted to return to the conventional Medicare system and may have also wanted to reinstate their prior Medigap coverage or buy a new policy.

According to Consumer Reports, which studied more than 1200 Medigap policies, premiums increased significantly between 1994 and 1998: an average of 35 percent higher for all the plans, and 41 percent higher for Plan C, the plan chosen by the greatest number of seniors.[6]

BASIC COVERAGE

The basic, bedrock Plan A provides the following benefits, which are also available under all the other plan forms:

- Coverage of Part A coinsurance for in-patient hospital days 61-90 in each benefit period (see Chapter 5 for a discussion of Medicare coverage of inpatient hospitalization);

- Coinsurance for the Part A lifetime reserve days;

- One hundred percent coverage of hospital costs that would be eligible for Part A coverage if it were not for the fact that the person has used up all 90 coverage days in the benefit period and has also used up all 60 of his or her lifetime reserve days (this Medigap benefit is limited to 365 additional lifetime reserve days);

- Three pints of blood or packed red blood cells per year; and
- Coverage of Part B coinsurance (generally 20 percent of the approved charge, after satisfaction of a $100 annual deductible for physician services; other services may have different coinsurance amounts).

Plan B covers the basic services of Plan A, plus the Part A deductible.

Plan C covers:

- The basic services of Plan A;
- The Medicare Part A deductible;
- The Medicare Part B deductible;
- The Skilled Nursing Facility (SNF) coinsurance; and
- Emergency care during travel outside the U.S., subject to a $250 deductible and 20 percent coinsurance up to a lifetime maximum benefit of $50,000 ("foreign emergency care").

Plan D covers:

- The basic services of Plan A;
- The Medicare Part A deductible (but not the Part B deductible);
- The SNF coinsurance;
- Foreign emergency care; and
- "At-home recovery"-a benefit of up to $1,600 a year for short-term home care assistance with activities of daily living (ADLs) (e.g., bathing, dressing, personal hygiene), as part of the process of recuperating from injury, an operation, or an illness.

Plan E covers:

- The basic services of Plan A;

- The Medicare Part A deductible;
- The SNF coinsurance;
- Foreign emergency care; and
- Up to $120 a year for preventive care and screening.

Plan F covers:

- The basic services of Plan A;
- The Medicare Part A deductible;
- The Medicare Part B deductible;
- SNF coinsurance;
- Foreign emergency care;
- One hundred percent of "excess charges" under Part B (excess charges are amounts greater than the schedule amount for the service, but within the permissible 15 percent limit over and above the schedule amount that providers are allowed to charge); and
- The possibility of using a high deductible insurance plan.

Plan G covers:

- The basic services of Plan A;
- The Medicare Part A deductible;
- SNF coinsurance;
- Eighty percent (not 100 percent) of Part B excess charges;
- Foreign emergency care; and
- At-home recovery.

Plan H covers:

- The basic services of Plan A;
- The Medicare Part A deductible;
- SNF coinsurance;
- Foreign emergency care; and
- An outpatient prescription drug benefit that covers 50 percent of such charges after a $250 deductible, with a $1,250 annual limit on benefits.

Plan I covers:

- The basic services of Plan A;
- The Medicare Part A deductible;
- SNF coinsurance;
- Foreign emergency care;
- At-home recovery;
- One hundred percent of Part B excess charges; and
- The prescription drug benefit of Plan H.

Plan J covers:

- The basic services of Plan A;
- The Medicare Part A deductible;
- The Medicare Part B deductible;
- SNF coinsurance;
- One hundred percent of Part B excess charges;
- At-home recovery;
- Foreign emergency care;

- Up to $120 a year for preventive care and screening;
- A prescription drug benefit like that of Plan H but with a $3,000 annual limit; and
- The possibility of using a high deductible insurance plan.

PREMIUMS

All post-1992 Medigap policies must be guaranteed renewable, meaning the insurer must allow the renewal of a policy unless a material misrepresentation has been made or if premiums are not paid. Some pre-1992 policies, which allow non-renewal for other reasons, still remain in force.

Although benefits are highly standardized, insurers are given discretion to determine how they will set the Medigap premium, whether it be by issue age, attained age, or a "no-age rating." Premiums set via the issue age method are set based on the age at time of purchase, and remain the same as long as the coverage is retained. Attained age premiums increase each year, as the insured grows older. No-age rating sets a single, uniform premium irrespective of age at purchase or attained age. Medigap premiums may increase due to inflation.

LOSS RATIOS

Federal law requires Medigap policies to have an overall loss ratio of at least 65 percent (i.e., at least 65 percent of premiums taken in must be returned in the form of benefits). The mandated loss ratio for group policies is 75 percent.

According to the GAO, the average loss ratio for 1995 was well above the requirement: 86 percent.[7] But there were some significant geographical differences, differences among insurers, and especially differences among the various Plans. Plan G, at 73.8%, had the lowest average loss ratio, while Plan A, at 102.3%, had the highest loss ratio (i.e., insurers lost money on this plan, but could not stop offering it because of federal mandates). Plan F is the most popular plan, even though it typically costs more than Plan C and has a lower loss ratio (an average of 75.5% for Plan F, versus 89.3% for Plan C). The only difference between the two is that Plan F provides coverage of physician's excess charges. However, few insureds ever collect on these charges, because more than 95 percent of Medicare claims are assigned, resulting in no excess charges.

MEDICARE SELECT

Medicare SELECT began as a pilot project in 15 states in 1992 but was extended nation-wide and made permanent in 1995. Medicare SELECT is a modification of the standard plans under which the purchaser agrees to obtain Medicare services within the insurance company's network of preferred providers. Going outside the network is also permitted in case of emergency. However, if an insured person obtains non-emergency care from a non-network provider, that person may not be entitled to Medigap coverage for the non-network provided services. The trade-off is that the premiums are generally lower for Medicare SELECT coverage than for ordinary Medigap insurance.

MEDIGAP OPEN ENROLLMENT

Individuals who become eligible for Medicare have a six-month open enrollment period, during which they have an absolute right to buy any Medigap plan offered by the insurer of their choice. An individual cannot be turned down (or charged a higher premium) on the basis of health or claims experience, although coverage of preexisting conditions (those in existence as of six months prior to the effective date of the policy) may be excluded or limited until the policy has been in effect for six months. Generally, the open enrollment period begins on the first date that the individual has both enrolled in Medicare Part B and attained the age of 65.

PLANNING TIP: Federal law imposes Medicare secondary payor provisions, which provide that Employer Group Health Plans (EGHPs) are generally the primary payor for persons (such as over-65 employees and their dependents) who are covered by both Medicare and the EGHP. That is, the senior citizen can choose to be covered primarily by Medicare, secondarily by the EGHP, but the employer cannot draft its plan to make Medicare the primary payor. The secondary payor provisions do not apply to employers with less than 20 employees.

People covered by an EGHP are usually better off if they delay enrolling in Part B until they are no longer covered by the EGHP. Those with EGHP coverage probably do not need a Medigap policy. The open enrollment period for Medigap runs from the date of Part B enrollment, so those who defer their Part B enrollment until they leave the EGHP can also delay their Medigap open enrollment period.

TRANSITIONS BETWEEN POLICIES

It should not be necessary for the same person to have more than one Medigap policy. In fact, NAIC rules and federal law require a presale inquiry as to whether the potential purchaser already has Medigap insurance. If so, the old policy must be dropped in order to purchase a new one. In general, if the old policy was held for more than six months, no new waiting period can be imposed to bar claims on the basis of pre-existing conditions. However, a second waiting period is legitimate if the purchaser of the second policy voluntarily chose to switch to a policy plan offering greater benefits.

Guaranteed Issue

Older individuals may be disadvantaged if they belong to an EGHP and the EGHP stops offering benefits that supplement Medicare, or if they own a Medigap policy and their Medigap insurer becomes insolvent. A significant problem in 1998 and 1999 was the plight of individuals whose HMO did not renew its contract with the HCFA, especially if those individuals did not have access to another HMO. Without a protective provision under federal law, they might find it difficult or impossible to find a Medigap carrier to insure them.

Under this protective provision, an insurer must allow the guaranteed issue of Plans A, B, C, or F.[8] Any Medigap insurer must sell Plan A on request, and it must sell B, C, or F if it normally sells that plan. A person who formerly had a Medigap policy, but who dropped it to buy a Medicare SELECT policy or to enroll in an HMO, and who then dropped the Medicare SELECT policy or dis-enrolled from the HMO within 12 months, can re-institute the same coverage with the prior Medigap insurer, as long as it still sells that plan. If the insurer does not still sell that plan, the individual is guaranteed the issue of plans A, B, C, or F. But senior citizens must act quickly because the guarantee issue time is 63 days between losing one form of health coverage and applying for a new Medigap policy.

A person who signed up for Medicare+Choice as soon as he became eligible for Medicare, and who then dis-enrolled from Medicare+Choice during the first 12 months of enrollment, is eligible to buy any Medigap policy form sold by the insurer of his choice.

Federal rules do not allow Medigap insurers to deny guaranteed-issue applicants or charge them a higher premium on the basis of health status, health history, or claims history. (However, if the insurer otherwise charges age-based premiums, it can properly take age into account.) Pre-existing condition exclusions cannot be applied to anyone who had six months of continuous health insurance. For persons with under six months of continuous insurance, the term of any prior insurance reduces the pre-existing condition waiting period.

Note: Because Massachusetts, Minnesota, and Wisconsin have opted out of the ordinary regulation of Medigap insurance, these states have special transition rules.

For the NAIC guaranteed-issue rules, see the September 28, 1998 draft of the NAIC Medicare Supplement Model Regulation section 12. (The latest drafts of NAIC's Model Act and Regulations can be found at www.naic.org).

MEDIGAP, MEDICAID, AND BUY-INS

Under federal law, it is unlawful to sell a Medigap policy to a person who is already a Medicaid recipient. If a person who owns a Medigap policy later becomes a Medicaid beneficiary, he has the option of having both premiums and benefits suspended for up to two years while Medicaid covers the cost of care. If that person later loses Medicaid eligibility (e.g., as a result of receiving an inheritance), he can demand reinstatement of the policy up to 90 days after losing Medicaid eligibility, but must then resume premium payments. States have the option of coordinating Medicaid with Medigap by purchasing Medigap insurance on behalf of Medicaid beneficiaries.

CHAPTER FOOTNOTES

1. Social Security Act §1882 makes it unlawful to sell Medigap policies that do not conform to federal regulations. On December 4, 1998, HCFA issued a Notice, published at 63 FR 67078, announcing that the NAIC Model Regulation as of April 29, 1998 determines which policies conform to federal regulations. A policy will also be in compliance if it satisfies a state standard that is at least as stringent as the April 29, 1998 NAIC rule.

2. This information comes from the Health Care Financing Association Web site: www.medicare.gov/publications.html.

3. Mary Jane Fisher, "Medigap Reform Ahead?" *National Underwriter,* Life and Health/Financial Services edition, January 11, 1999, p. 1.

4. See GAO/HEHS-98-66, "Medigap Insurance: Compliance with Federal Standards has Increased," March 6, 1998.

5. In 1997, three-quarters of Medigap insurers surveyed told the Lewin Group that their Medigap sales had decreased. Allison Bell, "Medigap Sales Could Gain from HMOs' Retreat," *National Underwriter,* Life and Health/Financial Services edition, October 19, 1998, p. 1.

6. Mary Jane Fisher, "Study Skewers Medigap Plans," *National Underwriter,* Life and Health/Financial Services edition, August 24, 1998, p. 1.

7. GAO/HEHS-98-66, supra.

8. The HCFA Notice appearing at 63 FR 67078 (December 4, 1998) clarifies that guaranteed issue of plans A, B, C, and F becomes effective July 1, 1998 and continues even after 2002 if a Medicare+Choice plan terminates or the enrollee moves outside the plan's service area.

Chapter 4

LONG-TERM CARE INSURANCE

It is obvious that Medicare cannot meet all the medical and care-related needs of senior citizens because it excludes precisely the kind of custodial care that so many need. It is also obvious that Medicaid planning has many deficiencies, both for individuals and for society as a whole. Given this situation, one might expect the private sector to step in and that's exactly how long-term care insurance (LTCI) came about: as a means for people to purchase affordable coverage for their own future care.

A person with LTCI coverage who needs nursing home or home care can enter the best available facility or sign up with the best local agency without having to worry about whether the facility or agency participates in Medicaid or has openings for Medicaid patients. Insured persons can plan their own financial lives, dispose of their assets, and make their own estate plans, as they choose, with no need to fit into Medicaid requirements or explain their transfers. Many people find this freedom and flexibility extremely worthwhile.[1]

While the peace of mind can be priceless, LTCI is often expensive. So, the older client should shop carefully and select the right policy. The right policy is one provided by an insurer of top-flight financial soundness and reputation for service and a company that plans to be in the LTCI market for the long haul. The older client must determine a basic financial objective (i.e., payment of the first dollar of expenses or of catastrophic expenses only) and select the desired benefits. The list of benefits available includes nursing home and home care as well as innovative benefits such as adult day care, care giver training, and assisted living facility housing.

One of the most important determinants of premium is the age of the insured individual at the time of purchase (because premiums usually remain level after purchase). The premium also depends on allocation of risk. The more risk the insured accepts (in the form of lower daily benefit levels, longer waiting periods, or shorter duration of benefits), the lower the premium will be. However, there is a meaningful possibility that the insured will have to make significant copayments once coverage is triggered.

As Chapter Three shows, Medigap insurance must conform to strict federal requirements. LTCI insurers are given more leeway in designing policies. However, certain LTCI policies are designed to meet certain tax requirements and thus be "tax-qualified." Purchasers may be entitled to a tax deduction for part of the premium and probably will get favorable income tax treatment when they collect benefits. It is perfectly acceptable to sell non-qualified policies (as long as they satisfy state licensing requirements) and, in fact, sometimes a non-qualified policy is the best choice for an individual purchaser.

This discussion revolves around the rules promulgated by the National Association of Insurance Commissioners (NAIC), especially the Long-Term Care Insurance Model Act and Model Regulation.[2] However, since the states play an important role in regulating long-term care insurance policies it is important to check what each individual state has done in this field as well as keep up with developments in the NAIC's thinking.

POLICY STRUCTURES

The central coverage of LTCI is nursing home coverage, typically expressed as $X a day, with a usual range of $50 to $275 per day. It is permissible to sell policies covering only nursing home treatment although not to sell a policy that is limited to skilled nursing home treatment. Given the preference of most elders for staying at home, coverage of home care, by policy or rider, is popular. Basic policies are often written with half as much home care as nursing home coverage: for example, $100 per day institutional benefit and $50 per day home care benefit. To an increasing extent, LTCI policies are adding coverage of other types of benefits, such as adult day care. Some policies blur the distinction between housing and health care by offering coverage for stays in assisted living facilities and continuing care retirement communities.

NAIC rules (see below) and state law usually require LTCI policies to provide at least one years' coverage and many state laws do not permit LTCI policies covering less than two years. Instead of a deductible, LTCI policies may have a waiting period (typically, 10, 21,

30, or 100 days), although "first-day" policies are also available. Naturally, the longer the waiting period, the smaller the premium.

By and large, LTCI policies are guaranteed renewable, so age at purchase and benefit package selected are the major determinants of premium. Further, premiums can usually only be increased on a class-wide basis, not for the individual. Creative options are also available in payment terms. For example, in 1998, one life insurance company began to offer two new payment options. Under the "age 65" option, the policyholder makes larger annual payments and owns a paid-up policy at age 65. Similarly, the "10-year" option calls for only 10 years of premium payments to receive a paid-up policy. Obviously, premiums for these two payment options will be higher than conventional premiums.[3] Target purchasers include mid-life executives who can pay out of salary during high-income working years and have a fully paid-up policy at or shortly after retirement.

One of the most controversial LTCI issues is whether the individual purchaser should elect inflation protection. If elected, the question is whether the purchaser should select the 5 percent simple inflation protection (which will increase the premium about 50 percent) or the 5 percent compound (which will more or less double the premium).[4] The younger the insurance buyer, the greater the significance of inflation protection. Affluence cuts both ways. The larger the individual's assets, the greater the ability to purchase even expensive coverage, but also the greater the ability to use those assets to pay for private care. A possible option is to increase the size of the policy benefit initially purchased and hope that it will continue to be adequate.

The question of benefit triggers is also significant. Some of the first generation of LTCI policies used a "medical necessity" trigger under which certification of medical need for the care was a prerequisite for insurance reimbursement. However, many elderly people suffer from many ailments at once, or from generalized frailty but not from a specific, identifiable ailment, and thus might not qualify for benefits under this trigger.

Qualified policies (see below) must have both an ADL trigger and a cognitive impairment trigger. That is, benefits must be available on the basis of the limitation of the insured individual to perform a certain number of the activities of daily living (ADLs) such as eating, dressing, and bathing. Benefits must also be available to cognitively impaired individuals, even if they retain a high degree of physical capacity. Insurers who sell non-qualified policies have greater flexibility and can use any trigger, or combination of triggers, permitted by state law.

NAIC: DEFINING LONG-TERM CARE INSURANCE

The National Association of Insurance Commissioners (NAIC) defines long-term care insurance as a policy or rider that covers at least 12 consecutive months of "necessary or medically necessary diagnostic, preventive, therapeutic, rehabilitative, maintenance or personal care services" in any setting outside an acute care hospital.[5] Therefore, LTCI definitely covers custodial care not just acute care eligible for Medicare reimbursement. LTCI policies also have the potential to cover care rendered at home or in a community setting such as an adult day health center not just institutional care in a nursing home. Although the most common method of providing benefits is indemnity, the Model Act also permits benefits to be made on an expense incurred, prepaid, or other basis.

Long-term care coverage can come from a stand-alone policy or a rider, either "qualified" for tax purposes or non-qualified. Annuities and life insurance that provide incidental long-term care benefits fall under the NAIC definition, but Medigap, hospital, major medical, disability, and accident insurance do not. Life insurance death benefits that can be accelerated based on terminal illness or institutionalization are not considered long-term care insurance.

A group policy is issued to one or more employer, labor organization, or professional or trade organization.[6] In such a circumstance, the entity holds the policy and the individuals who are covered under it receive certificates. However, because most LTCI policies are sold to individuals, the discussion in this chapter largely centers upon the individual policy, with references to the policy-holder rather than the certificate-holder.

NAIC standards[7] permit state commissioners to adopt disclosure regulations, dealing with issues such as:

- Terms of renewability;
- Eligibility;
- Non-duplication of coverage with other insurance;

- Dependent coverage;
- Treatment of preexisting conditions;
- Continuation, conversion or termination of policies;
- Waiting periods; and
- Limitations on coverage.

Banned Practices

The NAIC Model Act[8] forbids certain insurer practices:

- Using the insured's age or deterioration of mental or physical health as a reason for canceling, non-renewing, or otherwise terminating a policy;
- Imposing a new waiting period when coverage is converted or replaced within the same company — except if the insured has voluntarily chosen to increase the benefits under the policy; and
- Limiting coverage to skilled nursing facilities or providing significantly more coverage for institutional skilled care than custodial care.

The most restrictive definition of "preexisting condition" that the NAIC will allow for an individual policy is "a condition for which medical advice or treatment was recommended by, or received from a provider of health care services, within six (6) months preceding the effective date of coverage of an insured person."[9] Furthermore, the preexisting condition limitation can only be applied to losses and institutional confinements occurring within six months of the effective date of coverage.[10] The NAIC makes it clear that insurers can do medical underwriting based on their own standards and can legitimately use the application form to collect the applicant's complete medical history.

The NAIC forbids prior hospitalization and step-down requirements in LTCI policies. That is, benefits must be made available to individuals who live in the community, even if they have not been hospitalized, and even if they have not received a higher level of care before receiving a lower level of care.[11] This is an important advantage of LTCI over Medicare and is a better fit with the usual pattern of care in which senior citizens start out reasonably healthy and functional but require more and more care over time.

However, a prior institutionalization requirement can be imposed in certain limited contexts: waiver of premium; recuperative benefits; and benefits for post-confinement and post-acute care. Any such requirement must be clearly disclosed and benefits cannot be conditioned on a prior institutional stay of more than 30 days.[12]

The Model Regulation[13] requires all policies (whether qualified or not) to include both cognitive impairment and activities of daily living (ADL) triggers. The most restrictive permissible provision is dependency in three ADLs. The insurer must consider bathing, continence, dressing, eating, toileting, and transferring to be ADLs and can add more ADLs to the policy definition. But, a person dependent in three ADLs must be entitled to coverage. Dependency is defined as a need for the hands-on assistance of another person to perform the ADL.

Consumer Protection

LTCI buyers have the right to return their policies within 30 days of delivery for a full refund of premium no matter why the applicant is dissatisfied. This right must be disclosed on the first page of the policy.[14]

When the initial solicitation is made to a potential buyer, he or she must be given an outline of coverage in the standard format prescribed by the local commissioner. If the policy is solicited by an agent, the agent must provide the outline of coverage before offering an application or enrollment form. With direct response solicitations, the outline must be presented together with the application or enrollment form.[15]

The Model Act[16] requires the outline of coverage to include:

- A description of the policy's principal benefits and coverage;
- The policy's principal exclusions, reductions, and limitations;
- The insurer's terms for continuing the policy, including any reserved right to change the premiums;

- Terms for returning the policy and getting a premium refund;
- A brief description of the relationship of cost of care and benefits; and
- Disclosure that the outline is only a summary and that the full terms can be found in the policy itself.

Certificate-holders under a group policy receive a briefer summary, describing the principal benefits and coverage, exclusions, reductions, and limitations. This summary discloses that the group master policy contains the actual contract terms.[17]

When a policy is delivered, a policy summary must also be delivered for an individual life policy that provides long-term care benefits, either within the policy or through the use of a policy rider.[18] Some of the items that the summary must explain are:

- How the long-term care benefits interact with other aspects of the policy;
- The amount and duration of benefits and any guaranteed lifetime benefits;
- Any exclusions, reductions, or limitations on the long-term care benefits;
- Any guarantees as to the costs of insurance charges; and
- Current and projected maximum lifetime benefits.

The Model Act[19] requires a monthly report to the policyholder if and when accelerated death benefits are in pay status.

Incontestability

During the first six months an LTCI policy is in force, the insurer has the right to rescind the policy or deny a claim that would otherwise be valid, if it can show that the insured engaged in misrepresentation that was material to acceptance of the application. Once the policy has been in force for six months, but for less than two years, the policy can be rescinded and claims can be denied on proof of misrepresentation by the insured that was both material to acceptance of the application and also related to the actual condition for which the insured has applied for benefits. In other words, in this situation, a misrepresentation about the insured's cardiac condition will not affect an application for benefits required by a hip fracture, although the insurer would be justified in rejecting a claim for home care after an episode of heart failure.[20]

After two years, mere misrepresentation by the insured will not permit the insurer to contest the payment of benefits. The insurer needs to be able to show the insured's knowing and intentional misrepresentation of relevant facts about his or her health, a much higher standard.

The Model Act[21] also forbids "field underwriting" based on medical or health status. This means that the agent or third-party administrator is not allowed to issue a policy, only to have it rescinded later by the home office, once the applicant's true health status becomes known. In contrast, it is quite legitimate for the agent to accept applications that are contingent on satisfactory health underwriting.

Once benefits have actually been paid under the policy, the insurer may be able to rescind the policy (if the appropriate conditions are met), thus preventing future obligations, but does not have the right to recover benefit payments already made.

Nonforfeiture Provisions

Whether long-term care insurance policies should include nonforfeiture provisions is one of the most controversial areas in LTCI regulation. It is not known for certain what percentage of people in a particular age range will ever use home care or go to a nursing home and it certainly is not known which individuals within the group will do so. Generally, at any given time about five percent of senior citizens live in a nursing home and about 45 percent will spend time in a nursing home at some point. Certainly one reason for consumer reluctance to purchase LTCI is the belief (whether rational or not) that they will never need this coverage.

On one side of the controversy, it can be argued that it is unfair for insured persons who do not use the long-term care coverage to pay premiums and receive no return. It can also be argued that nonforfeiture features are an incentive to purchase. On the other side, it can be argued that insurers cannot stay in the LTCI market unless they can earn a reasonable profit which they will not be able to do if they must turn over a large percentage of their premium base.

The way the NAIC has resolved the debate is to require insurers to offer their customers the option of purchasing a policy or rider providing nonforfeiture benefits. That is to say, the benefit must always be offered, but need not be included in every policy. Policies that include nonforfeiture benefits must have the same coverage elements, eligibility rules, benefit triggers, benefit lengths, and loss ratios as policies purchased by individuals who have declined the nonforfeiture benefit.

The NAIC Model Regulation[22] defines the required nonforfeiture benefit as a "shortened benefit period providing paid-up long-term care insurance coverage after lapse." The amount and frequency of benefits must continue the same as prior to the lapse (but will not increase), but the maximum amount to be paid or days of benefits will be set to equal 100 percent of the premiums already paid. The standard nonforfeiture credit is 100 percent of premiums paid, but not less than 30 days' nursing home benefit (measured as of the time the policy lapses). Insurers can provide other shortened benefit period options, as long as they are at least as generous as the standard. Nonforfeiture credits can be applied to any covered services, not just nursing home care. However, the total of benefits provided while the policy was in premium-paying status, plus those offered when it is in paid-up status, should not exceed the maximum benefits that would have applied if the policy had remained in premium-paying status.

Policyholders who decide not to purchase this protection must be offered a contingent benefit upon lapse that can be used during a specified period after a "substantial" increase in the premium.[23] The younger the policyholder, the larger the premium increase that will be deemed substantial, ranging from 190 percent at ages 30 to 34 to 10 percent over age 90. That is, they must be given a chance to reduce their policy benefits or convert to reduced paid-up insurance so that coverage will continue, albeit at a lower level, without the need to pay the increased premium for full coverage.

LTCI UNDERWRITING

Theoretically, healthy senior citizens should find it easy to understand the benefits of buying LTCI. In practice, consideration of LTCI (and other potentially distressing topics) tends to be deferred, often until the individual's health has deteriorated enough to make long-term care a topic of increasing personal relevance. At that point, it might seem a waste of time even to try to purchase LTCI coverage. However, although detailed insurer-specific information is hard to find[24], there seems to be a wide variation in acceptance rates. In one survey, the average survey respondent accepted 47 percent of LTCI applications at the preferred rate, but the range within the respondents was from 3 percent to 74 percent.

A review of underwriting guidelines from 23 companies, found that AIDS, cirrhosis of the liver, multiple sclerosis, muscular dystrophy, and Parkinson's Disease were considered grounds for rejection of an application. However, companies varied widely in their attitude toward selling LTCI to diabetics. Some declined insulin-dependent diabetics while others declined only those requiring large insulin dosages or already suffering diabetes-related complications. Areas of increasing concern in underwriting are osteoporosis and cognitive decline in applicants.[25]

In short, giving clients accurate advice about LTCI requires an individualized inquiry into the availability of insurance at premium, standard, or sub-standard rates. Unless the client is already severely ill, it should not be assumed that insurance is unavailable.

LIFE INSURANCE LTC BENEFITS

Any life insurance policy or rider that is sold as long-term care or nursing home insurance has to comply with the NAIC Long-Term Care Insurance Model Act as well as with applicable life insurance regulation. The Model Act also deals with individual life insurance policies that provide long-term care coverage within the policy or by rider.

When the policy is delivered, it must be accompanied by a policy summary that explains the relationship between long-term care benefits and other components of the policy (e.g., by deduction from the eventual death benefits). The summary must show the amount of benefits, length of benefits, and any guaranteed lifetime benefits, as well as exclusions, reductions, and limitations of benefits.

If it is appropriate for the policy type, the summary must disclose the effect of exercising other rights under the policy, disclose guarantees affecting the long-term care costs of insurance charges, and the current and projected maximum lifetime benefits. Further, the summary must note that inflation protection is not available under the policy.

If and when the long-term care benefit is triggered and is in payment status, the policyholder must be given a monthly report explaining the LTC benefits paid during the month, any changes in the policy (typically, reduced cash values or death benefits) resulting from the payment of these benefits, and the remaining LTC benefits still available for future use.[26] When life insurance-based LTC claims are denied, the Model Act[27] requires the insurer to give a written explanation of the reason for the denial, backed up by all information "directly related to the denial," within 60 days of a written request from the policyholder or his or her representative (for example, a guardian).

QUALIFIED POLICIES

The Health Insurance Portability and Accountability Act of 1996 (HIPAA) cleared up some important tax questions about long-term care insurance and enacted a new Internal Revenue Code Section, 7702B, to provide favorable tax treatment for "qualified" policies.

Under Section 7702B, all qualified policies must meet certain standards for benefits and consumer protection as set forth in the NAIC Model Act and Model Regulation.

Nevertheless, insurers have fairly broad discretion in designing their policies. Congress did not use HIPAA to impose the same kind of standardization that it earlier imposed on Medigap policies. The Taxpayer Relief Act of 1997, IRS Notice 97-31, and long-term care regulations clarify the HIPAA rules and provide some guidance in applying them.[28]

A qualified policy is an individual or group policy that offers coverage of qualified long-term care services, but nothing else; it can also be a life insurance policy that has an LTCI rider. Qualified contracts must be guaranteed renewable. They may not have cash value. Any dividends or premium refunds must be used to increase future benefits or reduce future premiums, but refunds can be made when the insured person dies or the contract is surrendered or canceled.[29]

The purpose of an LTCI policy is to provide "qualified long-term care services" to a "chronically ill individual" (as defined under an ADL test, a severe cognitive impairment test, or other tests grandfathered in or allowed by statute). That is, all qualified policies must have both an ADL trigger and a cognitive impairment trigger, but may not impose other requirements, such as medical necessity, on benefits.[30]

Qualified long-term care services are "necessary diagnostic, preventive, therapeutic, curing, treating, mitigating and rehabilitative services, and maintenance or personal care services" furnished to a chronically ill individual under a health care professional's plan of care.[31] Note that there is no requirement that the services be able to cure or even improve the condition — maintenance and custodial care are covered.

A chronically ill individual is one who has suffered a loss of functional capacity so that, for a period of at least 90 days, he or she is unable to perform two or more ADLs without substantial assistance.[32] (The 90-day period is not a policy waiting period; it is intended to draw a distinction between temporary changes in ability that are within the domain of acute health insurance, and lasting or permanent changes that fall under LTCI.)

HIPAA includes a list of six standard ADLs (eating, toileting, transferring, bathing, dressing, and continence). Qualified policies must either refer to all six of these or pick five of them to determine whether or not a person is ADL-impaired.[33] Insurers who sell qualified policies cannot define their own ADLs. It should be noted that bathing is usually the first ADL with which older people experience difficulty, so excluding bathing from the list of covered ADLs would have the effect of significantly limiting claims. Substantial assistance means either the physical assistance of another person or having another person nearby in case of need for assistance.

A chronically ill individual is also one who suffers from severe cognitive impairment,[34] which is defined as Alzheimer's disease or other condition causing a comparable loss or deterioration of intellectual capacity, leading to impairment in memory or orientation that can be measured by scientific tests. Ability to perform ADLs is irrelevant to this test.

Qualified policies are not allowed to pay or reimburse any expenses that could be covered by Medicare (or that would be covered except for copayment responsibilities). However, qualified policies are allowed to cover expenses for which Medicare is a secondary payor. Medicare-eligible amounts can be covered by qualified policies that make periodic (e.g., per diem) payments that are not tied to actual expenses.

NONFORFEITURE BENEFITS

The Model Act[35] requires the nonforfeiture options for a qualified policy to include at least:

- a reduced paid-up insurance benefit;
- an extended term insurance benefit;
- a shortened benefit period; and
- other forms that have achieved regulatory approval.

The issuer of a qualified policy can refund the premiums when the insured dies or when the policy is surrendered or canceled. However, the refund cannot be an amount greater than the total premiums paid and there can be no adjustment for interest.

Nonforfeiture is addressed by the Model Regulation.[36] (Life insurance policies and riders containing accelerated LTC benefits are exempt from the nonforfeiture requirement). The offer of nonforfeiture benefits must be in writing if it is not otherwise set out in the disclosure materials (such as the Outline of Coverage) given to the applicant. Policies offered with nonforfeiture benefits must offer the same coverage elements, eligibility rules, duration of benefits, and benefit triggers as policies sold without nonforfeiture benefits, and the nonforfeiture credits can be used for all covered care and services up to the policy limits. (The insurer is not required to offer total benefits in premium paying status plus paid up status that exceed what would have been payable if the policy had remained in premium paying status and nonforfeiture had never been triggered.)

Even if the applicant rejects the nonforfeiture benefit, the insurer must provide a contingent benefit upon lapse, which is triggered every time the insurer raises the premium "substantially." Whether an increase is substantial depends on the insured's issue age, ranging from 200 percent for issue ages up to 29 to 10 percent for issue ages of 90 and over. For typical issue ages of 60 to 65, the trigger ranges between 50 and 70 percent. On or before the date of a "substantial" premium increase, the insurer must offer to reduce the policy benefits so that a lower level of coverage can be maintained with the current premium level.

BENEFIT TRIGGERS

The Model Regulation has two sections dealing with benefit triggers: one addressing the topic in general[37] and a second for qualified policies.[38] The general section requires both cognitive impairment and ADL triggers. The ADL trigger must not require deficiencies in more than three ADLs. Bathing, continence, dressing, eating, toileting, and transferring must be treated as ADLs. The insurer can add additional ADLs as long as they are defined in the policy. A person is deemed to be deficient in an ADL if the hands-on assistance of another person is needed to perform the activity. For the cognitive impairment trigger the test is whether verbal cueing from, or supervision by, another person is needed to perform the activity. ADL and cognitive impairment assessment must be made by professionals. The policy must clearly describe the appeals procedure for benefit determinations.

The section of the model regulation dealing with qualified policies adopts the HIPAA requirement of a cognitive trigger plus an ADL trigger, this time defined as inability to perform one or two ADLs for an expected period of at least 90 days, resulting from loss of functional capacity. Generally, an insured will be considered to have met the requirements if, within the preceding 12-month period, a licensed health care provider has certified that the insured has met the requirements and the provider has prescribed the qualified long-term care insurance services under a plan of care."[39] Only the statutory ADLs (bathing, continence, dressing, eating, toileting, transferring) can be used; the insurer cannot use different or additional ADLs to determine access to benefits under a qualified policy.

The payment of benefits under a qualified policy is triggered when the substantial assistance of another person is needed to perform the ADL or if substantial supervision is required to protect the health and safety of the insured. Once again, a clear description of the appeals process is required.

THE LTCI MARKETPLACE

As of March, 1998, the Health Insurance Association of America (HIAA) estimated the average cost of spending a year in a nursing home at $41,000 and noted that for the group of senior citizens who have out-of-pocket health costs over $2,000 a year, 80 percent of this spending goes to long-term care.[40]

So far, market penetration with LTCI has not been great. Less than 10 percent of senior citizens own LTCI and LTCI pays for less than six percent of all nursing home days.

1996, the last year for which HIAA has complete figures, was a strong year for LTCI sales. About 600,000 policies were sold — a

16 percent increase over 1995. Sales for employer-sponsored programs were up 33 percent, reaching 120,000, as average premiums decreased five percent. It is not surprising that sales were highest in states with large senior populations: Florida, California, Pennsylvania, Illinois, Texas, Ohio, and Washington. According to HIAA, average annual premiums for a "basic" policy ($100 per day nursing home, $50 per day home care benefit, four years of coverage, 20-day elimination period) and for the same coverage with the addition of five percent compounded inflation protection would be as follows[41]:

AGE	BASIC	BASIC + INFLATION
40	$247	$589
50	$364	$802
65	$980	$1,829
79	$3,907	$5,592

Several conclusions can be drawn from this table. First of all, these are average figures, so naturally some policies will be more, some will be less, expensive. Also, a $100 per day figure is adequate in some markets at the present time, but may be too low in the future. In high-cost markets, a $100 daily benefit is already far too low to provide complete protection. Naturally, the premium to secure a higher benefit will be higher.

Second, the cost of a basic policy is quite low at age 40 or even age 50, so middle and upper-income people would not find it difficult to find the cash to purchase at those ages. But costs are much higher with inflation protection and the younger the purchaser, the more that inflation protection will add to the cost of the policy, because protection is extended over a longer horizon. By age 65, the basic policy costs enough to be a major budget factor for low-income seniors (especially senior citizen couples, both of whom want to purchase coverage), and $3,600 (the approximate cost of two basic policies with inflation protection) would be a large budget item for a senior couple whose income is $20,000 or even $30,000 a year. However, a retired executive whose spouse is still working, and whose household income is $75,000 a year or more, would be more receptive to spending $3,600 a year — especially if, as is likely, the executive and spouse have substantial assets to protect.

HIAA figures[42] for the best-selling policies of 1996 were slightly different. For a policy with four years of coverage, a 20-day waiting period, and a base benefit of $100 per day for institutional and $50 per day for home care, premiums would be as follows (five percent CIP means five percent compounded inflation protection; NFB is nonforfeiture benefit; the last column shows a policy with both benefits):

AGE @ PURCHASE	BASIC	+5% CIP	+ NFB	+ CIP AND NFB
40	$250	$590	$340	$800
50	$385	$800	$520	$1,200
65	$1,000	$1,830	$1,320	$2,450
79	$4,000	$5,600	$5,200	$7,500

The benefits of purchasing early appear quite clearly in this table. The impact of inflation protection on premium is much greater at earlier purchase ages, which makes sense, because the protection must extend over more years. But at the later entry ages, the nonforfeiture benefit has the greater impact on premium. If purchase takes place at the conventional age of 65, the best-selling policies with CIP and NFB cost $2450, which could be a difficult price point for middle-income seniors, unless they are willing to sell some stock or other assets, or unless their children are willing to contribute. But it should be affordable for high-income seniors. (Don't forget, though, that the $100 per day benefit would not be high enough for care in a high-cost area unless the insured person makes significant copayments. In high-cost areas, the premium would probably be higher because a higher coverage level would probably be chosen.)

The American Council of Life Insurance (ACLI) looks at it from the other end of the telescope. They point out that someone who is 45 years old today can expect to spend $489,446 to spend two years in a nursing home in 2038 (when he or she is 85). To fund that stay out of personal resources, he or she would have to save and invest $3,557 a year (quite apart from saving to supplement the pension as a source of retirement income). That is about eight times the average premium for an LTCI policy with two years of coverage ($417). What about today's 60-year-old who might enter a nursing home at age 85 in 2023? ACLI estimates that two years in a nursing home would cost $235,432 at that time, requiring annual savings of $4,481 to pay out-of-pocket — about five times the $824 LTCI premium. Once again, the earlier the policy is purchased, the greater the savings.[43]

Although there are many companies offering LTCI, the marketplace is extremely concentrated. In 1996, only two companies (Conseco and General Electric Capital Corporation) secured close to half of the $2.2 billion in premium revenues. Conseco alone had $567 million in premium revenues — about as much as Travelers, Penn Treaty, Prudential, IDS Life, and Fortis combined. GE Capital had 1996 LTCI premium revenues of $485 million. The next-largest player, John Hancock, was far behind at $192 million. Apart from the 10 market leaders, there were 118 other LTCI insurers, but they had less than $80 million premium revenue in all, 3.5 percent of the market. Approximately two-thirds of premiums were generated by independent agents, with career agents, banks, and employer-sponsored plans comparatively minor factors in generating business.[44]

In HIAA's view, LTCI issuers make a wide breadth of policies available to an equally wide scope of potential purchasers. Age requirements have been liberalized, so that persons anywhere from 18 to 99 may be able to purchase an individual policy.

About 80 percent of the policies in force at the end of 1996 were individual policies, although one-third of the insurers did have an employer-sponsored or life-insurance-related LTCI product. Of the 20 percent non-individual policies, 13 percent were employer-sponsored. Life riders represented 7 percent of policies (a cumulative total of 340,000 policies sold as of the end of 1996). Employers did not begin to offer LTCI plans until 1987 when only two employers did so. The numbers grew very slowly (7 in 1988; 54 in 1989; 135 in 1990) until 1991, when there were 288 employer-sponsored plans. The number approximately doubled each year for two more years (to 508 in 1992 and 968 in 1993) when growth slowed. In 1994, 1028 employers offered these plans; 1260 in 1995; and 1532 in 1996.[45]

A 1998 survey containing details of 111 long-term care insurance products offered by 58 insurers found that, in addition to the conventional nursing home and home care coverages, most long-term care insurance policies cover assisted living, hospices, respite care (for relief of family care givers), case management and care coordination, durable medical equipment, and bed-holds (paying to maintain a nursing home bed while the nursing home resident is temporarily hospitalized).[46]

The same survey shows a long-term care insurance premium range of about $700 to $1560 for $120 per day lifetime coverage, no waiting period, including home health care, purchased at age 60. (Even lower premiums were available for slightly different plans.) For age-70 purchase, the range was from $1790 to $3864. In other words, the most expensive policy at a particular age range cost more than twice as much as its least expensive counterpart. However, a simple price comparison does not tell the whole story, because LTCI policies vary quite a bit in the non-core benefits they offer and insurers also vary significantly in reputation, financial soundness, and claims management.

It is interesting to note that, although the incidence of most employee benefits increases with the size of the firm, most employment-related LTCI plans are offered by small (under 500 employees) or very small (less than 100 employees) companies. Of the approximately 1500 plans in place in 1996, 432 plans had some degree of employer involvement in paying for the plan while the others were "employee-pay-all" plans. However, since the average age for purchasers under these group plans was 43, the premium was probably quite low. Employer-sponsored LTCI plans often permit employees to cover their spouses or their parents and parents-in-law. Thus, an older client who wants LTCI but feels unable to afford it may be able to find coverage through a child's (or child's spouse's) work-related policy.

INCOME TAX TREATMENT OF LTCI

Under appropriate circumstances, someone covered under a qualified LTCI policy can receive part or all of the benefits under the policy without encountering income tax liability. The amount received will be free of tax if the benefit paid to a chronically ill individual does not exceed a daily indemnity amount of $190 ($69,350 a year). These figures are for 1999 and are adjusted for inflation. The Internal Revenue Code makes it clear that benefits paid under qualified policies are tax-free (subject to these limits). However, the Code does not say that benefits paid from non-qualified policies are tax-free.[47]

There is also the potential for an income tax deduction for the purchase of a qualified LTCI policy. The Internal Revenue Code sets forth premium amounts, keyed to the taxpayer's age. LTCI premiums may be deducted up to these amounts. In 1999, the premium amounts are: $210 for persons age 40 or less; $400 for ages 41 through 50; $800 for ages 51 through 60; $2,120 for ages 61 through 70; and $2,660 for over age 70.[48] Like the benefit limitation amounts above, the premium amounts are indexed for inflation.

Unfortunately, these amounts are not deductible per se. Instead, they are treated as potential medical expense deductions. That is, they are aggregated with all other allowable medical expenses and the actual deduction is the difference between total allowable medical expenses and 7.5 percent of the taxpayer's adjusted gross income.[49] For example, assume that Donald and Jennifer Platt's adjusted gross income is $109,487 for 1999, a year in which they pay LTCI premiums of $2,750 each. Donald is age 71 while Jennifer is age 67. Therefore, Donald can treat $2,660 as a potential deduction; Jennifer can treat $2,120 as one. But if their out-of-pocket medical expenses other than LTCI do not exceed $3,431.52 they will not get any medical expense deduction, because their "floor" is $8,211.52 (7.5 percent of $109,487).

Because LTCI premiums for qualified policies are deemed to be health insurance premiums, self-employed persons qualify for a more generous rule. In 1999 through 2001, 60 percent of the premium is therefore automatically deductible (without regard to adjusted gross income or other health expenses).[50] The other 40 percent of the premium can be aggregated with other medical expenses and deducted to the extent that it exceeds 7.5% of adjusted gross income.

MARKETING PROBLEMS

No question, selling long-term care insurance is difficult. Even sophisticated insurance purchasers, who apparently can contemplate their own deaths with equanimity as they purchase life insurance, can shrink from thinking about depressing subjects such as mental incapacity and loss of ability to function normally. The coverage can be expensive, which creates its own resistance, even though the value of LTCI in preserving freedom of choice in long-term care, and preserving the estate, is indisputable. Prospects may have very unrealistic expectations about what Medicare will provide or about the ability to create a complete Medicaid plan on short notice. LTCI products are complex and policyholders must make a number of choices (i.e., which carrier, what benefits to be covered, the size of benefit, whether or not to add inflation protection and non-forfeiture features, how long of a waiting period, and the duration of benefits).

According to a 1997 survey, one-third of respondents thought they already owned LTCI (probably because they confused Medicare eligibility with private coverage). However, statistics show that only one percent of the country's population and less than six percent of those over age 65 actually own a LTCI policy. Few surveyed could describe long-term care insurance but 72 percent said they were aware of its existence.[51]

ASSESSING THE CLIENT'S OBJECTIVE

Not all middle-aged and older persons purchase LTCI for the same reason. There are several ways that LTCI can fit into an elder care plan. Selection of one objective over another is a matter of personal taste and style, rather than choosing a valid over an invalid objective.

Some purchasers are extremely interested in securing coverage of most or all LTCI costs. Clients having this "front-end" objective will want to select a policy with no waiting period or a short waiting period; a broad spectrum of benefits; and a high daily benefit (probably with the home care benefit close to or at 100 percent of the institutional benefit). Such purchasers may prefer a qualified policy because of its broader range of coverage triggers, especially if they qualify for tax benefits.

Clients with a "back-end" objective see the possibility of a prolonged nursing home stay or a need for extensive home care as a catastrophic financial event but believe that there is less than a 50 percent chance of it happening to them. Therefore, they are interested in limiting their LTCI premium by accepting a higher degree of risk but want to be prepared if their worst-case scenario comes true. They will therefore accept a longer waiting period (during which they will use savings to pay the full cost of care out-of-pocket) but will want a four-year or lifetime duration of coverage. They may also be willing to accept a smaller daily benefit on the theory that they can manage copayments but not the full cost of care. In many instances, the back-end objective will appeal to an individual who has significant assets (and perhaps a fairly low income for the level of assets) and is extremely interested in protecting those assets and in estate planning.

TO "Q" OR NOT TO "Q"?

Some prospective purchasers will find themselves faced with a choice between qualified and non-qualified policies in selecting their desired benefit package. The question then becomes whether to select the qualified or non-qualified plan. Qualified plans must furnish extensive disclosures to potential buyers and must offer certain forms of consumer protection. However, it is quite likely that issuers of nonqualified plans will furnish at least as much disclosure and a good insurance professional will respond to clients' questions and will provide them whatever information they need for an informed purchase even if it is not mandated by federal law.

The purchaser should try to forecast how and when the policy will be used, although admittedly this is difficult. The point is to determine how likely it is that a particular kind of care or service will be needed that is covered by the qualified policy but not by the non-qualified one, or vice versa. The next question is whether the individual client will obtain any tax benefit from purchasing a qualified policy and, if so, how large the benefit will be. The tax benefit (the potential deduction available in the client's income tax bracket) should be subtracted from the qualified policy's premium to compare the real cost of the two plans.

COORDINATING LTCI AND MEDICAID

Some clients embrace private LTCI as a superior alternative to Medicaid while others use LTCI as part of a Medicaid plan. Such clients estimate the length of the penalty period they will encounter as a result of asset transfers, estimate the amount of that penalty period that will occur subsequent to their need for long-term care and plan to use LTCI to fill the gap.

For instance, a person's health might deteriorate seriously in August, 2002, to the point that he or she needs to enter a nursing home. Yet asset transfers in late 1999 might have generated a penalty period extending until May, 2004. If that person owns an LTCI policy with no waiting period and two years of coverage, the insurance policy will provide coverage until the individual becomes Medicaid-eligible (assuming that the laws in 2004 are comparable to the current ones).

ROBERT WOOD JOHNSON PROGRAMS

The Robert Wood Johnson Foundation created a program of public-private partnership for the funding of long-term care. Under the partnership plan, individuals agree to purchase and maintain at least a minimum of LTCI coverage of specified types. The state agrees that, once this coverage is used up, the individual will automatically be Medicaid-eligible, whatever his or her asset level may be.

These plans were quite popular with state governments because they offered a chance to cut the Medicaid rolls and provide an incentive for individuals to pre-fund their own long-term care. As of 1993, five states (California, Connecticut, Indiana, Iowa, and New York) had partnership plans in existence and had secured federal approval. Several other states had passed their own laws authorizing partnership plans.

Unfortunately, Congress cut off development of partnership programs by enacting legislation, effective May 14, 1993, basically forbidding creation of new partnership programs. The five "grandfathered-in" states were able to keep their programs and do not have to seek estate recovery from the estates of decedents who had used the partnership. The other states would be required to apply ordinary Medicaid rules for eligibility and estate recovery to people who owned partnership policies. Obviously, then, there would be little incentive to buy these policies.

CHAPTER FOOTNOTES

1. Stephen A. Moses, "LTC Insurance Could Play Role in Solving Medicaid Woes," *National Underwriter*, Life and Health/Financial Services edition, January 11, 1999, p. 13.

2. NAIC Models are available on line: see http://www.naic.org.

3. News Brief, "UNUM Adds 'To Age 65' and '10-Year' LTC Payment Options," *National Underwriter*, Life and Health/Financial Services edition, August 24, 1998, p. 13. For product developments, also see Linda Koco, "LTCs For the Late '90s Hit the Streets," *National Underwriter*, Life and Health/Financial Services edition, August 3, 1998, p. 25 and "Companies Bring Out LTCs for Varied Reasons," *National Underwriter*, Life and Health/Financial Services edition, February 1, 1999, p. 27.

4. Allison Bell, "Agents Keep Wary Eye on Long Term Care Inflation," *National Underwriter*, Life and Health/Financial Services edition, August 3, 1998, p. 7.

5. NAIC Long-Term Care Insurance Model Act, Section 4A.

6. NAIC Long-Term Care Insurance Model Act, Section 4E.

7. NAIC Long-Term Care Insurance Model Act, Section 6A.

8. NAIC Long-Term Care Insurance Model Act, Section 6B.

9. NAIC Long-Term Care Insurance Model Act, Section 6C.

10. NAIC Long-Term Care Insurance Model Act, Section 6C.

11. NAIC Long-Term Care Insurance Model Act, Section 6D.

12. NAIC Long-Term Care Insurance Model Act, Section 6D.

13. NAIC Long-Term Care Insurance Model Regulation, Section 24.

14. NAIC Long-Term Care Insurance Model Act, Section 6F.

15. NAIC Long-Term Care Insurance Model Act, Section 6G.

16. NAIC Long-Term Care Insurance Model Act, Section 6G.

17. See NAIC Long-Term Care Insurance Model Act, Section 6H.

18. NAIC Long-Term Care Insurance Model Act, Section 6I.

19. NAIC Long-Term Care Insurance Model Act, Section 6J.

20. See NAIC Long-Term Care Insurance Model Act, Section 7.

21. NAIC Long-Term Care Insurance Model Act, Section 7.

22. NAIC Long-Term Care Insurance Model Regulation, Section 23E.

23. See NAIC Long-Term Care Insurance Model Regulation, Section 23D.

24. In their fall, 1998 survey, Ted Pass and Beverly Brenner asked 35 major LTCI insurers about their underwriting policies. Twenty refused to provide any numbers at all, so their results reflect only 15 insurers. See "LTC Survey Pinpoints Underwriting Issues," *National Underwriter*, Life and Health/Financial Services edition, November 16, 1998, p. 7.

25. Ted Pass and Beverly Brenner, "LTC Survey Pinpoints Underwriting Issues," *National Underwriter*, Life and Health/Financial Services edition, November 16, 1998, p. 7.

26. NAIC Long-Term Care Insurance Model Act, Section 6K.

27. NAIC Long-Term Care Insurance Model Act, Section 6L.

28. Notice 97-31, 1997-1 CB 417; Prop. Reg. §§1.7702B-1, 1.7702B-2.

29. IRC Sections 7702B(b), 7702B(e).

30. It has been argued that this requirement gives non-qualified policies an extra measure of flexibility and therefore they are better choices for some potential buyers.

31. IRC Section 7702B(c).

32. IRC Section 7702B(c).

33. IRC Section 7702B(c).

34. IRC Section 7702B(c).

35. NAIC Long-Term Care Insurance Model Act, Section 8D.

36. NAIC Long-Term Care Insurance Model Regulation, Section 23.

37. NAIC Long-Term Care Insurance Model Regulation, Section 24.

38. NAIC Long-Term Care Insurance Model Regulation, Section 25.

39. NAIC Long-Term Care Insurance Model Regulation, Section 25.

40. Figures come from HIAA's statement, "The Role of Private Long-Term Care Insurance in Financing Long-Term Care and the Importance of Offering Long-Term Care Insurance to all Federal Employees," March 27, 1998, available at http://www.hiaa.org/newsroom/ltctest.html.

41. Allison Bell, "HIAA Reports Strong Increase in LTC Sales for 1996," *National Underwriter*, Life and Health/Financial Services edition, October 5, 1998, p. 3.

42. From the 1997 LTC Market Survey as referenced in HIAA's statement, "The Role of Private Long-Term Care Insurance in Financing Long-Term Care and the Importance of Offering Long-Term Care Insurance to all Federal Employees," March 27, 1998, available at http://www.hiaa.org/newsroom/ltctest.html.

43. These somewhat startling figures come from Rick Pullen, "Lighting a Fire Under Long-Term Care," *Best's Review*, Life/Health Edition, June, 1998, p. 12.

44. Figures were compiled by McKinsey & Co. See Allison Bell, "Two Companies Collect Half of LTC Premium," *National Underwriter*, Life and Health/Financial Services edition, August 10, 1998, p. 3.

45. See HIAA's statement, "The Role of Private Long-Term Care Insurance in Financing Long-Term Care and the Importance of Offering Long-Term Care Insurance to all Federal Employees," March 27, 1998, available at http://www.hiaa.org/newsroom/ltctest.html.

46. "LAN's Twelfth Annual Long-Term Care Insurance Survey," *Life Association News*, October, 1998, pp. 70-88.

47. IRC Sections 7702B(a), 7702B(d).

48. IRC Section 213(d)(10)(A).

49. IRC Section 213(a).

50. IRC Section 162(l).

51. Linda Koco, "LTCs for the Late '90s Hit the Streets," *National Underwriter*, Life and Health/Financial Services edition, August 3, 1998, p. 25.

Chapter 5

MEDICARE

In 1965, the Medicare program was launched to address two problems: senior citizens had very poor access to health insurance, and they were spending more than 20 percent of their income on out-of-pocket payments for health care. Since it was launched over three decades ago, the Medicare program has become immense. It is one of the most significant factors in health care reimbursement. However, senior citizens are still spending more than 20 percent of their income on out-of-pocket payments, by paying deductibles and coinsurance, and supplementing Medicare's coverage.

Unfortunately, when it designed the Medicare program, Congress failed to understand the age-related differences in the way people use the nation's health system. Although senior citizens sometimes suffer accidents or acute illnesses (which Medicare and the supplemental private "Medigap" insurance do a pretty good job of covering), they also often suffer chronic conditions that cannot be cured. Medicare has very limited nursing home coverage (only 100 days, in a skilled nursing facility, when recuperating from an episode of acute illness) and no custodial nursing home coverage, although millions of older people need custodial care. Although Medicare has home care provisions, the amount of home care available is not enough for the needs of many impaired elders even though the cost of providing this benefit has grown tremendously in the 1990s.

Senior citizens use a high volume of prescription drugs. Many elders take more than a dozen costly prescription drugs at a time. Medicare does not cover outpatient prescription drugs,[1] although some of the more comprehensive Medigap plans and most managed care plans do. As Chapter 6 shows, many older people turn to Medicaid as a way to deal with the limitations of the Medicare program. Medicaid, also created in 1965, was intended as a way to provide health care for the "indigent:" people without any meaningful amount of resources.

Medicaid does include custodial nursing home coverage, and in many states includes a level of home care far greater than Medicare provides.

The Medicare program is administered by private companies (insurers) acting under contract with HCFA to process medical claims. Part A contracting companies are called "fiscal intermediaries;" those that administer Part B are called "medicare carriers."

MEDICARE ELIGIBILITY

Eligibility for Medicare depends on age (having reached one's 65th birthday) or disability (being totally disabled for two years or more). It is not related to whether the person is currently working, and has nothing to do with the person's level of income or assets. However, at least 40 credited calender quarters of work experience are required. Those who do not qualify for automatic Part A coverage can buy this coverage. People with at least 30, but less than 40, quarters of work experience can get Part A coverage for a premium of $170 a month (or $187 a month if they apply after their initial period of eligibility). Otherwise, the Part A premium is $309 a month or $339.90 a month for those who enroll late.

Therefore, people who retire before age 65, and are not disabled, are not entitled to Medicare coverage, so they need COBRA continuation coverage (see Chapter 8) or private insurance to fill this gap. Nor does Medicare have spousal coverage, so a person who retires at age 65 but whose spouse is age 61 is eligible for Medicare, but the spouse (unless disabled for two years) is not.

In 1967, shortly after the Medicare program began, it covered only 19.5 million people. By 1996, the Medicare population had nearly doubled, to 38.1 million people. In 1995, there were close to six million "dual eligibles": people entitled to both Medicare and Medicaid. See HCFA Statistics: Highlights, at www.hcfa.gov/stats/hstats96/stathili.htm.

MEDICARE SERVICES

The Medicare program is divided into three Parts. Part A helps pay for care in hospitals and skilled nursing facilities, and for home health and hospice care. Part B (also known as Supplementary Medical Insurance or SMI, not to be confused with private "Medigap" Medicare Supplement Insurance) helps to pay for physician services. Part C is Medicare managed care, which concerns the way services will be reimbursed, not with which services are covered.

Medicare's coverage of its services is calculated on the basis of "benefit periods." A benefit period begins on the first day of inpatient treatment in a hospital, and ends 60 days after the patient's discharge from the hospital or from a skilled nursing or rehabilitation facility. There is no limit on the number of benefit periods a Medicare patient can have. The same deductible applies to repeated hospitalizations during the same benefit period, but the patient must pay a new deductible if the second hospitalization occurs more than 60 days after the discharge from the first.

Part A coverage is limited to 90 days inpatient hospitalization per benefit period, but if a longer duration is required, each person has 60 "lifetime reserve days" which can be applied to any hospitalization. However, once the supply of lifetime reserve days is used up, it cannot be renewed. Medicare does not cover private nursing, telephone or television rental in hospital rooms, or care (other than emergency care) provided in a hospital that does not have a Medicare participation contract. With limited exceptions for urgent care rendered in Canada, Medicare does not cover any care rendered outside the United States.

Medicare Part A coverage includes:

- Up to 90 days inpatient hospitalization per benefit period (in a semi-private room, unless a private room is medically necessary);
- Up to 100 days recuperation in a Skilled Nursing Facility (SNF);
- Part-time or intermittent home care services rendered by skilled professionals or home health aides;
- Hospice services elected by terminally ill persons to replace all other Medicare services; and
- Blood, after the first three pints.

Part B coverage includes:

- Medically necessary services rendered by a physician;
- Outpatient hospital services;
- X-rays and laboratory tests;

- Certain Durable Medical Equipment (DME) (e.g., wheelchairs, hospital beds used at home);
- Home health care for people who are enrolled in Part B but not in Part A; and
- Blood, after the first three pints.

SNF Coverage

A Skilled Nursing Facility (SNF) is a facility, either free-standing or a separate part of a hospital, that provides skilled nursing and other professional services (such as physical or speech therapy) to persons who do not need a hospital level of care, but who do require skilled care every day and, as a practical matter, must get the care at an SNF rather than at home or in another setting. In this context (and with respect to Medicare home health services) skilled services are services that inherently require professional training for their proper performance. Caring for a surgical incision, giving an injection, or setting medication dosages are skilled services. Feeding patients, helping them to the bathroom, or helping them dress are not skilled services.

An SNF must have a state license, must have at least one physician on call at all times, and must have enough staff to offer 24-hour-a-day nursing services, with at least one full-time registered nurse on staff.

Medicare covers up to 100 days of care in an SNF per benefit period, but the SNF care must be closely related to a hospitalization during that same benefit period. The patient must have spent at least three consecutive days in the hospital (not counting the day of discharge) before being discharged to the SNF. The basic rule is that the patient must enter the SNF within 30 days of the hospital discharge. Furthermore, a physician must formally certify the need for the care. In practical terms, then, SNF care is available when a person is recovering from an acute illness (e.g., a stroke) or injury (typically, a hip fracture caused by a fall), but not when a person experiences a deterioration in condition.

In 1996, there were 13,444 SNFs participating in the Medicare program. In 1994, HCFA paid a total of $7.1 billion to SNFs. This amount increased significantly the next year, reaching $9.1 billion in 1995. HCFA estimated that more than 1.2 million people would be in Medicare SNF care in 1996.[2]

After the 100th day, no Medicare coverage is available. There is no deductible, and there is no copayment responsibility for the first 20 days of SNF treatment during a benefit period, but coinsurance of $95.50 per day (in 1999) is required for days 21-100. (All Medigap policies, other than Plans A and B, cover the coinsurance.)

Home Health Care

In order for a Home Health Agency (HHA) to be reimbursed for care of a person under Medicare, the agency must have a state license and a contract with the HCFA. Medicare will not reimburse care provided by individuals hired privately by a Medicare beneficiary, or care provided through an agency that has a state license if it does not have a contract with the HCFA.

HHAs provide services such as in-home nursing, physical therapy, occupational therapy, and home health aide services in the homes (or other community settings) of their patients. Medicare covers HHA services, with no deductibles or coinsurance. Medicare managed care beneficiaries face an additional requirement in that they must get their home care from a HHA that also has a contract with their own managed care plan.

However, the Medicare home health care benefit is strictly limited. The services must be part-time or intermittent (although full-time intermittent services, or continuing part-time, services are possible). Intermittent skilled care means care provided less than seven days a week, or less than eight hours a day for a period of up to 21 days. The 21-day period can be extended if the patient can prove that more care is needed, but on a finite and predictable basis. Part-time care means a combination of skilled nursing and home health aide services adding up to less than 8 hours a day and less than 28 hours a week, even if care is provided seven days a week. The local HCFA office can authorize 35 rather than 28 hours of care a week on a showing that the patient needs the extra care.

Someone who needs a nursing home level of care on a permanent basis does not qualify (but see Chapter 6 for a discussion of Medicaid programs that provide nursing home-level care in the patient's home). Medicare home health services must be rendered in accordance with a care plan drawn up and supervised by a physician.

Under the basic Medicare home health care plan, people who have only Part A get their home health services under Part A, while those who have Part B but not Part A (a very small group of people) get their home health services under Part B.

The Balanced Budget Act of 1997 introduced a new category of Medicare home health care called "post-institutional home health services" for Medicare beneficiaries enrolled in both Part A and Part B. Under this program, home health services must be prescribed by a medical professional and must start within 14 days of being discharged from a hospital where the patient spent at least 3 days, or within 14 days of leaving a Medicare SNF. Furthermore, only 100 home health visits are covered under this program.

Another requirement is that the recipient of Medicare home health services must be "homebound," meaning not necessarily bedridden, but definitely spending most of the time at home.

If the patient needs and requires skilled services, the care plan can legitimately include part-time or intermittent home health aide services consisting of personal care such as assistance with getting dressed, bathing, or using the toilet. However, the personal care services must be adjuncts to professional services. Someone who needs only personal care and not skilled services does not qualify for Medicare home care even if home-bound.

In 1996, there were 8,437 HHAs participating in the Medicare program, and HCFA payments to HHAs increased greatly, causing additional concern about the financial stability of the Medicare program. In 1994, Medicare HHAs received a total of $12 billion. The next year this amount increased 25.8% to $15.1 billion.

Hospice Services

Terminally ill Medicare beneficiaries (diagnosed as having six months or less to live) have the option of substituting hospice services, provided under Part A by a Medicare-certified hospice program, for all other Medicare services. If the beneficiary recovers, he can return to the regular Medicare program and Medicare will cover other illnesses or injuries that occur but are not related to the terminal illness (e.g., a cancer patient's heart problems).

Hospice services are primarily home care services. The hospice benefit includes: (1) care from doctors and nurses, (2) medical equipment and supplies, (3) pain medication, (4) medical social services, (5) physical, occupational, and speech therapy, and (6) home health aide and homemaker services. Although most services are rendered in the home, the patient can be hospitalized if medically required (e.g., a flare-up of pneumonia) or for up to five days to provide respite for a spouse or other family member who is significantly involved in the terminally ill person's care. Hospice benefits are not subject to a deductible, but small copayments are required for respite care and outpatient drugs.

Claims Administration and Hearings

Senior citizens are entitled to a notice whenever a benefit claim is denied. In most instances, they are also entitled to a hearing to appeal the denial.

On a day-to-day level, Medicare is administered by insurance companies known as "fiscal intermediaries" (intermediaries) for Part A and "Medicare carriers" (carriers) for Part B.

Health care providers send the claim form to the intermediary. The Medicare beneficiary is responsible for deductibles and coinsurance (or has Medigap insurance to cover it), but the provider cannot bill more than the rate schedule for the health care services.

Part B claims can be either assigned or unassigned. An assigned claim is handled in the same way as a Part A claim. The beneficiary or Medigap policy pays the deductible and coinsurance, and Medicare pays the rest. For unassigned Part B claims, the doctor is still responsible for submitting the paperwork, but the patient pays the doctor's fee and then is reimbursed by the HCFA (at the rate of 80 percent of the HCFA's schedule amount), and perhaps by Medigap insurance.

Once the health care provider submits a bill to the intermediary or carrier, the insurance company will review the claim and determine whether to approve the claim, deny it entirely, or approve it at a lower level than requested. If it approves the claim, the beneficiary will receive what is popularly known as an "Explanation of Medicare Benefits" or "EOMB."

PRACTICE TIP: Tell your clients to keep their EOMBs, because they are helpful for tracing deductibles and coinsurance that may be entitled to Medigap reimbursement. They also are useful for determining whether the expenses might be deductible as medical expenses. They may also be used to ascertain whether a caregiver child has the ability to claim the parent as a dependent.

If the claim is denied, the beneficiary will receive a disallowance notice.[3] Disallowance notices (and EOMBs in amounts lower than the amount claimed) contain an explanation of the appeals procedure. The beneficiary is always entitled to at least one hearing with the intermediary or carrier. Anyone designated by the Medicare beneficiary (not necessarily an attorney) can represent him at the hearing.

PRACTICE TIP: Many "initial determinations" are reversed at the hearing, so it is always worth protesting if there is evidence that a mistake was made. For instance, the patient's attending physician may not have used the right "buzz words" on the form, but the patient definitely qualified for the particular Medicare services.

Medicare beneficiaries always have the right to have the intermediary or carrier review the initial determination. The availability of other hearings involves subtle questions of administrative law, and depends on the type and amount of the claim. If the amount in controversy of a Part A denial is $100 or more, the beneficiary can appeal the intermediary's decision to an Administrative Law Judge (ALJ) who works for the Department of Health and Human Services (HHS). The case can go to federal court if the amount involved is at least $1,000. For Part B, the first step is reconsideration by the carrier, then a hearing by the carrier if the amount in controversy exceeds $100, and an HHS ALJ hearing if $500 or more is involved. Here, too, judicial review is available if $1,000 or more is at stake. See 42 USC section 1395ff, and 42 CFR Part 473.

If the claim is denied on the grounds that the services were custodial, that they were not "reasonable and necessary," or that home care was not warranted because the individual was not "homebound" (see above), it is possible to obtain a "waiver of liability." That is, as long as the patient did not know that Medicare would not cover the services, the patient will not have to pay for them out-of-pocket. (However, if a similar claim has already been denied in the past, the patient will know that the claim was invalid, and a waiver of liability will not be granted.) If the service provider knew the services were not covered by Medicare, the provider will be stuck with the bill. The HCFA will be stuck if neither the patient nor the provider knew the services were not covered. See 42 USC section 1395pp and 42 CFR section 411.400(a).

As a managed care system, Medicare+Choice carries the potential for conflict between gatekeepers and patients who are denied what they believe to be necessary care. Medicare+Choice organizations are required to have meaningful procedures for hearings and appeals (reviews of service entitlements or disputes about patients' copayment responsibilities). See 42 CFR section 422.562. All other disputes are called "grievances." The HCFA is still reviewing requirements for grievances.

Medicare+Choice patients must be given written notice if their claims are denied. The notice must provide specific reasons for the denial, in understandable language, and patients must be given notice of how to seek reconsideration of the denial. See 42 USC section 1395w-22(g)(1)(B) and 42 CFR section 422.568.

MEDICARE COPAYMENTS

Most Medicare enrollees receive Part A services without a premium, but those without the necessary quarters of Social Security coverage pay monthly premiums. Technically speaking, Parts A and B are independent, and it is possible for a Part A enrollee to turn down Part B coverage. Signing up for Part B requires a monthly premium of $45.50 (1999 level), although usually payment is made by deductions from the Social Security check, so the enrollee does not pay anything out-of-pocket. There is a single annual $100 deductible requirement for Part B. The fee-for-service Medicare system is essentially an indemnity system. Medicare generally pays 80 percent of its schedule amount for the particular medical service rendered. If the claim is assigned (see below), the doctor cannot charge more than the schedule amount.

Theoretically the patient would be responsible for the full balance of an unassigned claim, but Medicare forbids "balance billing" (making the patient responsible for more than 15 percent over and above the Medicare amount). The permitted 15 percent surcharge is known as the "limiting charge." Some states (such as New York and Massachusetts) impose even stricter limits on balance billing. See below for a discussion of physicians who opt out of the Medicare system and bill their patients privately.

The Part A hospital deductible (the amount the patient must pay before any Medicare payment is available) is $768 (in 1999) for each benefit period. If there is more than one hospitalization during a benefit period (which begins with initial hospitalization and ends 60 days after the person has been in the community without being an inpatient at a hospital or SNF), only one deductible is required. Once the patient has satisfied the deductible (whether out-of-pocket or by using Medigap insurance), the Medicare system pays the full costs of up to 60 days of inpatient hospitalization in each benefit period. Medicare covers up to 90 days hospitalization in each benefit period, not just 60, but for days 61 through 90, the patient becomes responsible for coinsurance of $192 per day. A person using lifetime reserve days is responsible for $384 per day coinsurance.

There is no deductible for Medicare SNF coverage (i.e., this is "first-day coverage," unlike many long-term care insurance policies, which have a waiting period; see Chapter 4). There is no copayment responsibility for days 1-20 of the stay. For days 21-100, the patient's copayment liability is $96 per day (in 1999). Medicare home health care is rendered without any deductible or coinsurance, except for a 20 percent coinsurance requirement imposed on most items of Durable Medical Equipment (DME).

The beneficiary is responsible for paying for the first three pints of blood used each year, although a few Medigap plans cover this "blood deductible."

Persons who receive outpatient hospital services under Part B are responsible for 20 percent of the actual hospital charge, for which there is no limit set by Medicare fee schedules. For outpatient mental health services, the patient is responsible for 50 percent of the Medicare schedule amount, rather than the 20 percent charged in other contexts.

Assigned and Unassigned Claims

Most doctors who take Medicare patients "accept assignment." They agree to bill Medicare directly for 80 percent of the schedule amount, and also agree not to charge more than the schedule amount. The patient must satisfy the $100 annual deductible, and must pay the physician directly for the 20 percent coinsurance. For an unassigned claim, the patient pays the doctor directly, and then seeks reimbursement from Medicare for 80 percent of the schedule amount. The patient is responsible for (1) the annual deductible, and (2) the difference between the actual charge or the greatest amount the doctor is allowed to charge (typically, 115 percent of the schedule amount) and 80 percent of the schedule amount.

In many instances, senior citizens will want to select a doctor who accepts assignment, so that they can benefit from the greater convenience and lower cost of assigned claims. The HCFA assists them in finding a doctor by publishing "The Medicare Directory of Participating Physicians and Suppliers," available from Social Security offices and State Offices on Aging. Part B carriers are obligated to send free copies on request.

PRACTICE TIP: For certain assigned claims, a patient who has Medigap insurance (see Chapter 3) can have the Medigap insurer make the copayment directly, instead of the patient co-paying and seeking reimbursement from the Medigap insurer. To do so, the patient must give the doctor the Medigap policy number, and ask the doctor to write it on the Medicare claim form. If the Medigap insurer has a "crossover" contract with the HCFA, all claims (assigned or unassigned) go directly to the insurer.

MEDICARE ENROLLMENT

People who start receiving Social Security benefits before age 65 are automatically enrolled in Medicare Part A. The HCFA mails their Medicare cards to arrive approximately three months before their 65th birthday. The Medicare card is also mailed automatically to persons who have satisfied the official definition of disability for two years.

People who remain in the labor force, or otherwise are not receiving Social Security benefits, must take steps to apply for Medicare. The optimum time to apply is three months before the 65th birthday, so the transition to Medicare coverage will be made smoothly.

All Part A enrollees automatically qualify for Part B unless they opt out. The initial enrollment period for Part B (or for buying into Part A) starts on the first day of the third month before the month of the enrollee's 65th birthday and ends seven months later. A person who fails to enroll during this period not only must pay extra for late enrollment, but will not be able to enroll until the next "general enrollment period" (January 1-March 31 of the following year), and coverage will not begin until July 1 of that year.

The Part A buy-in premium is 10 percent higher for late enrollment. The Part B premium increases 10 percent for every 12 months of late enrollment. However, there is no penalty for late Part B enrollment if the individual deferred enrollment because he was covered by an employer's group health plan (EGHP). (See immediately below for a discussion of the relationship between Medicare and EGHPs.)

Secondary Payor

For EGHPs maintained by employers who have 20 or more employees, the EGHP is required to be the primary payor. If the EGHP pays the full bill, Medicare has no theoretical responsibility for payment. (Theoretical, because Medicare often ends up paying bills that should have been covered by an EGHP.) Medicare is supposed to be a secondary payor for services that fall within Medicare coverage and which are not fully covered by the EGHP.

Employers are not allowed to draft their plans to exclude older employees from coverage, or even to make Medicare the primary payor and the EGHP merely a secondary payor. However, employees do have the option of rejecting the EGHP and electing to make Medicare their primary payor. Individuals who make this election, and who enroll in Part B, also start their six-month open enrollment period for Medigap insurance. If they do not also purchase Medigap insurance within this six-month time frame, they may find that coverage is denied or unaffordable.

MEDICARE MANAGED CARE: PRE-M+C

Given the tremendous increase in Medicare spending, and the importance of Medicare to the nation's ever-growing senior citizen population, it is natural that Congress and the HCFA have shown a great deal of interest in using managed care to cope with health care inflation. Unfortunately, the experiment has not been fully successful, and has created many problems for the government, insurers, health care providers, and patients.

In 1997, about one-seventh of Medicare beneficiaries (over 4.5 million people) received their care via managed care organizations. In that year, Medicare spent more than $26 billion on reimbursement to managed care organizations.

Although other forms of managed care organization are recognized under federal law,[4] the predominant form of Medicare managed care is the Health Maintenance Organization (HMO). HMOs enter into contracts with the HCFA, under which they are paid directly by the HCFA. The HCFA sets capitation levels based on 95 percent of the average cost of care for all Medicare beneficiaries in the relevant geographic area.

From the point of view of the Medicare beneficiary, if they sign up with an HMO, they in essence agree to obtain all their care (with limited exceptions for emergencies) from doctors and facilities that have contracted with the HMO. In return for surrendering their free choice of provider, they have lower out-of-pocket costs.

Most HMOs do not charge an explicit premium to their enrollees. Instead, the HCFA compensates the HMO directly. The HCFA will continue to deduct the Part B deductible from the enrollee's Social Security check, or will bill the enrollee directly for the Part B premium. In general, HMO enrollees do not pay deductibles or coinsurance when accessing Medicare-covered services from a network provider. Furthermore, many HMOs, at least during their initial marketing campaign, offer additional benefits, such as prescription drug coverage, glasses, and preventive medicine services as incentives to join. Managed care enrollment eliminates the need for a Medigap policy, which can result in hundreds of dollars (or even over $1,000) in savings per year. Under prior law, it was unlawful to sell a Medigap policy to an HMO enrollee. Such sales are now permitted, but HMO enrollees usually value the ability to dispense with Medigap coverage.

Whether or not HMOs engage in improper "cherry-picking" marketing practices (as some advocates have alleged), healthier senior citizens have an incentive to join HMOs, whereas sicker senior citizens usually will not join HMOs. Sicker seniors are more sensitive to health care issues, and are more likely to have existing relationships with doctors they like. The result is that HMOs end up with a fairly healthy caseload. However, some disabled under-65 Medicare beneficiaries, or even senior citizen beneficiaries, have an incentive to join HMOs that offer prescription drug coverage if they already have, or anticipate, expensive prescription drug needs.

Pre-Balanced Budget Act of 1997 rules (see below for BBA '97 changes) allowed managed care beneficiaries to disenroll from managed care and return to the fee-for-service Medicare program as often as they wanted. Often, they cost the Medicare program a great deal money by accessing services in the fee-for-service system that were denied by managed care gatekeepers.

Most Medicare HMOs have "risk" contracts, under which they receive a flat amount from the HCFA, and derive their profits from spending less to actually provide care than the HCFA payment. "Cost" HMOs are reimbursed by the HCFA on the basis of the actual cost of providing health care to enrollees.

The risk/cost distinction is very significant to HMO participants, because risk HMOs have "lock-in" provisions but cost HMOs do not. That is, if a patient obtains non-emergency care from a hospital, nursing home, physician, or other provider who does not have a contract with the HMO, the HMO will not pay for the care, and neither will Medicare. The patient will be responsible for the full amount of the bill.

However, if the risk HMO has a point of service (POS) option, patients can go outside the network for care, and the HCFA and the HMO will pay part of the cost, although the patient will still have a larger copayment responsibility than if he had remained within the network.[5] Participants in "cost" HMOs will not have to pay deductibles or coinsurance if they stay within the network. They will have to make those copayments for out-of-network care, but Medicare will cover 80 percent of the schedule amount.

MEDICARE+CHOICE

The Balanced Budget Act of 1997 (BBA '97) took a dramatically new approach to Medicare managed care. For one thing, it added a new Medicare Part C, which deals with managed care operations, to the existing Parts A and B. For another thing, the risk and cost HMO programs are being phased out in favor of the new Medicare+Choice (M+C) program. Although the HCFA will not renew HMO contracts, it should be easy for providers to receive new contracts as M+C plans.[6] Physician service organizations (groups of doctors that manage their own administrative tasks) and "risk-bearing entities" are eligible for M+C contracts. A risk-bearing entity is either a health insurance company, or another business that serves the same function of providing health care but takes the risk that the HCFA's payments will be lower than the actual cost of caring for their enrollees.

The Medicare+Choice program has been criticized from many perspectives. It has been criticized by senior health advocates concerned about the availability of quality care and the difficulty of understanding the new layer of bureaucratic requirements. It has also been criticized by provider advocates such as the Health Insurance Association of America (HIAA). As of February, 1999, very few applications to become M+C plans had been received by the HCFA.

HIAA points out that the BBA '97 limits rate increases for private plans to 2 percent per year, which will probably not be enough to keep up with cost increases. HIAA also criticized the rapid timetable required for making coverage decisions, finding the 14-day time frame too limiting for thoughtful consideration.[7]

In June, 1998, the HCFA published the M+C "mega-reg," covering more than 140 closely-printed pages explaining the M+C program.

You can find it at 63 FR 34968-35116 (June 26, 1998). It has also been printed as a pamphlet by health law publishers such as CCH and Aspen.

Under the BBA '97 and the mega-reg, the M+C program consists of three major parts:

- Coordinated care plans consisting of HMOs, HMOs with a POS option, Provider-Sponsored Organizations (PSOs), and Preferred Provider Organization (PPO) plans;

- Medicare+Choice Medical Savings Account (MSA) plans; and

- Medicare+Choice private fee-for-service plans.

M+C coordinated care plans are network plans, which involve signing up a network of physicians, hospitals, and other health care providers. Coordinated care plans are allowed to impose utilization review requirements and gatekeeper mechanisms, but are forbidden to offer any financial incentive to providers that could impair adequate treatment.

PRACTICE TIP: There are regulations that deal with hearing and appeal rights for M+C plan members who disagree with the plan's determination about the availability of a health service they want. See 42 CFR sections 422.560-.622.

Medicare MSAs

Outside the Medicare contexts, Medical Savings Accounts (MSAs) are IRA-type accounts. Certain persons who are covered by high-deductible health insurance policies can make deposits into the account with certain MSA contributions being tax-deductible. If the account holder has medical expenses that are not covered by insurance, he can withdraw funds from the MSA to pay the medical bills.

Medicare MSAs, however, are capitated plans funded by the HCFA's payments on behalf of the enrollee. (These payments are not taxable income for the beneficiary, and the beneficiary is not entitled to a medical expense deduction for expenses paid by the MSA.) Like other MSAs, they work in conjunction with high-deductible medical insurance policies, but in this instance, the HCFA makes the premium payments. Medicare MSA participants continue to pay the Part B premium.

MSA high-deductible policies can offer free choice of provider, or can have a network of preferred providers. It is up to the insurer to decide, and up to the Medicare beneficiary to choose the policy he prefers. Health care provided to an MSA participant is not subject to Medicare cost schedules, although the high-deductible policies may impose their own cost schedules. Otherwise, health care providers can legitimately charge any amount they see fit when treating a Medicare beneficiary who participates in an MSA.

The account holder can take money out of the MSA to pay medical bills that fall under the insurance policy's deductible. In practical terms, this is usually handled by giving the Medicare beneficiary an ID card or series of "checks" that can be used to draw down funds from the account. Withdrawals for other purposes constitute taxable income and may be subject to up to a 50 percent excise tax penalty. After the policy's deductible is satisfied, an insurance company makes payments for the account holder's care following normal Medicare rules. The insurance policy's premiums are paid by the HCFA.

For 1999, the first year in which Medicare MSAs will be available, the policy's deductible may not be greater than $6,000. This amount will be adjusted each subsequent year based on the "national per capita Medicare+Choice growth percentage." Federal law prohibits sale of Medigap insurance to Medicare MSA beneficiaries, because they are supposed to use the MSA rather than insurance funds to pay their out-of-pocket medical costs.

People are allowed to join an MSA as soon as they qualify for Medicare. If they do not enroll at this time, the enrollment period is November of each year, with MSA coverage becoming effective as of January 1 of the subsequent year. People who enroll in November have until December 15 of that year to disenroll and elect another form of Medicare coverage, otherwise, they are locked in to the MSA plan for a full year.

At the account holder's death, the HCFA is entitled to reimbursement from the account based on the number of months left in the calender year. Any sums remaining after the agency is reimbursed pass to the heirs of the account holder.

Private Fee-for Service Plans

Medicare+Choice Private Fee-for-Service Plans work much like conventional health insurance plans. The rules for these plans appear at 42 CFR section 422.4 and section 422.216. Private plans pay their providers on a fee-for-service basis (not a capitated basis), and set their own rate schedules. The plan cannot put health care providers at financial risk or give them financial incentives to restrict treatment, and cannot penalize them financially for ordering a large amount of health care services for very sick patients. These plans are market driven in that there are no federal limitations on the premium that can be charged by the Plan.

All M+C plans must provide the same range of benefits that fee-for-service Medicare beneficiaries receive, although the plan can require them to receive all their care within the network.

M+C Pros and Cons

Although the HCFA is doing a great deal to publicize the M+C program and inform Medicare beneficiaries of their options, it is understandable that many older people find the multiplicity of programs confusing. They may well turn to a planner for advice about what to do.

- If a client can comfortably afford Medigap insurance, and has a trusted group of doctors (especially if they accept assignment), he should probably stay within the conventional Medicare system.
- However, if purchasing Medigap insurance is a financial strain, or a client does not have attending physicians (or is not particularly satisfied with the doctors he has consulted), M+C may be the better choice, because managed care obviates the need for Medigap coverage.
- A person considering M+C should find out which doctors will participate in which managed care plans.
- Some managed care plans offer additional benefits (e.g., prescription coverage) as incentives for signing up, so if two plans are of equal quality, it could make sense to choose the one that offers incentives.
- Clients should be aware that it is harder to "disenroll" from M+C (i.e., to switch to another plan or go back to conventional fee-for-service Medicare) than it was to disenroll from a Medicare HMO, so choices should be made only after serious deliberation.

- As happened in late 1998, insurers may withdraw from the managed care marketplace if they are dissatisfied with reimbursement rates or administrative procedures, so make sure your clients know what to do (e.g., resume Medigap coverage) if they lose coverage due to withdrawal from the M+C system.

PRACTICE TIP: Check out the "Medicare Compare" database at www.medicare.gov for ongoing quality comparisons of M+C plans.

THE PRIVATE-PAY OPTION

The Balanced Budget Act of 1997 (BBA '97) clarified the status of private contracts between doctors and their senior citizen patients. Before BBA '97, it was uncertain whether it was legal for doctors to go outside the Medicare system and arrange to treat over-65 persons on a fee-for-service basis without reference to Medicare reimbursement provisions (including Medicare fee schedules), and with no necessity to complete the cumbersome Medicare paperwork.

Under the new law, a doctor may opt out of the Medicare system entirely, and charge patients whatever amount the doctor sees fit. However, Medicare will not make any reimbursement at all to opted-out physicians. Medigap insurers have no obligation to cover any part of the bills of such physicians. The patient must pay purely out of pocket (or use acute health insurance). Furthermore, the exit from Medicare must be complete. It is not permissible to treat Mr. Bigbucks as a private-pay patient and Mrs. Everyday as a Medicare patient.

A doctor who chooses to opt out of Medicare may not return to the Medicare system for two years. Legislation has been introduced in Congress to increase the amount of flexibility available to doctors, by allowing them to opt back in without having to wait for two years.

SUMMARY

Although it does not cover the kind of custodial care that is necessary for many senior citizens, Medicare does play a vital role in covering the acute health needs of the elderly and disabled. Older people should always be aware of the Medicare benefits available to them (especially the less known skilled nursing facility, home health, and hospice benefits), and should use their hearing and appeal rights to challenge rejection of meritorious benefit claims.

The Medicare+Choice system has the potential to shift a large proportion of beneficiaries into managed care plans, if enough plans are created, and if enough older people opt to get their care in this manner. Meanwhile, clients should only sign up with a managed care plan if it offers an adequate number of skillful, compassionate doctors in the right specialties and sub-specialties, if its gatekeeper policies are not unduly restrictive, and if there are assurances that the plan will remain in the managed care marketplace and not terminate its HCFA contract.

CHAPTER FOOTNOTES

1. In early 1999, the Clinton Administration proposed that Medicare begin to cover prescription drugs because the federal budget was operating at a surplus. Robert Pear, "Clinton's Plan to Have Medicare Cover Drugs Means a Big Debate Ahead in Congress," *New York Times*, January 24, 1999, p. A24, In contrast, a bipartisan commission making recommendations about the future soundness of the Medicare system called for sliding-scale premiums for Medicare beneficiaries, with those who had higher incomes paying higher premiums for the coverage. Robert Pear, "Income-Based Medicare Proposal is Offered," *New York Times*, January 23, 1999, p. A16.

2. These statistics are from the HCFA's website at www.hcfa.gov/stats/hstats96/stathili.htm.

3. If the issue is entitlement to Medicare benefits in general, rather than the amount of the benefit, the appeals process goes straight to the Social Security Administration. 20 CFR §404.900 et.seq.

4. 42 USC §1395mm and 42 CFR Part 417 have rules affecting "traditional" Medicare managed care plans (if anything that came into existence in 1982 can be called traditional).

5. The POS rules appear at 42 CFR §422.105.

6. A standard M+C contract with HCFA is part of HCFA's Website, www.hcfa.gov/medicare/2000cont.pdf.

7. For these and other criticisms, see Mary Jane Fisher, "HIAA Airs Concerns on Medicare+Choice," *National Underwriter*, Life and Health/Financial Services Edition, October 5, 1998, p. 42.

Chapter 6

MEDICAID PLANNING

Senior citizens and their families often find themselves between a rock and a hard place if they suffer a catastrophic medical event (such as a stroke or hip fracture) or a gradual decline in physical and mental capacity. The rock is the high cost of custodial care ($40,000 a year is a typical nation-wide average figure; $150,000 a year is possible in an area where real estate prices and health care costs are especially high). The hard place is Medicare's exclusion of custodial care. A small but growing number of senior citizens have provided for these risks by buying long-term care insurance (see Chapter 4), but coverage will certainly be unavailable once an older person's health has deteriorated.

The Medicaid program, however, does cover custodial nursing home services. States are required to provide some Medicaid home care, although in most states the amount and level of care will not be adequate to meet the needs of a seriously impaired person.

Medicaid rules are complex, confusing, and change frequently. Furthermore, there are really several overlapping sets of rules. There are rules that determine how states have to set up their Medicaid programs, rules that govern the eligibility of people who apply for Medicaid, and rules that govern financial transactions of Medicaid recipients and their spouses after the applicant has become eligible for Medicaid.

When a person applies for Medicaid, all of that person's financial transactions for three years before the application are scrutinized. Scrutiny goes back five years with respect to certain trusts (Medicaid planning with trusts is discussed later in this chapter). Furthermore, if the applicant is married, all of the spouse's financial transactions are also scrutinized under the same standards. It does not matter that there were sound reasons for the transactions such as re-balancing the portfolio, profit-taking on appreciated securities, saving income taxes, planning the estate, or helping a family member in financial distress. It does not even matter that the person did not know anything about Medicaid or had no intention of making a Medicaid plan until catastrophe struck.

It follows, therefore, that potential earnings from a transaction, or possible tax savings or beneficial estate tax consequences, must be balanced against potential loss of future Medicaid benefits. What makes this decision process so difficult is that current financial and tax consequences can be determined absolutely, but it is impossible to tell if a client will ever need nursing home care or extensive home care. If such care is needed it will not be known when this care will be needed, what the client's financial situation will be at that time, and what rules the Medicaid program will follow.

One important caution is that eligibility for benefits depends on following the Medicaid rules, not rules for other legal systems. The fact that something is tax-deductible, or has been removed from the potentially taxable estate, does not apply for Medicaid purposes. There is no Medicaid charitable deduction or annual exclusion, for instance, and although there is a kind of marital deduction, it does not work in the same way as it does for estate tax. Similarly, the fact that a transaction is permitted by Medicaid rules does not exempt it from income taxation or negative estate tax consequences. There is no substitute for careful planning based on all the alternatives, by considering what will be the income tax consequences of a proposed transaction, how it will affect a possible future Medicaid application, and how it will affect the administration and taxation of the estate.

To make sense of the tangled thicket of Medicaid rules,[1] it helps to divide the rules into four major categories:

- Treatment of income;
- Treatment of assets;
- Rules about transfers; and
- Protection for the community spouse.

THE MEDICAID GAMBLE

Most clients do not even think about Medicaid until they are in an emergency situation. Long-term care is needed and there is little or no insurance available. Medicare benefits are used up or close to exhaustion, and the cost of care is much more than can be afforded out of current income. Paying for the care out-of-pocket therefore requires digging into assets, and perhaps depleting them and leaving the spouse short of money or even destitute. The Medicaid system includes some built-in protection for healthy spouses, and does not require the sale of a homestead as long as a spouse or minor, blind or disabled children continue to live there. These protections are not available in the private-pay system.

However, as you will see in the balance of this chapter, Medicaid eligibility can be delayed or precluded by either spouse's transactions that occurred over a period of three or five years before the application. People who wait until the last minute often discover that they are Medicaid-ineligible because of harmless, or even intelligent, activities undertaken to increase investment returns, save taxes, or plan the estate. That is, they need care right away but their penalty period (see below) lasts for many years, or even past their predictable life expectancy.

Does that mean that the problem can be solved by engaging in Medicaid planning well before long-term care is needed? Well, yes and no. Yes, because transactions can be tailored to safeguard eligibility under current rules. But a Medicaid plan may turn out to be a bad choice for a person who does not require long-term care, such as someone who dies in an accident, suffers a catastrophic heart attack or stroke, or dies after a serious illness that is acute enough to be covered by Medicare and Medigap insurance. It is impossible to predict what Medicaid law will look like in five years. We have seen some recent, dramatic changes in estate tax law, and estate taxation is a subject that generally moves at the stately, slow pace of a glacier. Medicaid law is notoriously unstable.

Furthermore, tax and estate planning and Medicaid planning do not work well together. The interests of the Medicaid plan may require sales, transfers of assets, or creation of trusts at times or in ways that raise rather than lower the tax bill. Sound estate-planning moves (such as adding ascertainable standards powers to trusts) can have bad Medicaid consequences. We know for a fact that all our clients will die eventually (although we do not know how large the unified credit exemption will be at that time), so some kind of estate plan is mandatory. We do not know if our clients will ever apply for Medicaid, when they might apply, or what the rules will be at the time of application.

It is easy to be short-sighted, and make a plan that covers only one spouse's needs. In the short run, it may make sense for the sicker spouse to make large transfers to the healthier spouse, and for the healthier spouse then to make further transfers of those amounts. But if the comparatively healthy spouse falls ill or is injured during the three to five years after the re-transfer, he may lose or suffer a delay in Medicaid eligibility because of those re-transfers.

The tax consequences to the recipient are different depending on whether a lifetime gift or an inheritance is received. The parent's Medicaid plan may call for transferring excess assets to a child or other person who would actually prefer, and have a better tax outcome, from an inheritance.

If you add in the ethical quandaries, you can see why many people (not all of them inside the insurance industry) consider long-term care insurance a superior alternative to Medicaid planning, or want to integrate private insurance and Medicaid planning.

ETHICAL AND PRACTICAL ISSUES

There is no question that Medicaid was designed, and has always been operated, as a program for the indigent (that is, persons with very limited assets). At first blush, that is not the description of the average financial planning client. The baseline ethical issue, then, is whether it is morally appropriate to undertake steps that are permitted by law, but that take advantage of loopholes within the law. The lawyers who do Medicaid planning take the position that it is no different from tax planning or estate planning, which often require some very elaborate measures that would never be undertaken without a tax motivation.

However, other people find this exploitation of loopholes morally questionable, or simply a bad gamble. Those who take this position point out that the Medicaid program is very expensive, and places a heavy burden on the federal and state budgets, and thus it is very likely that Medicaid eligibility or services will undergo further restrictions. Today's elaborate planning steps could generate a big tax bill, without ever making Medicaid benefits available. Furthermore, the Medicaid system limits its recipients' freedom of choice.

Instead of being able to enter what is believed to be the best nursing home that has an available bed, the Medicaid recipient must accept the first available placement in a nursing home that has a Medicaid contract, even if the nursing home has quality problems, or is inconvenient for family visits. The simple solution to this problem is to retain enough funds to enter the preferred nursing home as a private-pay patient, then make a Medicaid application after those funds are exhausted. However, this will not work if the preferred nursing home does not participate in Medicaid.

MEDICAID HISTORY

Medicaid, like Medicare, was part of President Lyndon Johnson's Great Society program of social innovations. The two programs were supposed to take care of the medical needs of two groups of people who could not be accommodated by conventional health insurance: senior citizens (for Medicare) and the "indigent" (for Medicaid).

Medicare is a completely federal program. The federal government funds the program, using Medicare taxes paid as part of the Social Security tax on wages, as well as Part B premiums (and Part A premiums paid by a small group of people who would otherwise be ineligible for Medicare). Although the Medicare rules laid out in Chapter 5 may seem complex, at least there is only one set of rules for the whole country.

Medicaid works differently. The federal and the state governments collaborate. Medicaid programs are run by the states, and the individual states can customize their Medicaid programs (and set many of their own rules). The federal government subsidizes Medicaid by providing a Federal Medicaid Assistance Percentage (FMAP) to the states.

The poorer the state, the higher the level of FMAP. FMAP levels range from 50 to 75 percent of the cost of Medicaid. The state itself makes up the difference between the FMAP level and the actual cost of the program. In order to qualify for FMAP, state Medicaid programs must satisfy minimum standards set by the federal government. At the other end of the scale, certain programs are too generous for federal standards, and do not qualify for FMAP. If the state wants to provide such programs and services, it must pay 100 percent of the cost. The result is that each state has its own Medicaid rules and its own mix of Medicaid services.

Federal law provides for "waivers": situations in which a state obtains federal permission to create programs that receive FMAP even though they fail to satisfy the basic federal requirements. Waiver programs are especially important for provision of Medicaid home care.

The Medicaid program is Title XIX of the federal Social Security Act. Medicaid law is found at Title 42, United States Code Section 1396 *et seq.* Complete understanding of Medicaid also requires understanding of a state's policies. Unfortunately, in many states, important Medicaid rules are not enacted in the state's code of laws, where anyone can read them. Important issues are often settled by hard-to-find state and local regulations and internal rules of the Medicaid agency.

Although it is not an official regulation, and therefore neither the HCFA nor state Medicaid agencies are obligated to follow it, the HCFA's State Medicaid Manual (SMM) is an excellent, clearly-expressed resource for understanding Medicaid rules and their practical application. You may be able to obtain a printed copy from your local Medicaid office or from an elder law attorney with whom you work. The SMM can also be downloaded from Web sites such as the Kansas Elder Law Network or the HCFA's website.

MEDICAID VOCABULARY

A married person who needs long-term care is usually referred to as the "sick spouse" or "Medicaid spouse." Some Medicaid provisions affect both people who have already qualified for Medicaid and those who have applied (or might apply in the future), so the term "Medicaid A/R" (standing for "applicant or recipient") is often encountered. The date of institutionalization is the date on which the sick spouse enters a nursing home or begins to receive a comparable level of Medicaid home care.

One of the most important choices that state Medicaid programs can make is whether the state will be a "medically needy" state or a "cap" state. In a "medically needy" state, Medicaid services can be provided to a person who is "medically needy": whose assets are within the state eligibility limits, and who agrees to "spend down." "Spend down" means to pay all excess income to the nursing home or other long-term care provider, before Medicaid payments to the provider begin.

In a "cap" state, however, most Medicaid services (including nursing home care) will be denied to a person whose income exceeds the "income cap," even if that person has no assets and cannot afford to pay privately for nursing home care. A state's income cap may not exceed three times the benefit that the individual would receive if he were poor enough to receive Supplemental Security Income (SSI) benefits, which is a federal Welfare program for the aged, blind, and disabled. For 1998, the maximum income cap was $1,482 a month; the 1999 maximum income cap is $1,500.

Medicaid planning is very difficult in cap states, because for many people, their Social Security benefit plus their private pension will exceed the cap, and there is no way to anticipate these amounts or transfer them to someone else. Therefore, in a cap state, it is often advisable for people who have access to lump-sum pension payments to elect the lump sum (which can be transferred or placed into a trust) instead of a continuing stream of pension payments. Another possibility is to put the extra income into a trust. In some states or some circumstances, a court must approve the creation of the trust, and supervise trust administration.

Income Issues

The Medicaid definition of "income" generally includes anything, such as Social Security benefits or pension payments, that is paid on a one-time or continuing basis. "Assets" are financial assets such as bank accounts, securities, and real estate other than the homestead. Medicaid law has been revised to make it clear that barriers between income and assets are not absolute. For example, if income is received in a particular month, anything that is not spent in that month becomes an asset. Also, many kinds of income received by senior citizens cannot be "anticipated," meaning that it is not permitted to assign rights to future Social Security or pension benefits. For income that can be anticipated, transfers of income follow the same rules as transfers of assets (see below).

Protecting the Spouse at Home

Assets can be "available" for Medicaid purposes even if they are entitled to protection in other contexts. A New Jersey decision (*Mistrick v. Division of Medical Assistance & Health Servs.*, 712 A.2d 188 (N.J. 1998)) holds that one spouse's IRA is available to the other spouse for Medicaid purposes, even though IRA accounts have favorable tax treatment and are protected against the claims of creditors. A few months later, Ohio made a similar decision in *Martin v. Ohio Dep't of Human Servs.*, 1998 Ohio App. Lexis 5475 (Ohio Ct. App. Nov. 20, 1998).[2]

The Medicaid system makes provisions for the needs of the "community spouse" (also called the "healthy" or "well" spouse). The community spouse is the spouse of an institutionalized Medicaid recipient. Without these provisions, the financial condition of the community spouse would often be desperate, because of the need to pay the mortgage or rent and meet other personal financial needs, while the couple's entire financial resources were devoted to the care of the sick spouse. Because over three-quarters of nursing home residents are not married, these provisions are not available to many needy nursing home residents.

To protect the community spouse, the community spouse is allowed to have an amount of assets that will not cause the sick spouse to be ineligible for Medicaid. This amount is known as the Community Spouse Resource Allowance (CSRA). When the obligation of the sick spouse to "spend down" is computed, there is allowed a monthly payment to the community spouse, which reduces the amount that must be spent down. This monthly payment is referred to as the Community Spouse Income Allowance (CSIA).

States are allowed to set their own CSIA and CSRA levels, as long as they stay within federal guidelines. For 1999, the CSIA must be at least $1,357 a month, and may not be higher than $2,049 a month. Although there are some technical differences, the CSIA is similar to the concept of the "minimum monthly maintenance needs allowance" (MMMNA) for the community spouse. The MMMNA has two components: basic needs and housing needs.

The CSRA can be anywhere from $16,392 to $81,960, and states may use many different techniques for calculating the CSRA. Federal law provides that a state must allow at least the minimum CSRA, and may allow up to the maximum. Or, it can let the healthy spouse get either the "snapshot" spousal amount (see below) or the maximum, whichever is less. In addition to the generally applicable CSRA, if the healthy spouse can convince a Medicaid hearing officer to allow a larger amount, or can obtain a court order for a larger amount, that must be permitted as the CSRA.

Some of the states simply look at the personal assets of the community spouse, and if his assets are below this level, a transfer can be made. A more complex methodology compares half of the couple's joint resources to the CSRA level, and also compares the healthy spouse's personal assets. The community spouse can retain half of the combined assets, but can retain the minimum CSRA (even if it is more than half), but cannot retain more than the maximum (even if it is less than half).

See below for a more detailed discussion of "post-eligibility" financial issues.

Assets and the "Snapshot"

A Medicaid application triggers a one-time calculation of the "snapshot" amount. The applicant discloses all assets he owns (and his spouse owns, if the applicant is married). The assets are aggregated, and half the assets are considered to belong to each spouse. The spouses are entitled to require that an assessment be done as soon as one spouse enters a nursing home, even if the Medicaid application will not be made immediately. Having the assessment done in advance speeds up the application if and when it is made.

The snapshot is not very significant if the person enters the nursing home as a Medicaid recipient, or applies immediately after entry. Nor is it significant in states (such as New York and Pennsylvania) which have adopted the maximum CSRA. But it can make a big difference if the person enters the nursing home as a private-pay patient and does not apply for Medicaid until later, at a time when marital assets have declined significantly (probably as a result of paying privately for care.)

The State Medicaid Manual's (SMM) section 3262.2 adds the concept of the "spousal share" to the determination. The spousal share is half of the couple's combined non-exempt resources at the time the sick spouse enters a nursing home. The spousal share does not change, even if the actual amount of marital assets changes.

When the actual Medicaid application is made, the community spouse is entitled to the "protected amount," which is the highest of these four figures:

- The spousal share, but not more than the maximum CSRA (1999 figure: $81,960);
- The CSRA level actually adopted by the state;
- The enhanced CSRA allowed by a court support order (see below); or
- The enhanced CSRA permitted after a Medicaid fair hearing.

The sick spouse is eligible for Medicaid if his resources, after the community spouse receives the protected amount, are below the state's Medicaid resource level (usually set at $1,000 to $2,000).

The SMM gives the example of a couple whose non-exempt resources at the time the sick spouse enters the nursing home are $120,000. That makes the spousal share $60,000 (half the resources). The application for Medicaid does not occur until their resources have been reduced to $90,000.

Assume that the couple does not have a court order or fair hearing to enhance the CSRA. Also assume that the state has adopted a CSRA of $35,000. The state's Medicaid resource level is $2,000. From the $90,000 in combined resources, $60,000 is subtracted (the larger of the spousal share ($60,000) or the states CSRA ($35,000)). This remaining $30,000 is the amount used to determine the institutionalized spouse's eligibility. The sick spouse is not yet eligible for Medicaid because the remaining resources exceed $2,000. But as soon as the couple's combined resources fall below $62,000 (the spousal share plus the $2,000 limit), the sick spouse will become eligible.

What if the couple had started out with more resources? The spousal share could never be more than the maximum CSRA. If they had started out with less, then in all probability, all of the assets would be able to go to the community spouse. The SMM gives another example of a couple with combined resources of $20,000 when the sick spouse entered the nursing home, and resources of $10,000 at the time of the Medicaid application. The spousal share is $10,000 (half the resources upon entry into the nursing home). The community spouse would be entitled to the state's CSRA level of $30,000. The sick spouse would be entitled to retain the state's Medicaid resource level (the example assumes that it is $3,000). If his personal resources are $8,000 out of the couple's $10,000, he is immediately eligible and can transfer $5,000 of the $8,000 to the community spouse. Because the spousal share is lower than the CSRA, the CSRA rather than the spousal share is used in the calculation.

SPOUSAL REFUSAL

Theoretically, husbands and wives have an equal duty to support one another. In many instances, the spouse with more income and assets gets sick and enters a nursing home first. The CSRA and CSIA recognize this duty of support. However, it is perfectly possible that the sick spouse will have very limited personal income and resources. What is the obligation of the healthy, more affluent, community spouse?

Perhaps surprisingly, federal Medicaid law contains a "just say no" provision. That is, state Medicaid agencies are not allowed to deny

Medicaid benefits to patients on the grounds that their wealthier spouses refuse to support them or let any of their own income or resources be used. However, part of the Medicaid application process is an agreement to assign support rights to the Medicaid agency. The Medicaid agency then has a legal right to sue the community spouse for non-support. Whether this is a meaningful threat to individual community spouses depends on the local policy. Some Medicaid agencies are very active in this matter, but most bring few or no non-support suits.

Community spouses who want to preserve their own financial position, but who do not want to engage in outright "spousal refusal" can enter into an agreement with the state Medicaid agency. Usually, offering 25 percent of the difference between the community spouse's actual income and the MMMNA will be acceptable. For instance, a person with $3,000 a month income as compared to a $2,000 MMMNA will probably not be sued if he offers, and actually pays, $250 a month to the Medicaid agency for the care of the sick spouse.

PRACTICE TIP: Medicaid benefits can be denied to the spouse of a healthy person who refuses to provide information about his financial situation, so make sure that potential community spouses provide disclosure, even if they want to make a spousal refusal.

TRANSFER PENALTIES

The planner must never forget that Medicaid is a program for the indigent, so the level of non-exempt assets is crucial in determining eligibility. If it were possible simply to give away the excess assets, then everybody could qualify for Medicaid. To protect the financial stability of the system, Medicaid law imposes transfer penalties on people who give away assets and then apply for Medicaid nursing home care, or Medicaid home care provided under a waiver program.[3]

A transfer is either an outright gift, or selling an asset for less than its fair market value (in this instance, only the uncompensated part of the transaction is a transfer). The transfer-of-asset rules are found in 42 USC section 1396p(c). Before 1993, the transfer rules applied only to transfers of resources, but since then, transfers of income have also been subject to penalties.

Transfers that are exempt (they do not affect Medicaid eligibility) include the following:

- A transfer by one spouse to the other spouse;
- A transfer by one spouse to someone else, for the sole benefit of the other spouse;
- A transfer to the Medicaid applicant's blind or disabled child, or to a trust that benefits only blind or disabled children of the transferor;
- A transfer to a trust whose sole beneficiaries are one or more disabled persons under age 65;
- A transfer that was made only for a purpose other than qualifying for Medicaid;[4]
- A transfer by someone who intended to dispose of the assets at their fair market value;
- A transfer that is reversed, in that the property is given back to the transferor (even though there is no transfer penalty, the person may become ineligible because of possessing the additional property); and
- A hardship case, where denying Medicaid would be life-threatening (applicants who claim hardship must be given an administrative hearing to prove their case).

The exempt transfers of homesteads is discussed below.

Some transfers are so remote in time from the Medicaid application that they will not be taken into consideration. The "look-back" period is the amount of time during which a Medicaid agency can scrutinize financial transactions. The general look-back period is 36 months. That is, when a person applies for Medicaid, he must disclose information about all financial transactions, including gifts and charitable contributions, that occurred in the 36 months before the application. The look-back period is 60 months for certain transactions involving irrevocable trusts. Of course, the applicant may find this loss of privacy infuriating or humiliating, but it is part of the "cost of doing business" with the Medicaid system.

Apart from emotional factors, many older people lack the detailed financial records that the Medicaid application requires. This is especially true of people with poor eyesight, or some degree of mental confusion. In such cases, the planning team may have to hire a "daily money manager," accountant, or even a private investigator to straighten out the transaction history and present it in an acceptable form.

Once Medicaid eligibility is established, it runs three months retroactively. Therefore, if the applicant can prove that he paid out-of-pocket for health costs, or that a family member or friend paid these expenses, then the Medicaid agency has an obligation to reimburse the applicant. If the applicant reimburses someone who advanced funds for health expenses, this constitutes repayment of a loan, not a transfer. However, there must be contemporary (not after-the-fact) financial records to substantiate the reimbursement argument.

The Penalty Period

If non-exempt transfers did occur during the look-back period, Medicaid law requires the imposition of a "penalty period:" a number of months during which Medicaid services will be denied. The calculation involves dividing the non-exempt transfers made during the look-back period by an official figure used to represent the cost of private-pay nursing home care in the relevant geographic area of the state.

EXAMPLE: Gail Lespinasse made two transfers: a gift of $25,000 to her daughter, made 40 months before her Medicaid application, and a gift of $50,000 to her son, made 20 months before her Medicaid application. Because these are outright gifts, the look-back period is 36 months (not 60 months). The gift to her daughter occurred outside the look-back period, so it does not count. The gift to her son occurred during the look-back period, so it does count. If the official cost-of-care figure is $5,000 a month, then Mrs. Lespinasse's penalty period is 10 months. If there were no other factors involved, Mrs. Lespinasse would be eligible for Medicaid as soon as she applied, because her penalty period began 20 months ago (when the transfer was made) and ended 10 months later.

Until 1993, there was a maximum penalty period of 36 months. No matter how large the transfer, the penalty period would never be longer than 36 months. (It is just a coincidence that this is the same as the look-back period.) So anyone who had three years of long-term care insurance coverage could be certain of qualifying for Medicaid once the coverage was used up. However, a 1993 federal law removed the maximum, so that the theoretical penalty period might very well be 10 or even 20 years, if the transfer is large enough.

The penalty period is "theoretical," because a person who is able to make very large transfers has the option of transferring less, but retaining enough funds to delay the Medicaid application for more than 36 months after the last transfer. If a very large transfer was made with no consideration of Medicaid, such as by a healthy person engaging in estate planning, it is possible for some of the transferred assets to be returned, thus reversing the transfer and eliminating that part of the penalty period. These returned assets could then be used to pay privately for care.

The penalty period runs from the date of the transfer, which is simple enough to apply if there is only one transfer. If there is only one transfer, but it is less than one month's official cost of care, the state can choose between imposing a penalty for part of a month, or not imposing a penalty at all. If the penalty is not an even number of months, most states round down. A transfer of $40,000 and an official amount of $3,000 a month will generally give rise to a 13-month penalty (13⅓, rounded down).

If there are several transfers, the penalty periods must run consecutively. In the past, some states allowed "stacking" of transfers, so that the penalty for one transfer would expire in March, and the penalty for a second, smaller transfer would expire in February. Congress put a stop to that in 1993. Individuals cannot gain any advantage by splitting up transfers into an overlapping series, and a second penalty period does not begin until the first has been exhausted.

According to the State Medicaid Manual section 3258.5H, if assets are transferred in a way that the penalty periods would overlap, the A/R will be subject to a single penalty period that begins on the first day of the first month of the first transfer. For example, in a state where the official cost of care is $2,500, transfers of $10,000 each in January, February, and March would be treated as a single transfer on January 1, giving rise to a 12-month penalty ($30,000/$2,500). This is so because there would be a four-month penalty period for each individual transfer, so the periods would overlap. If there are multiple transfers but the penalty periods would not overlap, then each penalty period starts and ends, then the next one starts and ends. If the official cost-of-care figure is $4,000, and transfers of $8,000 each are made in January, August, and November, there will be three separate penalty periods: January and February (because of the two-month penalty generated by transferring $8,000 in January), August and September, and November and December.

Because a transfer by one spouse will affect the other spouse's eligibility, and if a penalty is assessed against the first spouse to enter a nursing home, the penalty period is divided between the spouses if the one-time community spouse makes a Medicaid application (i.e., the same transfer does not create two separate penalty periods). And if the same person receives both institutional and non-institutional Medicaid services, the penalty period will be apportioned between the two.

TREATMENT OF THE HOMESTEAD

Our legal system often makes special provisions for the family homestead (e.g., bankruptcy and debtor-creditor rules). Medicaid follows suit. The value of one principal residence is not included in determining the asset level for eligibility purposes no matter how large the home is, how large the grounds around it, how much it is worth, or even how recently it was purchased before the Medicaid application.

Therefore, a basic Medicaid planning technique for individuals who have excess assets, but who are not homeowners, is to use the excess assets to buy a home that can become a homestead. Homeowners can use excess assets to fix up the homestead, either in conventional ways to enhance its resale value, or in specific elder-friendly terms, such as adding a stair lift, making it wheelchair-accessible, or creating a separate apartment for a live-in caregiver. Because there is no limit on the value of the homestead, these changes will not impair eligibility.

Medicaid planning also affects planning for senior housing. Many seniors plan to sell their large, unwieldy, hard-to-heat homes and move to a more compact unit, whether or not that unit is specifically designed as senior housing. "Snowbirds" may flee areas with long, tough winters to find a warmer retirement environment. The home sale strategy is especially attractive now that a married couple may exclude up to $500,000 of certain home-sale gains from income taxation (see Chapter 7). However, from the Medicaid perspective, the outcome is that an exempt homestead (which does not affect eligibility) has been turned into non-exempt cash (which definitely does affect eligibility). This does not mean that senior citizens should avoid selling homes that may be inconvenient or even unsafe. All it means is that Medicaid consequences should be considered in making the decision.

The family home remains exempt for Medicaid eligibility purposes as long as it is a "homestead," meaning as long as the Medicaid beneficiary lives there and receives home care. It also remains exempt after the Medicaid beneficiary enters a nursing home, as long as a community spouse or a minor, blind, or disabled child continues to live there. But note that if the Medicaid beneficiary is a single, childless person (or has adult children who live elsewhere) and is permanently confined to an institution,[5] the home is no longer a homestead, and its value will be treated as an excess asset. Therefore, the single nursing home resident may have to sell the home and go off Medicaid until the excess amount has been spent down. Another possibility is to do a "half a loaf" plan (see below) and transfer some of the excess value and spend down the rest.

Homestead Transfers

Medicaid law contains some special, permissive provisions for transfers of homesteads. At this point, you may be shaking your head in disbelief. If the homestead is favored for Medicaid purposes, why transfer it? Because, unless it is transferred, the state Medicaid agency may be entitled to place a claim against the estate after the recipient dies (see below).

Certain transfers of the homestead to close family members can be made without penalty. No matter how large the value of the transfer, it does not give rise to a penalty period. The permitted transferees are:

- A spouse;
- A minor, blind, or disabled child;
- One or more siblings who already have partial ownership of the home, and who lived there for at least a year before the transferor entered the institution (this provision copes with the common situation of parents leaving the family home to a group of siblings); or
- A "caregiver child;" a son or daughter who, for a period of at least two years provided hands-on care to a parent that was able to delay the need for nursing home institutionalization. Caregiver child status is not available to a child who lives elsewhere, even if he provides significant financial support. See 42 USC section 1396p(c)(2)(A) for details.

Reverse Mortgages

In an ordinary mortgage, the lender advances a lump sum for purchase of the home and the homeowner then repays the lender in a series of monthly payments. The mortgage usually requires immediate repayment of the balance if the home is sold, unless the purchaser wants to and is allowed to assume the mortgage. However, the majority of senior citizens own homes that are fully or nearly mortgage-free.

A reverse mortgage, like a home equity loan, is a means of achieving liquidity in the home equity without selling the home. The lender agrees either to provide a lump sum or to make a stream of continuing payments (this is known as a reverse annuity mortgage, or RAM) to the homeowner. The lender is entitled to repayment at a stated rate of interest, but repayment is not required as long as the mortgagor or mortgagor's spouse continues to live there. Once the spouses are both deceased, in nursing homes, or moved out of the house, repayment is required. Some reverse mortgages also give the lender a share in the appreciation in value of the home.

The Medicaid planning significance of reverse mortgages is that federal rules consider the mortgage to be a transaction for value in which the Medicaid beneficiary assumes a debt obligation. Therefore, there is no transfer and no transfer penalty, and the money paid by the mortgagee-lender to the mortgagor-homeowner does not constitute income for Medicaid purposes.

The downside is that, sooner or later, the mortgage must be repaid, and this is usually done by selling the home and turning the proceeds over to the lender. So if the family intends for children to inherit and live in the house, or for them to receive the entire sale proceeds (not just whatever is left after the reverse mortgage is paid off), the reverse mortgage will conflict with this plan. But if there are no children to inherit or the children have homes of their own or have no intention of living in the area, or if it seems likely that a Medicaid application will be made in the near future (so transfers would create an unwieldy penalty period), the reverse mortgage can be a worthwhile device.

ESTATE RECOVERIES

Before 1993, Medicaid planning fit in well with conventional planning, because most transfers were made to spouses or family members, who would normally be the beneficiaries of the estate plan. Furthermore, if assets could be made unavailable (for instance, by placing them into trusts), in many cases they could be transmitted free of claims from the state Medicaid agency, because at that time, the only asset that could be claimed after the Medicaid recipient's death was an interest in the homestead.

When a Medicaid recipient dies, the state Medicaid agency is still entitled to place a claim against his or her homestead. However, if the recipient's surviving spouse or minor, blind, or disabled child lives in the homestead, the enforcement of the claim must be delayed until they die or move away. (This is similar, but not identical, to the list of people to whom the home can be transferred without penalty.) This provision protects vulnerable people who want to remain in their homes. But if they decide to sell the home, an estate recovery claim can be placed on the sales proceeds.

The estate recovery claim against a homestead is theoretically the amount that the Medicaid agency spent to provide nursing home care to the recipient, but it is limited by the deceased recipient's interest in the home.

EXAMPLE: Crystal Davis spent three years in a nursing home. The state Medicaid agency paid $40,000 a year for her care, or a total of $120,000. Before moving to the nursing home, she lived in a home that she inherited from her parents and owned with her sister Evelyn. After Crystal's death, Evelyn sold the home for $200,000. The state Medicaid agency could place a claim of $100,000 against the sale proceeds. Crystal was a one-half owner, so her share of the home (no longer a homestead, because Evelyn was not a spouse or minor, blind, or disabled child) was worth $100,000, which is less than the $120,000 expended on her behalf by the Medicaid agency. If Crystal had transferred the home to Evelyn before moving to the nursing home, the state Medicaid agency would not have been able to recover against Crystal's estate.

Since 1993, the state agency's recovery power has been extended, and now covers all of the deceased recipient's interests in financial assets. Under most circumstances, the Medicaid beneficiary would have transferred all financial assets in order to qualify. However, there may be interests in items like income-only trusts.

Federal Medicaid law defines the "estate" to include the decedent's entire interest in all kinds of assets. However, some state statutes limit the state's recovery power to the probate estate, with the result that jointly owned property and revocable trusts are not subject to estate recovery, because they do not enter the probate estate.

If the state decides to pursue estate recovery, it must wait not only until the Medicaid recipient has died, but, if there is a surviving spouse, until the surviving spouse has died, too. But the state can only assert its claim against the estate of the Medicaid beneficiary, not the estate of a surviving spouse.

States vary greatly in their attitude toward estate recovery. Some states actively pursue all recoveries, and have even out-sourced collection to private companies. Many states, however, seldom or never take steps to recover against estates. But it is very unwise to assume that today's passivity will necessarily continue at the time it might affect a client's family.

The general rule is that estate recovery applies only to the estate of the Medicaid recipient, not the estate of a surviving spouse. However, some recent cases permit states to apply their own statutes, calling for recovery against the estate of the surviving spouse[6] despite arguments from attorneys that these state laws contradict the Social Security Act. The moral? Make sure that you understand the local Medicaid rules.

HALF A LOAF: A BASIC STRATEGY

Although a full understanding of all the complexities of Medicaid is a matter for specialists, there are a few basic tools that any financial planner can understand and use or keep in mind when significant financial steps are undertaken.

Wise homestead planning is critical. Depending on the circumstances, it may make sense to buy or improve a homestead, thus reducing the amount of excess assets. However, if there is a risk of estate recovery, transferring the homestead could be worthwhile, especially if an exempt transfer is possible.

The "half a loaf" theory is based on the old proverb that "half a loaf is better than no bread." As discussed above, making non-exempt transfers gives rise to a theoretical penalty period. The penalty period is only theoretical if the Medicaid application is delayed until after the penalty period has expired. But what if, instead of transferring enough resources to create a 20-month penalty period, a person transfers only enough resources to create a 10-month penalty period, and retains the rest of the assets? True, the person would be ineligible during those 10 months. On the other hand, there would be enough funds to pay privately for nursing home care during the period of ineligibility.

When the funds ran out, so would the penalty period, and he would then be eligible for Medicaid.

EXAMPLE: Hiram Wiswell is a widower. He lives in a state where the officially published cost of care is $4,000 a month. A non-exempt transfer of $50,000 in March, 1999 would create a 12-month period of ineligibility (most states disregard fractional months): $50,000/$4,000 = 12, so he would be ineligible until April 1, 2000. But if he transferred only $25,000 and kept the rest, his period of ineligibility would be only six months, and he would have $25,000 available to pay privately for treatment during that time. It might make sense for him to transfer only $20,000 and keep $30,000 in case the actual cost of private payment was higher than the official figure used in calculating penalty periods.

Medicaid beneficiaries have a duty to collect any funds they are entitled to, even if this has the result of terminating their Medicaid eligibility. See below for a discussion of the exercise of a waiver of the right of election in the estate of the beneficiary's spouse.

As discussed below, there are some complex planning strategies that can be undertaken involving trusts. The basic strategy is to make assets unavailable by placing them into an "income-only" trust, that is, a trust from which the Medicaid beneficiary can never get any distributions of principal, under any circumstances. Under Medicaid rules, that principal is fully insulated from the beneficiary, and therefore does not affect eligibility. However, the look-back period for such a transfer to trust is 60 months, not 36, and the beneficiary's interest in the trust corpus is subject to estate recovery after death.

MEDICAID AND INSURANCE

A small (not over $1,500) burial fund is considered an exempt asset. A life insurance policy with cash value of up to $1,500 is exempt, but a policy with a higher cash value is not exempt. Because of cash-value life insurance, many Medicaid applicants will have significant assets they were not aware of. It stands to reason that buying additional cash-value insurance should be approached with caution if the potential purchaser is likely to make a Medicaid application.

However, term insurance does not have cash value. One strategy that might work in emergency Medicaid planning would be to shed excess non-exempt assets by purchasing term insurance benefiting the spouse. There is no transfer, because the insurance has been purchased for value in an arm's length transaction. Of course, the insurance will probably be quite expensive, if obtainable at all, because of the insured's age and deteriorated health. The advantage of this strategy over simply giving the funds to the community spouse is that, although there is no penalty period on an interspousal transfer, the assets will still be reflected in the snapshot.

MEDICAID PLANNING WITH TRUSTS

Trusts are an important elder planning vehicle, because they create an income stream and relieve the senior citizen of financial planning responsibility for the trust corpus. Trusts can save taxes, and can make it easier to carry out a complex estate plan after the trust grantor's death. Also, revocable trusts can serve as will substitutes. You cannot escape application of Medicaid rules by calling the arrangement something other than a "trust." Any legal arrangement with trust-like consequences will be treated as a trust. If the trust contains assets of several persons, only the part traceable to the Medicaid beneficiary will affect eligibility.

PLANNING TIP: These Medicaid rules apply only to inter vivos trusts. Testamentary trusts under which a Medicaid applicant or recipient is a beneficiary are not covered. See 42 USC section 1396p(d) for trust rules.

Trusts that are already in force will naturally have Medicaid consequences, and individuals making a long-range Medicaid plan may create new trusts as part of the plan. There are several Medicaid questions to be considered in reviewing any trust: how its income will be treated; whether part or all of the trust corpus is an "available" asset for Medicaid purposes; whether creating the trust is a transfer and, if so, how long the penalty period will be; and whether the remaining corpus, at the time of the Medicaid recipient's death, is subject to estate recovery. An important point to remember is that a trust set up by either spouse will affect the eligibility of the other spouse, even if the applicant spouse is not a trust beneficiary or remainderman.

Trust Income

The basic Medicaid rule is that income actually received from a trust, or that the beneficiary has a right to receive but rejects, is available for Medicaid purposes, whether the beneficiary is the grantor of the trust or not. In a medically needy state, the income will increase the spend-down obligation. In a cap state, it may render the person ineligible for Medicaid.

If income could be paid to the beneficiary, but instead is paid to someone else, those funds are considered transfers by the beneficiary to the recipient. However, if the trust is drafted to allow the trustee to invest in unproductive assets, and the trustee does so, thus reducing the income, this will not have negative Medicaid consequences.

This must be contrasted with a "trigger trust," a trust whose terms change (such as to terminate the beneficiary's status) when a beneficiary applies for Medicaid or enters a nursing home. Trigger trusts are considered contrary to public policy, and are void for Medicaid purposes. If the Medicaid recipient is a beneficiary under a testamentary trust created under the will of someone else, the testamentary trust is not considered an improper trigger trust even if it contains provisions that would be invalid in an inter vivos trust created by the recipient.

Availability of Corpus

The next question is availability of the trust corpus. For Medicaid purposes, trust principal is available if the terms of the trust say it is available, as well as to the extent that a person is a trustee or can otherwise determine how the principal will be disposed of.

Revocable trust corpus is always fully available, because the grantor can amend or terminate the trust at any time, or can withdraw funds from it. When it comes to irrevocable trusts, even if there is an independent, neutral trustee, or even a trustee with an adverse interest, any amount of principal that the trustee could remove from the trust for a patient's benefit, using his or her maximum powers of discretion, is available to the patient. This is true even if, in fact, the trustee never does invade the principal. Remember that tax rules do not apply to Medicaid, so the trustee's neutrality or adverse interest is irrelevant.

In many situations, attorneys who are oriented toward estate planning but unfamiliar with Medicaid rules will draft trusts containing a "HEWS" power. A HEWS power (it stands for Health, Education, Welfare, and Support, also called an "ascertainable standards" power) limits invasion of the trust to instances that satisfy an objective, ascertainable standard such as the health or support needs of the trust beneficiary, to prevent trust amounts from being included in the grantor or beneficiary's taxable estate.

Of course, an excellent argument could be made that anyone sick enough to need nursing home care needs invasion of trust principal to pay for the care. Therefore, HEWS powers are a problem in Medicaid planning. It does not mean they should never be used, only that the potential estate tax saving should be balanced against potential loss of Medicaid benefits, bearing in mind that most estates can be free of estate tax for other reasons such as the marital deduction and credit shelter trusts. See Chapter 13.

The HCFA itself has agreed to the acceptability of "income-only" trusts in Medicaid planning. If the patient is entitled to receive income from the trust, but there is no circumstance under which the patient can require the trustee to invade the principal on his behalf, and if the trustee has no discretion to invade corpus on the patient's behalf, then trust income is available, but trust corpus is not.[7]

Transfer Issues

The next Medicaid question is whether there has been a transfer that will give rise to a penalty period. If the trust was created more than 36 months before the Medicaid application (or more than 60 months, for an irrevocable trust from which the patient cannot receive invasions of principal under any circumstances), then the transaction was too remote in time, and will not affect Medicaid eligibility. But if the trust was created or added to during the look-back period, then a transfer occurred to the extent that funds were removed from the patient's control. The transfer is exempt to the extent that it was made to or for the benefit of the patient's spouse, or to or for a minor, blind, or disabled child. Otherwise, a penalty period will be created, calculated as discussed above.

The HCFA's position is that the look-back period for income-only trusts should be 60 months, even though the language of the statute refers to trusts from which the patient cannot receive funds of any kind. (See footnote seven above.) HCFA also uses a 60-month look-back in situations where funds are transferred out of a revocable trust and to someone other than the patient (such as a son or daughter). There is no additional penalty when assets are transferred out of an irrevocable trust that is not available to the patient to a third party, because the penalty period was imposed when the trust was created. However, if a transfer is made to a third party from a revocable trust whose principal could be invaded for the patient's behalf, the look-back period for the transfer is 60 months.

SNTs

In some areas, SNT stands for "special needs trust;" other areas use the phrase "supplemental needs trust." In either case, the meaning is the same: a trust that can be used to provide comforts of life for a person who receives Medicaid or other public benefits, but whose corpus is not available for Medicaid purposes and therefore does not impair eligibility for public benefits. SNTs are a very significant part of the planning process for accident victims (who are critically injured enough to need long-term care), and for the process under which adults plan for the future of their disabled children.

They are much less significant in elder care planning, because it is difficult or impossible to set up an SNT to benefit oneself or one's spouse. One exception is a testamentary trust created under the will of one spouse, to take care of the supplemental needs of the other spouse after the testator's death. Medicaid law does allow one special kind of self-settled SNT (a trust set up for a person's own benefit). This is called a "pooled fund" or a "d(4)" trust; "d(4)" is shorthand for the section of the statute that makes these trusts possible. The full citation is 42 USC section 1396p(d)(4)(C). Details are in the State Medicaid Manual section 3259.7B.

In one type of d(4) trust arrangement, the elderly person contributes to a fund administered by a charitable organization and benefiting a large number of persons. The individual's share of income from the fund can be used to provide the same small comforts that an SNT would provide, but the contribution to the fund is not available for Medicaid purposes. When the person who contributed to the fund dies, first the charity receives an agreed-upon amount for managing the fund. Next, the state Medicaid agency is entitled to estate recovery until it has recovered the full amount it expended for the Medicaid recipient's care. If anything is left over, it becomes part of the decedent's estate and can be distributed according to the estate plan.

MEDICAID PLANNING WITH ANNUITIES

As discussed above, having too many non-exempt assets will prevent Medicaid eligibility. Sometimes transferring the assets to someone else will work, but often (especially in an emergency situation), the transferor will fall afoul of the transfer-of-asset rules and will be ineligible for Medicaid benefits when they are needed. Sometimes, placing the assets into an income-only trust will work. Yet, in many Medicaid plans, it is necessary to find a way to convert assets into income without making a transfer.

The definition of "transfer" depends on a change in ownership that is partially or totally uncompensated. Buying products, services, or financial goods at their fair market value is not a transfer, because there is no uncompensated element. Therefore, some interesting planning techniques involve annuities, either commercial annuities purchased from an insurance company (see Chapter 12) or private annuities (non-commercial arrangements, such as with a family member).[8]

Some annuity transactions do have a transfer element, because the annuity is not "actuarially sound" because it does not represent a reasonable estimate of the annuitant's life expectancy. If, based on tables issued by the HCFA (not the IRS tables used in other annuity contexts), the annuitant's life expectancy is 10 years, a 12 year annuity would represent a transfer of two years worth of payments to the remainderman.

Actuarially sound annuities must satisfy another requirement. The amount that the annuitant would receive under an immediate annuity, over the course of the predicted remaining life expectancy, must be at least as great as the purchase price of the annuity. If there is a shortfall, that represents a transfer to the insurance company or the person providing the private annuity.

One important Medicaid annuity planning technique is for the community spouse to take assets over and above the CSRA and use them to purchase an actuarially sound immediate annuity.[9] That way, the couple's resources will be reduced, there will not have been any transfer, and the income that the healthy spouse receives from the annuity will not be considered available to the sick spouse. However, if the community spouse later needs institutional care, the income from the annuity will have to be spent down (in a medically-needy state), or could block eligibility (in a cap state). Another problem is that the more income the healthy spouse has, the less income the sick spouse can transfer as part of the CSIA, and the more that the local Medicaid agency is likely to demand as an income contribution from the healthy spouse.

Buying an annuity is one of the few Medicaid planning options available to a single person. Once again, excess resources are turned into income, which can be used as long as the individual making the plan can remain in the community. After institutionalization in a medically-needy state, the annuity income will have to be spent down.

If the single person has children or other heirs he wants to benefit, a limited amount of estate planning can be done as part of the Medicaid plan. The individual buys an actuarially sound term-certain annuity, naming the potential heirs as beneficiaries. If he dies before the term ends, the balance goes to the beneficiaries. But, of course, the beneficiaries will not receive anything if the individual lives at least as long as the term certain. If the main objective is transmitting assets to heirs, not enhancing current income, it makes more sense to do a half-a-loaf transfer. The annuity plan works better if estate planning is only a subsidiary objective to extra income.

Private Annuities and SCINs

In most families, the Medicaid applicant will be receptive to the idea of transferring excess assets to a spouse or children, because those are the people he wants to benefit, and the people who would figure in his estate plan. Unfortunately, the Medicaid consequences of a transfer can be negative.

A private annuity can come to the rescue. Instead of giving the surplus funds to the children, the applicant can enter into an arrangement under which the excess funds are exchanged for the child's promise to make regular annuity payments which represent an appropriate actuarial return on the investment, in light of the parent's life expectancy (in the Medicaid context, the Medicaid actuarial tables, not the IRS tables, must be used).

The child must continue making the payments even if the parent outlives the predicted life expectancy. In this case, the child has made a poor financial bargain, but let us hope that he is glad that the parent's lifespan is long. If, on the contrary, the parent dies before the entire investment in the annuity contract is recovered from the annuity payments, Internal Revenue Code (IRC) section 72(b)(3) allows the decedent's final income tax return to include a corresponding loss deduction. In most family private annuity situations, a life annuity will be desirable, because the older person is critically interested in securing income. However, if the individual is unusually healthy, the child may prefer an annuity for a term of years, because this limits the exposure if a life annuity would require payments much in excess of the original consideration paid for the annuity.

An important feature that distinguishes the private annuity from the commercial annuity is that an insurance company insists on being paid in cash for the annuity. Family members may very well be willing to accept property (such as a homestead or other real estate, shares in the family business, or art works) that would otherwise become the subject of transfer or inheritance.[10] In many cases, the private annuity will be purchased with appreciated property. The purchaser will not have to pay capital gains taxes when the annuity is purchased, provided that the annuity is unsecured, meaning that the parent must accept the risk that the child will fail to make the scheduled payments.

A self-canceling installment note (SCIN) or death terminating installment note, is another intrafamily planning device. A SCIN might be preferred to a private annuity by the child, because the tax consequences for the child are better. The parent makes an installment sale of property to the child, receiving back an installment note. Unlike an ordinary commercial transaction, however, the note's terms provide that the obligation to pay the remaining installments will be canceled when the parent dies. The term of the note must be shorter than the parent's life expectancy. Also, the SCIN must provide benefits to the parent, either by paying an above-market interest rate or by paying more than fair market value for the purchased property.

The self-canceling feature means that there is nothing in the parent's estate after death, and therefore there is nothing for Medicaid estate recovery to operate on.

MEDICAID IMPLICATIONS OF JOINT PROPERTY

Older people often have joint bank or brokerage accounts, but these accounts can be classified either as "true" joint accounts or "convenience" accounts. In a true joint account, each joint owner has an equal right to the money in the account and, when one joint owner dies, the other automatically inherits the balance. Such accounts often, but not always, involve spouses or cohabitants, and in many cases both parties have deposited funds into the account.

A convenience account adds the name of a child, friend, or employee to the account, so that a more mobile person can perform banking transactions on the older person's behalf. People sometimes try to dispose of these convenience accounts by will. Whether the will provision can take effect depends on state law, and whether it was made clear that the account was not a true joint account, only one for convenience.

The Medicaid implications of joint accounts begin with the presumption that all the money in the account belongs to the patient and is available to him. But if the other joint tenant deposited funds into the account, the patient is entitled to a hearing to prove this point. Part of the process of getting ready to make a Medicaid application is compiling bank records to prove how funds entered and left the joint account during the look-back period.

The tricky part about joint accounts is that anything that has the effect of reducing the patient's share of the joint account is treated as a transfer made by the patient. That is, if the other joint tenant withdraws money from the account, this is considered a transfer by the patient, even if the patient did not authorize or even know about the withdrawal, and even if it was part of a pattern of financial elder abuse victimizing the patient. See the State Medicaid Manual section 3258.7 for more guidance.

PLANNING IN SPECIAL SITUATIONS

The rules and strategies described above work best for married couples, only one of whom requires Medicaid benefits, living in a "medically needy" state where excess income can always be spent down. This discussion also assumes that the need for Medicaid is caused by age-related illness or frailty. The rules are somewhat different when the care is required because of injuries due to an accident, medical malpractice, or other cause for which someone can be held financially liable. In this situation, it is likely that a tort settlement will be reached. An important part of structuring the settlement is to make sure that the Medicaid agency that has provided benefits in the interim will be repaid. States differ in their approach to how high a priority the repayment takes. Some states are more generous than others in allowing the injured person and family to benefit from the settlement.

A person who has never married, a divorced person, or a widow or widower will not be able to make use of the spousal protection provisions. For them, placing assets into an income-only trust or purchasing an actuarially sound annuity (commercial or private) is likely to be the best route to take.

In the "cap" states, planning advantages can be achieved by using a Miller trust, named after the case of *Miller v. Ibarra*, 746 F. Supp. 19 (D. Colo. 1990), and also referred to as a Qualified Income Trust. See 42 USC sections 1396p(d)(4)(A) and (B), and HCFA Transmittal 64. To make use of such a trust, the Medicaid patient must receive the income, then deposit it into a special trust. Funds from the trust can only be used to pay the patient's personal needs allowance, allowances to the spouse and dependents, medical expenses that are not covered by Medicaid, or (if the state has rules allowing this use), maintenance of the homestead. The terms of the trust must provide specifically that, when the patient dies, the Medicaid agency will have the right to recover from the estate, up to the full amount of benefits paid. Of course, in many cases the estate will be smaller than the benefits, so the agency will not be able to get a full recovery, but there will also be no assets available to be inherited by the decedent's family.

In many families, financial planning revolves around planning for the needs of a disabled child. The child may no longer be able to work, because of physical or mental illness or injury, or the child may never have been able to work because of life-long disability. Until the disabled child reaches the age of majority, his parents have a duty to support him. But once the child reaches majority, financial efforts by parents and grandparents are deemed voluntary.

Attempts to benefit a disabled child should be structured carefully to avoid limiting the individual's access to SSI (Supplemental Security Income) and Medicaid benefits. This can often be done by:

- Making the disabled person just one of a class of potential beneficiaries under a "sprinkle" trust and tailoring the amount actually paid to that person to his needs and public-benefit eligibility;
- By setting up a Supplemental Needs Trust as the limitations on self-settled trusts do not apply if the trust is created by a parent or grandparent who has no duty to support the disabled person; or
- By creating a trust for the benefit of the child that is a "discretionary" trust (one where the trustee has complete discretion to distribute income and principal) rather than a "support" trust which is obligated to satisfy the beneficiary's support needs, even if the result is loss of valuable public benefits.

Once the disabled person dies, the state Medicaid agency is entitled to seek estate recovery, but only for benefits paid after age 55. Part of the estate (or all of it, for a person who died before reaching age 55) will thus be exempt from estate recovery.

In some families, there are two generations of benefit eligibility to think about: an elderly parent and a disabled child. From the parent's perspective, remember that the homestead can be transferred to or for the sole benefit of a minor, blind, or disabled child without penalty.

HOME CARE

Although most of this discussion has revolved around nursing home care, which is the service that people usually think of when they engage in Medicaid planning. However, institutionalization is usually a last resort. Clearly, most impaired elderly people would prefer to remain at home and most caregivers and other family members would prefer that care be available there.

All of the states have at least one "waiver" program for providing home care. See www.hcfa.gov/medicaid/obs7.htm for more discussion of the waiver process and its significance. State Medicaid agencies are allowed to offer home care services without having to conform to all of the federal requirements that would otherwise apply. Most importantly, a waiver program can be made available only to certain Medicaid beneficiaries, such as sufferers from a specific disease, or elderly people who need a nursing home level of care, without being made available to all Medicaid beneficiaries. Waiver programs can also be limited to only part of a state. The financial eligibility rules for waiver programs, including transfer penalties, are the same as for Medicaid nursing home care.

Everyone benefits from waiver programs. Sick people can stay at home instead of being placed in institutions. The Medicaid agency benefits, because it costs less to provide care under a waiver program than to place the patient in a nursing home.

PACE Programs

In the mid-1980s, On Lok Senior Health Services of San Francisco developed a model for providing high-level, intensive home care to the frail elderly. In 1997, Congress authorized the Program of All-Inclusive Care for the Elderly (PACE), a demonstration program that pays providers a capitated rate for delivering home care to people who would otherwise have to be institutionalized. In 1998, there were 12 PACE demonstration programs, with 36 more sites considering joining the program.

PACE is based on an interdisciplinary team that assesses the needs of the frail elderly, develops a care plan for them, then furnishes the necessary services at adult day health centers and home care.

PACE patients who are Medicare-eligible pay a monthly premium with the state Medicaid agency paying for the care of Medicaid-eligible patients. See www.hcfa.gov/medicaid/bbapace.htm for more information.

MEDICAID AND DIVORCE

There are plenty of legitimate criticisms that can be raised against Medicaid as a whole, and against Medicaid planning, but the Medicaid system is sometimes unjustly accused of forcing harmonious senior citizen couples to divorce. In fact, Medicaid rules favor married couples. Medicaid-motivated divorce (as distinct from couples who are genuinely unhappy, or where one partner wants to remarry) is usually a bad idea.

When a couple divorces, either their property is community property, which is equally divided between them, or it is marital property which must be "equitably" divided. There are many factors in equitable distribution, but the needs of the parties are considered more important than who owned the property originally, or who contributed the funds used to purchase it. Therefore, it is possible that a large percentage of the couple's property will be distributed to the sick spouse, with resulting negative consequences for Medicaid planning.

Similarly, divorce courts have the power to order spousal support, depending on the relative needs of the parties. Clearly, a person who needs extensive long-term care is incapable of self-support, so it is possible that the divorce court will order the healthy spouse to provide income to the sick spouse.

What if the person who needs medical care is in a stronger financial position that the healthy spouse? While the Medicaid system provides for protection of the community spouse, an ex-spouse is not a community spouse. Not only can the Medicaid patient not transfer the CSRA or CSIA to the ex-spouse, but many states take the position that court-ordered alimony does not reduce the spend-down obligation. So the divorced person residing in a nursing home would in effect have to spend down all income other than the personal needs allowance (because no CSIA could be transferred), but would still have to make payments under the separation agreement or court-ordered alimony payments.

There are also technical legal problems that can complicate or prevent senior citizens' divorces. If the state allows no-fault divorce, it is not necessary to prove any marital wrongdoing, but it is usually necessary for a period of time to elapse between separation and the grant of a divorce.

If the state does not allow no-fault divorce, or if the waiting period is inconveniently long, the spouse seeking the divorce has to be able to prove some kind of marital fault by the other spouse. It is possible that illness-related behavior will count as "insanity" or "mental cruelty" entitling the healthy spouse to a divorce, but also possible that such matters will be treated as beyond the control of the sick person and therefore not "fault."

Capacity is also a problem. Legal capacity is required to sue or be sued, and a person suffering from Alzheimer's Disease or other dementing illness may lack such capacity. If a guardian has already been appointed, the guardian may be able to handle the divorce case (or a special "guardian ad litem" might be appointed just for the suit). On the other hand, some states have taken the position that divorce litigation is so inherently personal that a guardian cannot take part in it. In those states, a demented person's marriage is effectively permanent, because there's no way to dissolve it by divorce.

GUARDIANS' PLANNING POWERS

There is a high correlation between the need for the kind of lengthy custodial care that Medicaid provides, and mental incapacity. Some people apply for Medicaid because they are physically frail although cognitively intact, but in many cases, the real need for institutionalization comes from loss of mental capacity. If the elderly person has a well-drafted contingency plan that copes with possible loss of capacity as well as Medicaid eligibility, it is likely that the plan can be brought into operation and will be effective. Unfortunately, the vast majority of the elderly do not have such a plan.

As discussed in Chapter 13, the legal system's response to capacity loss is either guardianship or guardianship alternatives. When a guardian is appointed, one of the basic tasks is to figure out what the ward (impaired person) owns, and take steps to collect any amounts owed to the ward. Some courts interpret this to mean that the guardian must be proactive, even if gathering additional resources would impair the ward's Medicaid eligibility. Other courts are more permissive, recognizing that in the long run the ward is better off qualifying for Medicaid than receiving a sum that is less valuable than the health care.

Some courts are very hostile to Medicaid planning in general, and see their role as protecting the public treasury. In these courts, guardians who ask permission to make Medicaid-oriented transfers, create trusts, or do half-a-loaf planning are likely to be turned down.

Other courts, however, conceptualize the guardian as taking the ward's place. Under this theory, the guardian can do anything that the ward would have been able to do personally if he still had capacity, including creating a Medicaid plan. These courts see Medicaid planning as the equivalent of income tax or estate planning, in that a person can undertake any lawful measures, however complex they are, to take advantage of the system's loopholes to save money or obtain other financial benefits.

An intermediate position is also possible, under which the guardian is allowed to carry out the intentions already shown by the ward during capacity (including gifts to charities and family members), but cannot implement new tactics on the ward's behalf. Thus, a sound incapacity plan either includes Medicaid planning as well, or establishes a pattern during capacity that can be followed if and when incapacity occurs.

CONTRACTS FOR SERVICES

Medicaid law explicitly recognizes one kind of payment for care provided by family members: the gift of a homestead to a "caregiver child" (see above). Such a gift is not penalized as a transfer, because in effect the child has assisted the Medicaid system by deferring the parent's need for nursing home care.

Otherwise, the HCFA's position is that it will be presumed that family caregivers perform their services without expecting to get paid. However, the presumption can be rebutted if, at the time the care was provided (but not after the fact), the elderly person and the caregiver entered into a written contract under which reasonable payment would be made for services.[11]

The elder law attorney in the planning team should be able to draw up a simple contract, spelling out what the caregiver will do, the cash or property that the caregiver will receive, and that the compensation is fair based on market rates for similar services, or is based on the financial sacrifice that the caregiver made to provide the services.

Note that the compensation does constitute taxable income to the caregiver. The caregiver may be covered by the "Nanny tax" rules (i.e., the simplified procedure for remitting FICA taxes). Under the Nanny tax rules, the employer of a household employee reports the FICA tax on his own tax return. The employer has a choice to either withhold the employee's share of Social Security tax from the employee's wages, or to assume responsibility for paying the entire FICA tax (15.3% of the household worker's wages). Household employers do not have to withhold federal income tax on household worker's wages, unless the employee asks the employer to withhold, and the employer agrees to do so.

POST-ELIGIBILITY ISSUES

Before 1988, Medicaid had a policy of "deeming," meaning that all of a couple's income and resources were considered available to pay for the sick spouse's nursing home care, with no provision for the needs of the community spouse. Given the high cost of nursing home care, this policy often caused both a sick spouse's Medicaid application to be denied (on the basis of excess funds), and required most, if not all, of a couple's combined funds to be applied to the sick spouse's care needs. In 1988, the Medicare Catastrophic Coverage Act (MCCA) added provisions for safeguarding at least some assets and income for the healthy spouse, so that he can continue to maintain a home and pay his own living expenses.

The Spend-Down Process

Once Medicaid eligibility has been established, and the sick person has been placed in a nursing home or begins to receive Medicaid home care, he has an obligation to "spend down" each month. First the individual's income is calculated.[12] The patient must be allowed to retain a "personal needs allowance" set by the state. Federal rules require the state to set the allowance (used, for example, to buy shampoo and toothpaste) at a level of at least $30 a month.

If the Medicaid recipient continues to pay health insurance premiums or pays or makes co-payments for health care, funds used for this purpose are excluded from income. (However, once an individual enters a nursing home, LTCI premiums will probably be suspended, and once a person qualifies for Medicaid, LTCI benefits will probably also be suspended.) Finally, the CSIA, and any allowance for dependent children, is subtracted. The result (known as the "share of cost" or "patient pay amount") is the amount that must be spent down. The Medicaid system pays the nursing home the difference between the Medicaid payment rate and the amount spent down by the nursing home resident.

EXAMPLE: Claire Finneran is a 76-year-old nursing home resident. Her income, from pensions and Social Security, is $1,700 a month. Her husband Frank's income is $1,200 a month, and the CSIA for their state is $1,400. Because Frank's income is $200 short of the CSIA, Claire can transfer $200 a month to him for his own needs. After this $200 transfer and her personal needs allowance of $50 a month, Claire's patient pay amount is $1,450 ($1,700-$200-$50). If the Medicaid nursing home rate is $3,000 a month, the state Medicaid agency pays the nursing home $1,550 a month ($3,000 - the $1,450 paid by Claire).

As this example shows, the spend-down obligation can be quite substantial. Is it worth it to apply for Medicaid? Yes, if it is possible to transfer assets before the application, thus preventing the need to liquidate the assets to pay privately for care. Furthermore, as this example shows, Mrs. Finneran pays about half the Medicaid rate each month for her care. It is very likely that the private-pay rate for the same nursing home bed is $4,500 or more. Without Medicaid, Ms. Finneran would need to pay $4,500 a month, with income of only $1,700, requiring her to liquidate $2,800 of assets a month.

Enhancing the CSRA and CSIA

An important legal principle is that even if a basic rule is fair, many systems provide a "relief valve" for cases where application of the rules would be unfair. Accordingly, the Medicaid system includes provisions for adjustments, which may be based on court orders, such as family court orders directing the institutionalized spouse to increase the level of support provided to the healthy, as well as for administrative hearings (called "fair hearings") within the Medicaid system itself.[13]

A fair hearing can also grant a higher than normal CSIA level, especially in states where housing costs are high and a special housing allowance can be provided.[14] However the concept of fairness merely requires that the community spouse be protected from dire poverty. It is not necessary to preserve the lifestyle the community spouse enjoyed before the nursing home spouse became sick.[15]

The CSRA can also be adjusted if a Medicaid fair hearing, or a court order, allows a higher level to be transferred to the healthy spouse. The adjustments are only to be made in exceptional circumstances, and to prevent unusual financial duress. If the judge or hearing officer accepts the argument and orders a higher CSRA level, then the institutionalized spouse may transfer this additional amount without penalty.

PRACTICE TIP: If there is evidence to support a higher level, going through a hearing can be very worthwhile. Any person who has knowledge of the facts (the person need not be a lawyer) can represent a Medicaid claimant. Because the ordinary CSIA and CSRA levels are guaranteed by federal law, the community spouse will not lose by requesting a hearing, because the provisions for the community spouse may not be cut back because of the hearing.

If the community spouse's income is below the CSIA, can the sick spouse transfer additional resources to the community spouse, so that the community spouse can invest these resources in order to gain additional income? This argument may achieve some degree of success, especially if the extra resources are used to purchase a commercial annuity for the community spouse. Under conditions where interest rates paid to investors are low, it would be possible to transfer.

However, the Sixth Circuit decided, in *Chambers v. Ohio Dep't of Human Services*, 145 F.3d 793 (6th Cir. 1998), *cert. denied*, 119 S.Ct. 408 (1998), that an "income-first," not a "resource-first" approach, could be used. As long as the sick spouse has income that could be transferred to the healthy spouse, the CSRA should not be increased.

New York's highest court, the Court of Appeals, made a similar decision in *Golf v. New York State Dep't of Social Services*, 697 N.E.2d 555 (N.Y. 1998). In the Golf case, the husband entered a nursing home while his wife continued to live at home. Their resources totaled $105,763, of which $86,855.25 belonged to Mrs. Golf, and $18,908.35 belonged to Mr. Golf. At that time, New York's CSRA was $70,740, and the MMMNA was set at $1,769. Mrs. Golf's actual income was only $1,319. Mr. Golf would have been Medicaid-eligible if he could have transferred the excess resources to Mrs. Golf to make up for her shortfall in income. If he could not, he would be ineligible because he had about $13,000 in excess resources. Mrs. Golf had some success in New York's lower courts. The Appellate Division required a "resources first" method, but the Court of Appeals reversed, allowing the New York rule to be "income first."

This is also the rule in the Third Circuit. See *Cleary v. Waldman*, 167 F.3d 801 (3rd Cir. 1999).

Right of Election

A general estate planning rule (see Chapter 13) is that spouses cannot be disinherited against their will. In most circumstances, if a married person dies without a will, the surviving spouse is entitled to a share (typically, one-third to one-half) of the decedent's estate. If the decedent did leave a valid will, but that will provides less than the statutory "elective share," the surviving spouse has the right to "elect against the will" by filing an election to receive the statutory share. This share will be granted at the expense of the bequests in the will.

What if a Medicaid recipient's spouse dies, leaving less than the statutory share? Part of the process of applying for Medicaid is a promise to garner all funds to which the applicant is entitled, so the spouse must elect against the deceased spouse's will, even though the likely result is the loss of Medicaid eligibility after receiving the funds. What usually happens with a post-eligibility inheritance is that the Medicaid recipient takes the funds, makes arrangements to go off Medicaid and re-apply, and either spends down the funds or does a half-a-loaf transfer. Refusing to elect against the will is treated as a transfer of assets. See *Tannler v. Wis. Dep't of Health and Human Servs.*, 564 N.W.2d 735 (Wis. 1997).

A strategy that usually works is, while a Medicaid plan is being made but before the application, the spouses waive their rights of inheritance and election. Waivers of the right of election are often made as part of a pre-nuptial agreement, but they can also be made after marriage. Usually the best move is for each spouse to renounce rights in the other's estate. This is legally sufficient, even though in practice one spouse may have much more money than the other. Then, by the time one spouse is a Medicaid recipient and the other one dies, the existing waiver of the right of election will control.

This strategy "usually" works, but not always. The New York case of *Estate of Dionisio v. Westchester DSS*, 665 N.Y.S.2d 904 (AD 2d Dept 1997), involved a couple who signed mutual waivers of the right of election two weeks before Mrs. Dionisio went into a nursing home, but 20 months before she applied for Medicaid. After she had been in the nursing home for only four months, Mr. Dionisio died, leaving an estate of close to half a million dollars with none of it left to Mrs. Dionisio.

Mrs. Dionisio's Medicaid application was denied, on the grounds that she had transferred $156,500, which was the one-third share of the estate she would have received by electing against the will.

Although her lawyer claimed that the waivers of the right of election were made to save estate tax, and not for Medicaid purposes, the court rejected this argument. The Dionisio case highlights the kind of problems that often arise after hurried, last-minute plans. Perhaps the result would have been different if the waiver had occurred not only long before the Medicaid application, but long before nursing home admission.[16]

Income Issues Post-Eligibility

If income is payable in the name of just one spouse, it is considered to belong to that person. If income is paid jointly to both spouses, the income is considered to belong in equal shares to each of them. Income paid to a spouse and someone else is assigned proportionately to the spouse. For example, if 50 percent to Joseph (the spouse) and 50 percent to his sister Kathleen, only Joseph's 50 percent affects his eligibility. If there is no written document establishing ownership of income, it is considered to belong equally to both spouses. If the income derives from a trust, then the terms of the trust govern assignment of income. If the trust is not specific, then the rules above apply. State Medicaid Manual section 3261.

Post-Eligibility Assets: Head 'em Off At the Pass?

In some circumstances, a Medicaid recipient will become entitled to new assets after eligibility. The most common case is an inheritance or insurance benefits on the life of someone who has died after the person became Medicaid-eligible. The usual result is that the person will lose Medicaid eligibility, and will not be eligible again until the funds have been spent, or until they have been transferred and the penalty period has ended.

PRACTICE TIP: Most states have a fairly simple procedure for going off Medicaid, paying privately for a while, and going back on Medicaid. It is not necessary to go through a full-scale application process each time, or to move out of the nursing home and into another nursing home as a private-pay patient.

It is not enough for the Medicaid recipient simply to turn down the assets, because part of the Medicaid application is an ongoing promise to collect all funds to which the recipient is entitled. The problem is that accepting the assets leads to termination of Medicaid eligibility, but rejecting them is a transfer subject to a penalty period. Therefore, wherever possible, a person contemplating a Medicaid application should limit the amount of assets that will come into his possession after eligibility.

See above for a discussion of electing against the will of a deceased spouse. Potential Medicaid recipients can discuss this issue with family members, other than the spouse, who might make bequests, and ask them to leave the money to someone else. There is no obligation to leave money to a non-spouse, and no right of election against a non-spouse's will. But this will not work where a relative dies intestate, and the Medicaid recipient becomes a distributee (a person who receives an inheritance from a person who died without a will). Medicaid patients can also ask family members to remove them as insurance beneficiaries, and substitute someone who is not likely to be a Medicaid recipient.

CRIMINAL PENALTIES FOR PLANNERS?

Not only did the Health Insurance Portability and Accessibility Act of 1996 (HIPAA) revolutionize the tax treatment of long-term care insurance (see Chapter 4), it had dramatic but short-lived impact on Medicaid planning. A HIPAA provision, nicknamed the "Send Granny to Jail Bill," made it a federal misdemeanor for an individual to transfer assets in order to become eligible for Medicaid, followed by an application for Medicaid made during the penalty period. This was not a politically popular provision. There are lots of senior citizens, they vote, and their relatives are very interested in their well-being.

The Balanced Budget Act of 1997 amended this HIPAA provision, this time affecting a much less popular group of Americans. It was no longer a crime for individuals to transfer assets and then apply during a penalty period. Instead, the federal misdemeanor (punishable by up to a year's imprisonment and/or a $10,000 fine) was re-defined as advising someone else to make transfers (if the adviser was paid to render advice), if that person later applied for Medicaid during a penalty period. Potentially, criminal liability could have been applied to lawyers, accountants, financial planners, insurance professionals selling annuities, or anybody else who gave professional advice about Medicaid planning. This provision was nicknamed the "Send Granny's Lawyer to Jail Bill."

As you can imagine, lawyers soon rallied to get rid of this provision, and suits were brought in federal courts in New York and Rhode Island. In the spring of 1998, the New York Court issued a permanent injunction to prevent the Department of Justice from ever enforcing the provision. In a letter to Congress, Attorney General Janet Reno informed Congress that the Department of Justice would not prosecute any paid advisers on the basis of their clients' Medicaid applications. This letter sets policy nationwide, not just in New York, so there is no real risk of prosecution for giving your clients advice about Medicaid planning.

BUY-IN PROGRAMS

Many individuals are "dual eligibles." Dual eligibles are senior citizens or disabled persons who qualify for both Medicare and Medicaid. The Balanced Budget Act of 1997 changed previous law by making it clear that states are not required to pay Medicare deductibles or co-payments to the extent that the total payment to a health care provider would exceed the Medicaid rate. This has practical as well as philosophical consequences. In nearly all circumstances, Medicare pays more for services than Medicaid does, so health care providers often receive less for treating dual eligibles than they would for treating the same people if they were only Medicare beneficiaries.

Another group of senior citizens do not qualify for full-scale Medicaid benefits, but they need some financial assistance with health care costs. There are three federal programs to assist persons in this category: Qualified Medicare Beneficiary (QMB), Specified Low-Income Medicare Beneficiary (SLMB), and Qualifying Individuals (QI).

The Qualified Medicare Beneficiary (QMB) program pays part or all of the Medicare cost-sharing (deductibles, coinsurance, and Part B premiums) for elderly persons who are enrolled in Medicare Part A. To qualify as a QMB in 1999, a person must have income below $707 a month ($942 for a married couple), and resources below $4,000 for a single person, or $6,000 for a couple. Income limits are higher in Alaska and Hawaii.

The Specified Low-Income Medicare Beneficiary (SLMB) program covers the Part B premium (about $45 a month), but otherwise the enrollee is responsible for other Medicare cost-sharing. In 1999, SLMB monthly income limits are $844 per month for an individual, and $1,126 per month for a couple. Once again, higher levels are allowed in Alaska and Hawaii.

Qualifying Individuals (QIs) are eligible for partial or full payment of their Part B premium. QIs are eligible for full payments if monthly income falls below $947 for a single person, or $1,265 for a couple. They are eligible for partial payments if monthly income is below $1,222 for a single person, or $1,633 for a couple (all figures are for 1999).

Note that the income figures for buy-in programs change once a year, based on changes in the official federal poverty line. Usually the new poverty line is announced in February, unlike Social Security and Medicare changes, which are usually announced in late October. Figures can found in "Medicare and You" at www.medicare.gov/publications/mandy.pdf.

CHAPTER FOOTNOTES

1. A good current introduction to Medicaid law can be found on-line at www.nsclc.org/ltcod398.html, published by the National Senior Citizens Law Center.

2. For discussion of these issues, see "Community Spouse's IRA Is a Countable Resource," *Elder Law Report*, February, 1999, p. 6.

3. Theoretically, states have the option of providing non-waivered Medicaid home care, although few states have decided to do so. In order to receive FMAP, states must impose the same transfer penalties on waivered home care as on nursing home care. States can, but are not required to, impose transfer penalties on non-waivered home care. In fact, in New York State, it is possible to qualify for non-waivered home care immediately after transferring all non-exempt assets, but the CSRA and CSIA are transfer-related rules, and are not available to a recipient of non-waivered home care.

4. This is a tricky one. It is not good enough that Medicaid was not the only motivation. Usually, financial planning clients have several motivations, including helping family members, saving income taxes, and estate planning.

5. Some states use a subjective test: whether the nursing home resident wants to return home. Others use an objective standard: whether it is reasonable to believe that a return home is possible.

6. For instance, *North Dakota DSS v. Thompson*, 586 N.W.2d 847 (N.D. 1998).

7. HCFA's Robert A. Streimer, Director of Disabled and Elderly Health Programs, made this point in a letter dated February 25, 1998 and addressed to Dana E. Rozansky, Esq. See Thomas D. Begley, Jr., "Income Only Trusts: Having Your Cake and Eating It Too," *ElderLaw Report*, October 1998, p.1.

8. See Harry S. Margolis and Eric R. Oalican, "The Use of Annuities in Long-Term Care Planning," *ElderLaw Report*, November 1998, p. 1, for an excellent review of these strategies.

9. A deferred annuity could be purchased as part of a long-range plan, but there may be heavy penalties on premature withdrawals from such an annuity, and these funds may be required to pay long-term care expenses. *Id.*

10. These strategies are discussed in Alexander A. Bove, Jr., "Making Resources Disappear: The Magic of PANs and SCINs," *ElderLaw Report*, October 1997, p. 1.

11. For tax implications of contracts for care, see *Estate of Stern v. Treasury*, 98-1 USTC ¶60,299 (S.D. Ind. 1998), in which an estate was allowed to deduct $182,500 from the $1 million estate inherited by a caregiver, on the theory that this money was reasonable payment for her protracted services as caregiver. The court accepted an "implied contract" theory, under which a person who agrees to pay for care but does not clarify the amount is deemed to be liable for paying a reasonable amount comparable to the market rate. (In this case, reducing the taxable estate also reduced the estate tax and thus increased the net amount inherited by the caregiver.)

12. If the Medicaid recipient receives World War II reparations, the reparation money is not considered income.

13. See Ron M. Landsman, "Going to Court to Improve Spousal Benefits," Parts 1 and 2, *ElderLaw Report*, September and December 1998.

14. Fair hearing provisions are in 42 USC §1396r-5(e).

15. Cases such as *Schachner v. Perales*, 648 N.E.2d 1321 (N.Y. 1995), *Gomprecht v. Sabol*, 652 N.E.2d 936 (N.Y. 1995) and *Jenkins v. Fields*, 1996 U.S. Dist. Lexis 5852 (S.D.N.Y. 1996) make this point.

16. Also see *Matter of Mattei*, 647 N.Y.S.2d 415 (1996), in which a Medicaid recipient's daughter was appointed as guardian for her mother specifically in order to satisfy the mother's obligation as a Medicaid recipient to elect against her deceased husband's will, and to use the funds to pay for her mother's care while she was rendered ineligible for Medicaid by the inheritance.

Chapter 7

THE FAMILY HOME: A SPECIAL RESOURCE

The family home has undoubted sentimental value. Owning a home is an important part of most financial plans, and most senior citizens prefer to receive their long term care at home instead of moving to specialized housing or a health care facility.

Most senior citizens are homeowners, and most of their homes are mortgage-free. Furthermore, except for very wealthy people, the home is one of the largest (if not the single largest) financial assets in the financial plan. For all these reasons, planning for the home and its financial value looms large in the elderplan, and home equity is a major asset that must be handled wisely.

Sometimes remaining in the same home is the right strategy. Sometimes it makes sense to choose a different, more suitable home. The existing home may:

- need too much maintenance;
- be too hard to take care of;
- cost too much to heat and cool;
- be too far away from recreational and medical resources (especially for senior citizens who can no longer drive safely, and have little access to public transportation);
- be located in a neighborhood that has deteriorated and become dangerous;
- not be handicap accessible; or
- be too large for "empty nesters."

It may make sense to stay in the larger home if grown children are likely to move back in, or if space is needed for a home sharer or live-in home health care worker.

A traditional strategy is for older people to sell their home, take advantage of the tax exclusion for certain home sale gains (see below), and move to (1) rented accommodations, (2) a smaller, more convenient home, or (3) a retirement community or health care facility. Investing the home sale proceeds actively, or using them to purchase an annuity, can generate a gratifying stream of additional income for post-retirement needs. Whether this is the best strategy depends on emotional as well as practical (e.g., cash-flow, Medicaid, tax) factors.

OLDER CLIENT HOME STRATEGIES

- Stay in the home and plan to leave it to a child or grandchild. One problem with this is that the heirs may already be homeowners, or otherwise not interested in living in the older client's home. This also is not very practical if the intent is to divide the ownership among a large group of heirs. The simple alternative might be to direct the executor to sell the property and divide the proceeds. This brings up the problem of hurried "estate sales" that do not always generate optimum prices, especially if the death happens to occur shortly before a slump in the real estate market.

- Stay in the home and fix it up to make it more suitable for the needs of an older person, such as by replacing loose rugs with bare floors or carpeting, enhancing the lighting, adding security features including a response system for health emergencies, adding a lift on the staircase, widening doorways, and retrofitting bathrooms and kitchens for a wheelchair user.

- Stay in the home but transfer ownership of the home to a trust (see below) or transfer ownership as part of a Medicaid plan (see Chapter 6). It is also possible to do a sale-leaseback or gift-leaseback within the family, but these "split-interest" transactions are difficult, sophisticated, and mandate current advice from a top-flight tax advisor.

- Share living quarters with the parent moving in with a son or daughter, or vice versa. Also a possibility is an informal "home sharing" arrangement, which can provide companionship and perhaps some household services in return for rent-free or low-rent accommodations.

- Obtain a home equity loan or reverse mortgage. The funds can be used to pay for home care, nursing home care of a spouse who remains at home, or for travel or ordinary living expenses.

- Sell the home and use the proceeds of the sale to buy admission to a retirement community or a continuing care retirement community that does not offer equity ownership. The advantage of this strategy is that a person with a small taxable estate may be able to move enough funds out of the estate to avoid federal estate taxation, while making sure that he will have a comfortable, appropriate living environment, or access to quality health and custodial care, or both. This can work especially well for a single or widowed person who is unable to use the estate tax marital deduction.

CAPITAL GAINS EXCLUSION

The Taxpayer Relief Act of 1997 (TRA '97) liberalized the capital gains exclusion available for the sale of a homestead. As part of TRA '97, Congress enacted a single Code provision to replace two earlier provisions. These earlier provisions dealt with the "rollover" of gain when a home seller purchased a more expensive home within two years of the sale transaction and with sales by individuals over the age of 55. The current provision, which is effective for sales taking place on or after May 7, 1997, can be used by taxpayers of any age.[1]

If both the "use test" and the "ownership test" are met, up to $250,000 in capital gains (i.e., gross home sale proceeds minus the basis of the property) on home sales can be excluded from income. Furthermore, gains of up to $500,000 can be excluded by a married person who files a joint return for the year of the sale, where both spouses satisfy the "use test" and at least one spouse satisfies the "ownership test," provided that neither of them has excluded home-sale gain in the previous two years, not taking into account sales before May 7, 1997.

The ownership test requires owning the property for at least two of the five years prior to the sale. The use test requires having used that property as the taxpayer's principal residence for at least two of the five years prior to the sale. (The use test is modified to generally allow the exclusion if absence from the home was caused by living in a nursing home and the taxpayer used the residence for one year as a principal residence.) The ownership and use tests need not be satisfied in the same two years.

A widow or widower is deemed to satisfy the ownership or use test if the deceased spouse satisfied the test prior to the home sale. If an individual marries in a year in which he has already sold a home, that individual can exclude up to $250,000 if the use and ownership requirements are met by that spouse. If each spouse satisfies the tests as to a different home, each can exclude up to $250,000. See IRS Publication 523, "Selling Your Home," for more details.

The IRS Restructuring and Reform Act of 1998 (IRSRRA '98) clarified the availability of a partial exclusion to taxpayers who could not satisfy the full-scale ownership and use tests. In other words, someone who owned or used the property for only one year out of the five can exclude up to $125,000 (single person) or up to $250,000 (married person filing jointly) if they satisfy other conditions required by the Code.

ACCESSING HOME EQUITY

In many instances, home equity can be a promising source of funds by either obtaining a conventional home equity loan or line of credit, or through a "reverse mortgage," which is a special type of financial instrument usually used by senior citizens. However, it should be noted that using home equity reduces the value of the home that is available for inheritance, thus altering or defeating the estate plan.

Under a reverse mortgage, the elderly homeowner enters into an agreement with a lender. Usually the lender will be a financial institution such as a bank, but sometimes an insurance company. Some states have guarantee programs to provide incentives for banks to make such loans, and a few state agencies write the mortgages directly, without bank involvement. As part of the reverse mortgage, the senior citizen receives regular payments. If these payments take the form of an annuity, the arrangement is known as a Reverse Annuity Mortgage (RAM). In return, the lender receives an equity interest in the home. Usually, the interest is limited to the amount advanced, plus interest. However, if the deal includes an "equity kicker," the lender will be entitled to a share of the appreciation in value of the property.

Payments continue for a term of years, or for the lifetime of the homeowner. If the homeowner decides to sell the home, the loan becomes due and payable immediately. The loan also becomes payable on the death of the survivor of a home-owning couple. One advantage for homeowners who want to make a Medicaid plan is that for Medicaid and Supplemental Security Income (SSI) purposes, the funds paid by the lender to the homeowner are not considered income. The arrangement is considered a loan, not an income-generating investment. The typical reverse mortgage yields payments of under $8,000 a year, which is certainly not enough to pay for nursing home care, but may be enough to assist in paying for home care.

Whether the advantages outweigh the disadvantages depends on the facts of the case. See www.reverse.org, the Website for the National Center for Home Equity Conversion, for more information about reverse mortgages, and on-line calculators for determining the amount that a particular person could raise via a reverse mortgage. The American Association for Retired Persons (AARP) has a Home Equity Information Center that is also a valuable source of objective information.

According to federal statutes (specifically 15 USC section 1602(bb)), a reverse mortgage is a nonrecourse transaction that secures one or more advances of credit from the lender to the homeowner. Repayment has to wait until the consumer dies, vacates the home, or transfers ownership of the dwelling. Truth in Lending disclosures for adjustable-rate mortgages must be made to the homeowner.

If the lender offers an annuity as part of the deal, or arranges an annuity transaction or helps the borrower set up the annuity transaction, 12 CFR section 226.33 requires the lender to include the cost of the annuity in its disclosure of the cost of the transaction.

Under the Home Equity Conversion Mortgage (HECM) program, the FHA insures five types of mortgages for homeowners aged 62 or over. HECMs are not limited to single-family houses: duplexes, triplexes, and four-family homes, as well as certain condominium units, can qualify.

"Tenure plan" FHA-insured mortgages provide a fixed annuity for the life of the homeowner, as long as the purchaser remains in the home; the annuity ends if he moves away. "Term plan" mortgages offer a fixed annuity for a term of years. Funds are not made available immediately under the "line of credit plan," but funds will be made available on request, once eligibility has been established. The other two plans combine various features of these three plans.

The percentage of the value of the home that can be borrowed under a FHA-approved plan depends on the homeowner's age. The older he is, the larger the percentage that can be borrowed. The percentage increases rather than decreases with age because the older the person, the shorter the life expectancy and the shorter the time horizon over which the lender extends credit. The maximum size of the loan is set regionally, and ranges from $115,200 to $208,800 for single family homes. See entp.hud.gov/cgi-bin/websql/idapp/html/hicostlook.hts for the amounts for each county.

The Federal National Mortgage Association ("Fannie Mae") also has a reverse mortgage program, the Home Keeper Mortgage, available up to a maximum of $240,000 for a single-family home. (This is the nationwide figure for 1999.) Fannie Mae maintains a toll-free number, (800) 572-4562, for information on reverse mortgages and a directory of participating lenders.

A suit was filed in California in July, 1998 against Transamerica Corporation and Metropolitan Life Insurance, alleging that their "House Money Lifetime" reverse annuity mortgage product was unconscionably unfair, involving onerous terms and multiple fees, to the extent of constituting financial elder abuse.[2] The suit alleges that this product was sometimes sold to mentally impaired, very aged persons who were unable to understand the disclosures and who ended up owing two to six times the amount of proceeds that they received from the insurer. This particular product required customers to purchase a deferred annuity that will make payments to especially long-lived customers who outlive the equivalent of the value of their housing equity. It also gave the mortgagees a 50 percent interest in the appreciation of the value of the home after the arrangement was entered into, and required a "maturity fee," payable at the termination of the arrangement, equal to 2% of the appreciated value of the property. (The House Money product is no longer sold, although the issuers say that the discontinuance was due to market factors, not the lawsuit.) When this edition went to press, the suit had not been resolved.

HOUSE TRUSTS: PRTs AND QPRTs

In some circumstances, transferring ownership of a personal residence to a trust can be beneficial. The Code includes provisions for two related types of house trusts: the Personal Residence Trust (PRT) and the Qualified Personal Residence Trust (QPRT). The main difference between them is that a PRT contains nothing but the house, while a QPRT can contain a limited amount of other assets that can throw off enough income to pay taxes and other expenses of the house. Any home (whether principal residence or vacation home, and whether free-standing or condominium or co-op unit) can be placed into trust. The advantage is that ownership of the home can be transferred to the couple's children for far less than fair market value, thus removing the house and its potential appreciation from the parents' estate.

The parents can keep using the property for a term of years. The downside? If the parents are still alive at the end of the term (and the optimum term should be shorter than the parents' predictable life expectancy), the children get full ownership, and if the parents want to keep living there, they have to rent the house at a fair market rental. If they use the house and pay less than fair market value, the value of the house goes back into the estate, because the transaction then becomes a transfer with a retained life estate, which is part of the estate. Both a PRT or QPRT must be drafted to forbid the trust grantor and/or his spouse to re-purchase the home when the term ends.

If both parents die during the term of a PRT or QPRT, then the value of the home will be included in their estates. If one dies during the trust term but the other survives, then only the half interest of the deceased parent will be included in his estate, so the trust will achieve only half of its objectives. Just as second-to-die insurance is often used to shore up estate plans, life insurance can be used to make sure that a PRT or QPRT will achieve its objectives even if one or both of the former-owner spouses dies during the term.

INTRAFAMILY TRANSACTIONS

The higher the tax bracket of the senior citizen client, the more important tax planning becomes, and the more likelihood that there might be a federally taxable estate. Intrafamily transactions involving the family home may come to the rescue.

One possibility is for the older generation to sell (not give) their home to the younger generation. In a sale-leaseback transaction, the elders continue to live in the home and pay rent to the new owners. The home is removed from the potentially taxable estate. Although the older generation must pay rent, they receive a large sum of money for the sale (or continuing income payments if they grant a purchase-money mortgage).

But for the transaction to achieve the desired tax consequences, it must have real economic consequences. Structuring it as a "wash" (where each generation's financial obligation offsets that of the other), or failure to actually make or demand payments as required, will result in disregard for tax purposes. See *Maxwell v. Comm.*, 3 F.3d 591 (2nd Cir. 1993). Do not forget that capital gain on a home sale within the family must be recognized (although it will probably escape taxation because of the capital gains exclusion for home-sale profits), but loss on the sale of a home (whether to a family member or third party) is considered personal and thus is not tax-deductible.

A gift-leaseback involves the gift of a residence, while the donor continues to live there and pay rent. Probably, this will use up part of the unified credit against gift and estate taxes (see Chapter 13) or even, in extreme cases, lead to the need to pay gift tax. Internal Revenue Code Chapter 14 should also be consulted for large gifts. See above for a discussion of residence trusts.

Sometimes a home will be transferred to a family member, friend, or other unpaid caregiver based on past provision of care, or an agreement to provide care in the future. If the recipient is the child of the homeowner, and the child lives in the house for at least two years before the transfer, providing care that defers institutionalization, then the transfer to the "caregiver child" will not carry a Medicaid penalty (see Chapter 6). The transfer will also escape penalties if it is made more than 36 months before the Medicaid application, or if it can be proved that the value of the care was at least equal to the value of the home, so there was no gratuitous element in the transaction. For this purpose, the contract should be in writing, and must have existed before the care was rendered, not afterwards.

MEDICAID TREATMENT OF HOMESTEADS

As Chapter 6 explains in more detail, the Medicaid system treats the homestead as an asset entitled to favorable treatment. The value of the homestead, no matter how great, is not considered in determining initial Medicaid eligibility, because it is an exempt asset. Furthermore, funds used to fix up the property (for medical purposes or otherwise) are not transfers, because there is no "give-away" element.

A property remains a homestead as long as a nursing home resident's spouse or dependent relative continues to lives there. Property ceases to be a homestead if it is owned by a single person who is in a nursing home and is too sick to return home.

CHAPTER FOOTNOTES

1. IRC Sec. 121.

2. Ralph T. King Jr., "Insurers Face 'Elder Abuse' Charge in Mortgage Suit," *Wall Street Journal*, October 15, 1998, p. B1; Amanda Levin, "Insurers Sued Over Reverse Mortgages," *National Underwriter*, Life and Health/Financial Services Edition, September 14, 1998, p. 28.

Chapter 8

RETIREMENT PLANNING

An older client base will probably consist of three groups: persons in their 50s and 60s who are contemplating retirement (the largest group), those who have already retired, and a small group of those who have retired and want to return to the workforce. Therefore, the planner's task includes giving advice about the best timing for retirement, the tax- and Medicaid-wise ways to handle retirement benefits (whether to be selected or already in pay status) and how the estate plan should deal with these funds.

There are some factors that work in favor of older people remaining in the workforce. The Age Discrimination in Employment Act makes it illegal to force any person over age 40, who is still qualified to perform the job, to retire when he prefers to keep working. (There is an exception for "bona fide policymakers," who can be required to retire at 70, if their job functions during working life included significant management responsibility, and if they are entitled to a pension of $44,000 or more per year when they retire. There is also an exception for tenured university faculty.) So theoretically, almost anyone who can still tackle the job can keep working. In 1996 and 1997, Congress changed the tax laws (see below) to make them more favorable to continued employment. Many employers not only tolerate but actively recruit older workers, because of their skills and a work ethic that can be hard to find in younger employees.

With or without these incentives, most people prefer to retire before age 70, and many prefer to retire before the traditional retirement age of 65. In 1996, according to Census Bureau figures, only 18% of male senior citizens were still in the workforce, as were 9% of married female senior citizens and 12% of unmarried female senior citizens.

Sound retirement plans must take a long-range perspective, because according to Census Bureau figures, the average 65-year-old

American had a life expectancy of 17.4 years and the average white female 65-year-old had a life expectancy of 19.1 years. On a personal level, the retiree must find interesting and satisfying activities for this time period, including activities that can be pursued if health deteriorates. On the financial planning level, they must have an adequate level of income that will not be outlived. Furthermore, since the retirement plan can be expected to continue for decades, the planner might want to adjust the portfolio to maintain or add at least some growth investments, instead of having a pure income orientation.

The planning challenge is to make sure that adequate income is available, and is not outlived. However, there may be circumstances in which *less* income is better than *more*. Sometimes additional income places its recipient in a higher tax bracket, so adding more income does not necessarily result in a corresponding amount of after-tax income. Income that is not needed may accumulate, making the potentially taxable estate larger. And, as Chapter 6 indicates, additional income is a negative rather than desirable factor for a person who receives Medicaid or is going to make a Medicaid application.

This chapter deals with qualified and nonqualified retirement plans provided by an employer; see Chapter 10 for a discussion of Individual Retirement Accounts (IRAs). A plan is "qualified" if the employer that furnishes the plan follows an elaborate set of tax and labor law rules. In return, generally the employer can deduct the cost of sponsoring the plan, and the employees don't have to pay taxes on their pension accounts until they retire and start to draw the benefits.

Qualified plans are not allowed to discriminate in favor of highly compensated employees. Some companies that don't want to offer a qualified plan, or that want to provide extra benefits for top management, sponsor nonqualified deferred compensation plans. The tax consequences of these plans, as discussed below, are less favorable to both employer and employee than qualified plans.

SOURCES OF POST-RETIREMENT INCOME

After retirement, income typically derives from several sources:

- Qualified plan benefits provided by the employer
- Nonqualified plan benefits provided by the employer
- Individual Retirement Accounts (IRAs)

- Social Security benefits
- Employment income—either from post-retirement employment (see below) or earned by one spouse who has not yet retired
- Investment income, including annuity income and income from mutual funds, stock dividends, bond interest, rental from investment real estate, etc.
- Income from trusts set up by the retiree or by others for the retiree's behalf

In some instances, the retiree will also inherit funds or become the beneficiary of life insurance on the life of a spouse or relative. Some of these income sources are regular, others intermittent. Some are predictable, some fluctuate. Some continue for life, others for a period of years. Income may become available at various times in the post-retirement period; for instance, a deferred annuity may begin payments several years after Social Security benefits and qualified plan distributions become available.

PATTERNS AND PERSONALITIES

In its 1998 Retirement Confidence Survey, the Employee Benefits Research Institute (EBRI)[1] groups workers into six categories, reflecting differing views of how to fund retirement. This survey is useful to planners because, by characterizing their clients, they can highlight clients' real vulnerabilities and help them shift from financially self-destructive behaviors to more productive behaviors.

The "Deniers" group, representing 10% of the population, say that there's no point in saving for retirement because it's too far away, they can't estimate their future needs, and retirement planning is too difficult. Only 39% of this group have in fact done any retirement saving. Not surprisingly, 56% of this group (as compared to only 36% of the U.S. population in general) don't expect to have enough money for a comfortable retirement. Furthermore, after retirement, Deniers are more likely than others to describe retirement as "worse than they expected." Two-thirds of Deniers are over 45, so their perceptions of having plenty of time to plan are not accurate. In fact, 42% are already retired.

The “Strugglers” group (9% of the population) constantly encounter financial setbacks that sabotage their financial plans. Fifty-nine percent of this group are not saving for retirement, usually because they feel unable to divert any money from current needs, or because they intend to keep working throughout their lifetime. Half of them are not confident that they will have enough money to live on after retirement. Most fall into the 35-54 age category.

One-fifth of the population are described as “Impulsives,” and 60% of them are under 45. Impulsives usually hope to retire early, but few of them have started a savings program, and those who have usually have under $10,000 accumulated. They count on qualified plan distributions, perhaps in conjunction with late-life employment, to take care of them. Half of them are “somewhat” confident of being able to afford retirement, but few are confident of being able to afford long term care.

The “Cautious Savers” (21% of population), most of them 35-44 years old, are quite likely to have begun retirement saving; 61% have already done so. Most of them are confident that they are doing a good job, but 39% say that they don’t enjoy the planning process. Only half are confident of being able to afford retirement; many are anxious about being able to afford long term care.

Twenty-three percent of the population fall into the “Planners” group. Nine-tenths of them believe that anyone can have a comfortable retirement as long as adequate provisions are made in advance. Nine-tenths of this group also have faith in their own ability to save for retirement, and half of them expect to be prosperous enough to retire at 60. This is the group that is most risk tolerant, as long as they have a reasonable expectation of being rewarded for the risk. Eighty-one percent of this group expect to have enough income for a comfortable retirement, and about the same percentage are confident about every specific element of retirement. This group tends to be aged 35-54.

The highest point of the pyramid, the “Retiring Savers” (17% of the population), have a demonstrated history of accumulation for retirement (84% already have put aside money for retirement). More than one-third (38%) have already retired, and many more are close to retirement age. Most of them are more oriented toward saving than investing, and only about half are confident that they are doing a good job of investing their retirement funds. Overall, however, this group is confident about retirement (75% feel this way), and many of those who have already retired say that retirement is better than they anticipated.

A planner who can analyze where clients fit with respect to these groups can help them steer between the extremes of inappropriate lack of confidence ("Why bother—it's hopeless anyway") and excessive confidence ("I don't need a retirement savings program—something will turn up"). Furthermore, the planner can help clients develop better saving habits and can recommend investment alternatives that are prudent but not so stodgy as to deprive them of needed returns.

CHALLENGES TO RETIREMENT SECURITY

Traditionally, under conventional defined benefit pension plans, the retiree was assured of a predictable, fixed pension. In times of high inflation, this could create severe problems, as the fixed income failed to adapt to inflationary conditions. Current trends have shown a move away from the defined benefit plan to more market-responsive, defined contribution plans, including the extremely popular 401(k) plan. However, the problem with such plans is that they shift market risk to the retiree; in other words, if retirement occurs at a time when stock market conditions are unfavorable, the value of the retirement account may decline, and an annuity purchased with that account may consequently be smaller than anticipated. If the retiree has also made below-average investment decisions in managing the account, poor returns could further depress the size of the account.

Over 300 large companies have converted traditional defined benefit pension plans to a hybrid plan known as the "cash balance" plan.[2] It is anticipated that by the first decade of the twenty-first century, the cash balance plan will become the dominant form for large corporate plans. Unfortunately, however, the cash balance form favors younger workers and can seriously reduce the benefits available to older workers (those closest to retirement). The pension might be reduced 20%, or even cut in half, as compared to a traditional defined benefit plan.

It is common for a defined benefit plan to be designed so that the pension is based on years of service times a set percentage (e.g., 1.5%). This amount is then multiplied by the employee's average salary in either the last few years of employment or the highest-paid years of employment, to determine a dollar benefit amount. The result is that a large part of the pension—perhaps as much as half—accrues during the last five years of service. Some plans offer especially generous late-year accruals to motivate early retirement.

In contrast, the cash balance plan is a defined benefit plan that creates a portable pension account for each employee. (The account is merely hypothetical; unlike a defined contribution plan, there is no separate account for each employee.) A percentage of the employee's salary is contributed to the plan (4% is common). A cash balance plan is a "career-average" plan; in other words, the pension depends on earnings over the whole career. The accrual percentage does not change over time to increase the accrual rate in later years.

The actual pension amount is determined by the annuity that can be purchased with the account at the time of retirement, taking into account the interest rate (typically, 5%) promised by the plan. Unlike a 401(k) plan, where the employee often has some control over investment of the account, the employer controls investment of the cash balance pension account.

In practice, this means that younger employees receive a larger pension accrual each year than they would in a traditional defined benefit plan, but those who are close to retirement receive much less. The younger employees are motivated by the change, but the older workers no longer have the incentive of remaining in the workforce in the hope that a few extra years of service will significantly enhance their pension entitlement. (If it wishes to, the employer can cushion the effect of the change by allowing older workers to retain their benefits under the former plan, or can increase their accruals.) Some employers that switch to a cash balance plan at least increase their 401(k) match, so the employee has the potential of a larger 401(k) plan to help offset the smaller pension.

The employer is entitled to keep any earnings on the account balances over and above the plan's promised interest rate, and can use these earnings to make contributions to the plan in future years, so the net cost of the plan can be quite low if the employer can earn significantly more than the interest rate it promises. In effect, the plan can become a profit center for the company.

Another benefit to the company—but a risk to the employee—is that the cash balance plan may use different actuarial assumptions from those used in the old plan. At the time of conversion, the employer calculates the present value of the pension credits earned by each employee prior to conversion, but may adjust the value downward if the assumptions change.

Interest rates are also a potent factor. At the time of conversion, the employer calculates the accrued benefit already earned. Although this amount is a constant, its present value will change depending on interest rates. As interest rates fall, the accrued benefit is worth *more* because its present value is discounted less. Correspondingly, as interest rates rise, the accrued benefit must be discounted more heavily and thus decreases in value. This is yet another negative for older workers. Since current (1999) interest rates are very low, it would not be surprising if they increased meaningfully in the next few years, depressing the present value of the balances.

Of course, with a lower balance and lower accruals each year (or no accruals, if the employer believes that it has already satisfied its obligations, based on its own calculations), the eventual pension will be much lower. This phenomenon is known as "wearaway" or "plateauing"; in other words, it can take several years for the older employee's pension account under the new assumptions to reach its level under the old assumptions. A number of employee lawsuits have been filed to challenge conversions to cash balance plans, but several such suits have already been dismissed at early stages of litigation.

It might seem surprising that, given the minutely detailed regulation of pensions under the Internal Revenue Code and ERISA, employers would be permitted to do this. However, so long as the workers are entitled to receive their full vested balances if they change jobs (which is required under ERISA and the Code); the employer is given wide discretion to value the opening balances in a cash balance plan. It's possible that federal courts will find that these plans satisfy ERISA requirements, but violate the Age Discrimination in Employment Act, at least that is the theory being pursued by attorneys for some disgruntled participants.

Federal law requires employers to issue a "204(h) notice" (i.e., a notice of reduction of benefits, as set forth in ERISA Section 204(h)) to workers whose benefits will be reduced. If the client has received such a notice, it is important that the planner try to determine the level of their future pension. Participants in a cash balance plan should automatically be issued quarterly balance statements, which can be used to predict the amount of the pension. Any plan participant is entitled to receive a statement of his "vested accrued benefit" once a year, by making a written request to the plan, and the employer is required to disclose the amount of a single-life annuity payment the employee would receive for retirement at age 65. Most cash balance plans (but less than half of traditional defined benefit plans) permit lump sum payouts, so an analysis should be made of the desirability of taking the plan payout as a lump sum.

In January of 1999, the Supreme Court decided a case involving GM's Hughes Electronics subsidiary.[3] The plan in that case was funded in approximately equal shares by contributions from employees and from the employer. In 1986, the plan's investments were so successful that the plan was operating at a surplus. At that point, the company stopped making contributions; workers continued making contributions until 1991. The suit arose when a group of retirees sued, claiming that the changes in the plan's operations were drastic enough to constitute termination of the plan. (When a plan terminates, participants gain full, immediate rights to their account balances.)

The Supreme Court accepted the employer's argument that its sole obligation was to make the pension payments called for by the plan. As long as it did that, it was entitled to use the pension surplus to reduce the employer's contributions on behalf of other workers. In other words, the plan surpluses did not belong to the employees and retirees, even though their contributions created some of the surplus.

In practical terms, however, this case won't affect very many people, because most defined benefit plans (i.e., plans that promise a specific pension check instead of whatever annuity can be purchased with the value of the employee's account at the time of retirement) do not require employee contributions. Employers that want employees to contribute usually use 401(k) plans, not defined benefit plans.

RETIREMENT TIMING

When is the best time for older working clients to retire? There are many factors to consider:

- Pension formulas
- Early retirement incentives
- Stock market conditions
- Tax effects
- Career opportunities

- Payment for health care
- Personal, family factors

Some retirement plans define the benefit as an unchanging percentage of each year's compensation, but others include "stairsteps," so that working slightly longer may qualify the individual for a more favorable pension formula. If the benefit is based on the highest-paid three or five years, or on average compensation for a certain number of years, it may make sense to retire soon after an especially successful year—or to keep working after an especially unsuccessful year in the hope of a turnaround!

The *maximum* benefit available under a defined benefit plan (i.e., $130,000 in 1999) must be reduced for early retirement, and increased for late retirement. In this context, "early" or "late" means before or after Social Security retirement age. A person who retires early knows exactly how many pension payments will be made between actual retirement and the normal retirement age, but a person who retires late takes the risk of dying before the increased size of each pension check compensates for the reduced number of checks.

Employers who want to reduce their workforce often prefer to induce early retirement instead of laying off workers who want to keep their jobs. For instance, a person who accepts early retirement after 17 years at the company may be offered a pension as if he had worked for 20 years, or other more favorable formulas might be applied.

The traditional, defined benefit pension is paid based on the plan's formulas. Unfavorable stock market conditions may affect the amount the employer must pay to fund the plan, but they do not affect the pensions received by retirees. Today, however, the majority of plans are defined contribution plans, where the investment risk is shifted to the employee. The size of the employee's pension depends on the size of the annuity that can be purchased with the account proceeds at the time of retirement. Naturally, it's better to retire with a defined contribution plan when the stock market is at a high point rather than a low point.

As this book has often emphasized, senior citizens must plan for their medical care needs, and this is an important factor in the retirement calculation. Medicare benefits are not available until age 65 (unless the person has been disabled for two years), so a person who retires early cannot necessarily apply for Medicare right away.

A number of employers offer retiree health benefits; that is, the employer continues to insure retirees as well as active workers. This is especially true if the employer wants to create incentives for early retirement. However, if the employer has drafted its health insurance plan so that it retains the right to modify the plan (almost all employers adopt such provisions), it is perfectly legal for the employer to terminate its retiree health plan, to require retirees to pay part of the premium, to make them pay for coverage of their dependents, or to make them pay higher deductibles and coinsurance. (In technical terms, this is possible because health insurance is a "welfare benefit," not a pension. Consequently, it doesn't vest and the employer can lawfully alter the plan.) Therefore, retiree health benefits can't be relied on as a complete solution to the problem of paying for senior citizens' health care.

Later on in this chapter, tax issues will be discussed more fully. It should be noted that unless Congress amends the Internal Revenue Code, a person who takes his or pension in the form of a lump sum rather than an annuity will have more options by retiring in 1999 rather than in later years.

One personal factor that is often ignored is that spouses may be at different stages in their careers. A common scenario is that the husband is somewhat older than his wife, and has been employed continuously. The wife has often interrupted her career to accommodate childrearing needs. The upshot is that when he's ready to retire, she may just be hitting her stride. That tends to work against a plan that calls for an immediate move to a retirement community. Even if there is no planned move, there can be tensions between a retiree spouse who wants to travel or wants company on the golf course or tennis court, and a workaholic spouse who puts in long hours.

The summer of 1998 brought a dormant consideration back to center stage: the effect of stock market forces on retirement planning. The traditional defined benefit pension plan, which provides a fixed income, is ill-adapted to periods of high inflation. In many companies, it has been supplemented or replaced by a defined contribution plan, which shifts the investment risk to the employee/potential retiree. The August, 1998 market break served as a reminder that while prices may recover fairly soon, bull markets cannot be expected to last forever. If a potential retirement date occurs at a time when stock market conditions are poor, it might make sense to defer retirement for six months or a year in the hope that the market will spring back. (Of course, it could sink further into the mire in the interim!)

Retirement Planning Issues for Women

Although it is not inevitably true, it is very common for married women to survive their husbands. The period of widowhood can be prolonged, because not only do women have a longer life expectancy than men, but women tend to marry men who are older than they are. If, for instance, a couple marries when he is 28 and she is 23, and he lives to be 75, she will be widowed at age 70. If she lives to be 81 and does not remarry, she will be a widow for 11 years.

During those 11 years, her financial security will depend on her own pension and Social Security benefits, as well as provisions the couple has made for the surviving spouse.

The basic form of pension payment is the qualified joint and survivor annuity (QJSA, see below), and the payment from a QJSA is often cut in half when the first spouse dies. Many women do not qualify for pensions in their own right. Maybe they were full-time homemakers who never held paid jobs, or they might have worked for companies that didn't sponsor a pension plan. Perhaps they worked only part-time. The Retirement Equity Act of 1984 made it easier for workers to accumulate vested pension benefits despite interrupted work histories (such as years spent raising children), but many of today's senior citizen women spent a significant part of their working life employed before 1984.

Even women who put many years in the work force usually accumulate smaller pensions than their male counterparts, because:

- they often hold lower-paid jobs,
- they are less likely to have access to nonqualified deferred compensation, and
- in plans that let employees control investment of their accounts, women often lose out because of extreme conservatism in investing; many pick safer but low-yielding options.[4]

PAYMENT FORMS

All defined benefit plans have to make benefits available to married plan participants in "qualified joint and survivor annuity" (QJSA) form. This requirement does *not* apply to all defined contribution plans; target and money purchase plans, for example, must provide a QJSA benefit, but 401(k) plans are not required to do so. Under a QJSA, benefits are paid (usually each month) for the lifetime of the employee and spouse, whichever lives longer. See IRC Sec. 401(a)(11). The basic form is a 50% survivor annuity; in other words, the benefit is cut in half when one spouse dies. However, employers are allowed to subsidize the survivor annuity at any level from 51-100% of the initial payment. If a married employee wants to elect payments for 10 years or 20 years, or a lump sum, or any form other than the qualified joint and survivor annuity (QJSA), the consent of the other spouse is required. For unmarried employees, the basic pension form is the single life annuity.

The “pension max” strategy calls for increasing income for the period just after retirement by electing a 10- or 20-year annuity rather than a QJSA, and using some of the additional income to purchase life insurance that will benefit the surviving spouse.

Plans that are required to provide the QJSA benefit must also provide a qualified preretirement survivor annuity (QPSA) for the surviving spouse of any employee who dies before becoming entitled to retirement benefits.

Although plans have no obligation to permit lump sum withdrawals, many plans do so. For one thing, it’s a convenience for the plan: it just has to make one payment and close the file. (However, the option primarily belongs to the employee; a plan is not allowed to “cash out” a participant involuntarily, unless the account balance is under $5,000, in which case it is deemed too small to administer.) If a client receives a notice that a small balance will be cashed out, the client should be informed that the cashed out amount can be rolled over into an IRA account without a tax penalty, as long as the rollover takes place within 60 days of receipt of the cashout. (If a direct rollover is not elected, the employer must withhold 20% of the cashed-out sum, because the Internal Revenue Code requires income tax withholding from such distributions.)

In addition, lump sum withdrawals are desired by many plan participants. As fiduciaries, plan managers must be quite conservative in their investment strategies. Many participants believe that they can achieve higher returns on their own, or with good professional advice. That doesn’t mean that they’re right—or that their ability to administer money will continue forever.

Lump sums can be especially useful in elder planning because, in addition to traditional financial planning objectives, the older person can use a lump sum to:

- Create a trust that will be used in incapacity planning
- Create an income-only trust (useful in Medicaid planning)
- Set up a giving program to divest assets that are excessive, from the standpoint of Medicaid planning and/or estate planning. This is especially important in "cap" states (see Chapter 6), where the income from a pension in ordinary annuity form is likely to be high enough to preclude Medicaid eligibility
- Purchase a home that can become a Medicaid "homestead," or elder-proof an existing home, or
- Pay the admission fee to a continuing care retirement community.

401(k) PLANS

The 401(k) plan (its rules are found in IRC Section 401(k)[5]) is also known as a CODA (Cash or Deferred Arrangement) because it is funded through an employee's choice to have a portion of compensation paid into the 401(k) account rather than paid currently. Many 401(k) plans offer employer matches (e.g., for every $2 or $3 deferred by the employee, the employer contributes an additional $1) as an incentive. For 1999, the maximum permitted deferral is $10,000. The deferred amount is not taxed as income to the employee until it is withdrawn, nor is the appreciation in the value of the account taxed until retirement.

The employee always has the option of taking the money currently instead of adding it to the account. It is understandable—though unfortunate—that the rate of 401(k) participation and the amounts deferred tend to vary in direct proportion to the employee's income. Although low-income workers are in the most serious need of additional savings for retirement, they are the least likely to defer much if they have a 401(k) account at all.

In some situations, especially in small companies, lack of participation by low-income workers limits the ability of more affluent clients to defer the full 401(k) amount. This happens because 401(k) plans are required to be nondiscriminatory, and the Internal Revenue Code generally mandates nondiscrimination testing of them on the basis of comparing contribution rates for highly compensated to those of rank-and-file employees. If the plan fails the test, deferrals by high-income employees must be cut back (and usually returned to them as taxable compensation). However, design-based safe harbors are available that exempt a 401(k) plan from nondiscrimination testing.

The last two decades have shown a steady shift from traditional defined benefit plans toward defined contribution plans, particularly 401(k) plans. Employers like 401(k) plans because they are funded at least in part by the employee's own salary. The employer's administrative and contribution burdens are much lower under a 401(k) plan than under a pension plan. Close to 90% of employers who have 401(k) plans make matching contributions to the plan; the average "match" rate is about 60 cents for every dollar deferred by the employee.

Although employee deferrals are always 100% vested (i.e., the employee is always entitled to 100% of the balance), the employer match is considered a qualified plan contribution, so the vesting of the match amount is subject to the vesting schedule set forth in the plan document. It is permissible, and quite common, for the employer to require five years of plan participation for 100% vesting in the employer contribution. Employees who leave (or are laid off or fired) before the five years are up are entitled only to that portion of the funds attributable to the employee deferrals, and earnings on them. Furthermore, the employer may provide higher match levels where the employee invests in the employer's stock, or may offer higher match levels as a bonus or employee incentive.

The typical 401(k) plan offers several different investment alternatives from which the employee can choose, such as various equity and income-oriented mutual funds. Some plans, especially those of large corporations, include investment in the employer corporation's stock as one of the choices. In many cases, those clients who are contemplating retirement should be warned about the risk of concentrating too much of the 401(k) account in employer stock; more diversification could yield better post-retirement results.

Probably only 15-20% should be invested in the employer's stock; however, employer stock often makes up one-third or more of the 401(k) portfolio. The closer the employee is to retirement, the greater the risk from failure to diversify; the employee might retire at a time when the employer stock, or other dominant investment, is at low tide. Of course, sometimes the employee is simply lucky, or is able to time retirement based on investment factors, and leaves the workforce when the value of the retirement fund is at a peak.

Plan loans are permitted by many 401(k) plans—that is, the account holder is allowed to borrow up to one-half of the account balance (usually subject to a dollar limit), and to repay the loan over a period of at least five years, with longer repayment terms available for those who use the funds to buy a home. The interest paid by the borrower (at rates close to prime) is redeposited into the account. Account holders should be careful not to abuse plan loans. Failure to repay can result in the borrowed amounts being treated as withdrawals from the plan; if they occur before age 59½, the 10% penalty on premature withdrawals will apply. And, of course, outstanding loans will decrease the size of the account that will be available at retirement.

A plan loan can be very worthwhile if there is a health emergency that is not covered by Medicare or private insurance, but the real cash flow and tax impact of the loan should be compared with the outcome of using other sources of money for the care needs (such as taking out a home equity loan, liquidating investments and profit-taking, or borrowing against life insurance cash value).

SUCCESSION PLANNING FOR THE FAMILY BUSINESS

One of the greatest causes of failure, or of involuntary takeover, of family businesses is the lack of succession planning. Individuals in top management, unwilling to consider the possibility of their own death, incapacity, or even retirement, sometimes refuse to name a successor, provide appropriate training for potential successors, or develop a plan to gradually turn over the reins. As a neutral outsider, the financial planner can play an important part in stressing the value of a practical succession plan to the business and the post-retirement financial well-being of the top management.

The financial planner can also point out the common situation in which the business owner's estate is much too concentrated in shares of the business, and indicate the need for diversification, as well as for life insurance and other means of providing liquidity.

Often, disaster occurs because of the praiseworthy desire to be fair. A parent who owns a majority interest in a close corporation, or a large plurality interest, may divide that interest among his or her children in equal shares. The result is that each heir owns a block of stock that is difficult to sell and may not pay dividends. (This is especially true if the Board of Directors is controlled by other family members who work in the business and want to cut back on dividends and reinvest earnings in corporate needs—including higher salaries for top management!) This is a recipe for corporate deadlock.

An effective planner can help the entire management team and Board of Directors develop a plan (possibly including recapitalization) for an orderly increase in the responsibilities of heirs, or a buyout of some family interests by nonfamily managers. A buy-sell agreement serves many purposes; not only does it set terms for the transition, but, if properly drafted to reflect meaningful values, can establish the value of otherwise hard-to-value stock for estate tax purposes. In a stock redemption agreement, the corporation itself redeems stock belonging to a major stockholder. In a cross-purchase transaction, the other major stockholders buy out the retiring stockholder or the estate of a deceased stockholder.

Retirement planning for the founder can also be a good time to evaluate the corporation's life insurance portfolio. Key-person insurance can compensate the corporation for the loss it sustains when a leader dies. Life insurance purchased by the corporation (entity purchase) or by the designated successor (cross-purchase) can be used to fund payments to the decedent's family under the buy-sell agreement. Disability insurance can be used to fund buyouts premised on the founder's inability to continue leading, rather than upon his death; however, such insurance would not cover payouts resulting from the voluntary retirement by the founder, since this is not an insurable event.

See Chapter 13 for a discussion of the estate tax laws governing succession issues in the family business.

"UN-RETIREMENT": RE-EMPLOYMENT

The decision to retire is not always irreversible. Sometimes a job will open up with the former employer; the retiree already understands the corporate culture, and has a highly relevant track record with the same company. Part-time or full-time employment with another company, or signing on with a temporary agency, are other possibilities. An increasing number of older people take advantage of early retirement incentives or lump sum pension payouts to turn long-cherished entrepreneurial dreams into reality.

Going back to the workforce is a necessity for those who can't maintain a comfortable lifestyle on their retirement income, and is desirable for those who feel stultified without the challenges of work. However, the financial consequences of re-employment are not simple, and retirees should consider all the implications before getting a new job.

As Chapter 9 explains, work performed after Social Security benefits begin, and before age 70, will result in a reduction of Social Security benefits by 33 or 50 cents for every dollar earned in excess of the permitted amount. Of course, the earnings are also subject to income tax and FICA tax, so there may not be much left over after all the reductions are taken into account.

If the employment is short-term, the senior employee may not even qualify for participation in the pension plan, because employers can impose a requirement of one year's tenure (three years if the plan provides immediate vesting) before a new hire can participate in the plan. Even after participation, the plan typically will require either seven-year graded vesting (i.e., the employee's final entitlement to the pension account phases in over time) or five-year cliff vesting (no vesting for five years, then immediate 100% vesting).

A plan can set its normal retirement age as the later of 65 or the fifth year of plan participation (see IRC Sec. 411(a)(8)), so a late hire might have a personal normal retirement age of, for instance, 68 or 73. Thus, the older employee will probably not earn a pension, or at least will not become fully vested in it, on the basis of the new position. (However, it is unlawful for a qualified plan to impose a maximum age for participation in the plan (IRC Sec. 410(a)(2)) or to cease accruals to the plan because of age (IRC Sec. 411(b)(1)(G)).)

It should also be noted that an employer may defer the initial pension payment until 10 years after the date of initial participation, so even an earned and vested pension may not come into pay status until the older individual is quite aged—or deceased. See IRC Sec. 401(a)(14)(B).

TAXATION OF RETIREMENT BENEFITS

Pension plans are a form of deferred compensation; that is, instead of the employee receiving all compensation currently in the year it is earned, part of the compensation is placed into a pension plan. When the employee retires, he will presumably be in a lower tax bracket than during working life, and so will be able to save taxes by receiving the money post-retirement instead of earlier. (This advantage is less pronounced than in the pre-1986 years, when the tax brackets were both more numerous and further apart than under the current system.) Pre-1997 tax laws also penalized the accumulation of "excess" retirement benefits; the assumption was that people were supposed to consume their pension assets, not accumulate them for inheritance. But Congress revised those rules in the Tax Reform Act of 1997, making estate planning for qualified plan assets somewhat easier.

The enactment of the Small Business Job Protection Act of 1996 (SBJPA '96) made 1996 a watershed year in the taxation of pensions. Although the rules of SBJPA '96, as well as amendments added in 1997 and 1998 legislation, are complex, they are by and large quite favorable to taxpayers, and make it easier to fund a financially comfortable retirement.

Before 1996, a tax penalty was imposed on those who continued working beyond age 70½ and neglected to take their first plan distribution by April 1 of the year after the year in which they reached age 70½ (i.e., the required beginning date for qualified plans). A 50% penalty is imposed on individuals who take less than the required minimum distribution (basically, a distribution sufficient to liquidate the entire fund over the lifetime of the retiree, or the joint lifetimes of the retiree and a chosen beneficiary).

One of the changes made by SBJPA '96 was to change the required beginning date for most qualified plan participants to April 1 following *the later of* (1) the year in which the participant reaches age 70½, or (2) the year in which the participant retires. See IRC Sec. 401(a)(9)(C)(i). This change does not apply to more-than-5% owners of the employer sponsoring the plan, nor to distributions from IRAs. However, rank-and-file employees who remain employed after age 70 can generally defer the first plan distribution until they actually retire.[6]

The majority of pension payments (i.e., those taking the form of a continuing stream of monthly payments) are annuities. The taxation of annuities requires a distinction between the tax-free return of the taxpayer's capital and taxable sums that represent investment appreciation or contributions made by the employer. Therefore, an exclusion ratio must be calculated for the annuity.

Before SBJPA '96, this was somewhat complex, involving actuarial calculations. For annuity starting dates after November 18, 1996, a simplified schedule is available for life annuities. (If the annuity is provided for a term of years, the actual number of payments, e.g., 120 payments for a 10-year annuity, is used to calculate the exclusion ratio.) See IRC Sec. 72(d)(1)(B). The annuity is taxed as if the following number of payments will be made, based on the age at retirement:

Age	**Number of Payments**
55 or less	360
56-60	310
61-65	260
66-70	210
71 or over	160

For individuals who defer retirement for many years, note that in the case of an annuitant whose annuity starting date occurs after age 75, this table can be used only there are fewer than five years of payments guaranteed under the annuity.

The Taxpayer Relief Act of 1997 extended this concept by enacting another schedule, this time for the number of payments that can be expected under a joint and survivor annuity. This schedule is available for annuity starting dates beginning after December 31, 1997.

Combined Age for Both Annuitants	**Number of Payments**
110 or less	410
111-120	360
121-130	310
131-140	260
141 or over	210

With either table, the calculation is performed by dividing the employee's basis in the retirement annuity, measured as of the retirement date, by the applicable number of payments. The result is the excludable portion of each monthly payment.

Lump Sum Distributions

Without special relief provisions, taking a lump sum distribution would not be feasible for most retirees because the entire amount of the lump sum, typically in five or six figures, would be taxable income for the year of receipt. Before SBJPA '96, two forms of income averaging were permitted. The taxpayer would still have to pay the tax in the year of receipt of the lump sum, but the amount of tax would be calculated as if the lump sum were received in five or ten installments.

Although in general, SBJPA '96 was helpful to taxpayers, it repealed five-year averaging, effective for distributions occurring after December 31, 1999. Ten-year averaging continues to be permitted, but only for individuals born before 1936; thus, the large baby boom cohort is excluded from using 10-year averaging. Therefore, persons who are contemplating retiring in either 1999 or 2000 and who, all other things being equal, would receive their pension in lump sum form, might wish to accelerate retirement to 1999 in order to take advantage of the special averaging provisions while they are still available.

These limitations are not always onerous, however, because an IRA rollover can be used to defer taxation of all or part of a lump sum distribution. Any portion of a lump sum that is not desired for immediate use (and immediate taxation) can be placed in an IRA. Qualifying individuals may be able to convert a traditional IRA to a Roth IRA; however, such a conversion will result in immediate tax consequences (see Chapter 10). Once rolled over, the funds become part of the IRA, and are subject to the minimum distribution requirements applicable to traditional IRAs. Roth IRAs are not subject to these requirements.

PRACTICAL AND TAX CONSEQUENCES OF NONQUALIFIED PLANS

For a corporation to receive a current tax deduction for sums contributed to its qualified plans, the corporation generally must make benefits available on a nondiscriminatory basis to those employees who have worked long enough to be eligible for plan participation. Employees do not recognize taxable income as a result of contributions made to the plan on their behalf, nor are they taxed on the appreciation in the value of the account as it grows during their working life.

Qualified plans are subject to detailed and often onerous requirements imposed by the Internal Revenue Code and ERISA.

Some businesses (especially small businesses) may find it impossible to fund and manage qualified plans. For others, it may be possible to maintain a plan, but the benefit level that top management would receive is not high enough to have a motivating effect. In these situations, it makes sense to have a nonqualified plan instead of, or as a supplement to, the qualified plan.

The hallmark of nonqualified plans is that they are permitted to discriminate. Instead of covering all employees who have stayed with the company for a few years, the plan can be limited to only one executive, or a small group of executives. Or, the plan can have broader coverage, but provide unequal benefits. The tradeoff for this additional flexibility is that tax consequences are less favorable.

The employee is taxed as soon as he has "constructively received" benefits under the nonqualified plan. In general, income is constructively received when it is available, regardless of whether the employee actually receives it. However, income is not constructively received as long as the employee's rights are forfeitable, such as where the employee's control of its receipt is subject to substantial limitations or restrictions, or a contingency which might result in forfeiture of the employee's rights to the future payments. However, the IRS has ruled that there is no constructive receipt where the employee's rights are nonforfeitable, provided that (1) the agreement to defer compensation is entered into before the compensation is earned, and (2) the employer's promise to pay is not secured in any way.

A common strategy is for the corporation to avoid funding the nonqualified deferred compensation plan in advance. (This is not permitted for qualified plans; contributions must be made on a regular basis.) The executive is therefore subject to the risk that the corporation's creditors will be entitled to funds that would otherwise have been used to pay the nonqualified plan benefits.

The employer's tax deduction is deferred until the employee becomes taxable on the contributions. Of course, the employee will prefer not to have constructive receipt until after retirement, when presumably he will be in a lower tax bracket. The worst-case scenario occurs when the employee is deemed to have constructively received the income, but has not received any cash with which to pay the tax liability.

Even if the plan allows gifts of the benefits (most plans forbid such gifts), this is bad tax planning. The employee is still considered the recipient of the income, and therefore still has to pay income tax on it, despite also having made a taxable gift of a future interest that doesn't even qualify for the annual exclusion.

Generally, any unpaid balance of nonqualified compensation remaining at the executive's death will become part of the taxable estate. Furthermore, benefits remaining unpaid at the time of the executive's death will be subject to income tax, as income in respect of a decedent; however, the recipient of the income is then allowed to take a corresponding deduction for estate and generation-skipping tax paid on the income. See IRC Sec. 691.

Types of Nonqualified Plans

Employers have developed various ways to structure nonqualified plans:

- A Salary Continuation Formula plan provides a specified deferred amount, payable in the future, in addition to benefits provided under other plans and requires no reduction in the covered employee's salary. It generally uses a defined benefit type of formula. Such a plan for a selected group of executives is sometimes referred to as a "SERP" (for "supplemental executive retirement plan").

- A Salary Reduction Formula plan involves an election to defer a specified amount of the employee's compensation, similar to a 401(k) plan. Actual reduction of salary is not required; the contribution can be in the form of a "bonus."

- An Excess Benefit plan provides benefits for executives whose qualified plan benefits are limited under the Internal Revenue Code, making up the difference between the amounts payable under their qualified plan and the amount they would have received if there were no benefit limitations.

- Stock appreciation rights (SARs) and phantom stock formulas use a benefit formula determined on the basis of the value of a specified number of shares of employer stock, or stated in terms of shares of employer stock rather than cash.

- A Rabbi trust is an irrevocable trust set up by an employer for advance funding of nonqualified deferred compensation. The employer is not allowed to recoup assets from the trust until all deferred compensation obligations are satisfied. However, the employees covered by the nonqualified plan are subject to the risk that the corporation's general creditors will be able to place claims against the rabbi trust assets. (This risk yields tax benefits, because executives covered by the plan do not recognize income at the time funds are placed into the rabbi trust.) Rabbi trusts are so named because the first one was created to benefit the clergyman of a synagogue.

- Secular trust: A variation on a rabbi trust that protects trust assets from the claims of the corporation's general and bankruptcy creditors. However, the executive covered by a secular trust must recognize current income (which is taxed under the Internal Revenue Code's Section 72 annuity rules) from the contributions to the trust and perhaps the income earned by those contributions.

For unfunded plans, the following methods may be used:

- An Employer Reserve Account is an actual investment account where funds remain available to the employer and its creditors.

- An Employer Reserve Account with employee investment direction gives the employee the right to "direct" the investment of his account among broad types of investments, such as a family of mutual funds. However, a choice of specific investments may result in constructive receipt, as will direction that is binding and not merely advisory.

- Corporate-owned life insurance policies on the employee's life, owned by and payable to the employer corporation, provide a substantial death benefit even in the early years of the plan, which can be quite valuable to younger employees.

RETIREE HEALTH BENEFITS

At one time, it was common for employers, especially large corporations, to promise their retirees "lifetime health coverage, at no cost to you." Companies that want to downsize may offer a generous health benefit package as an incentive for early retirement. However, a common result is that the employees most interested in early retirement are often those employees with health problems. So, the company may end up paying high insurance or medical costs for many years.

During the last several decades, employers have been hard-pressed by rising health costs. Therefore, it is less likely than before that companies will offer new retiree health benefits and more likely that they will cut back or terminate benefits.[7] It is possible for employers to alter their retiree health benefit programs (or, to look at it the other way around, potential retirees are at risk of losing health benefits) because, for legal purposes, retiree health benefits are deemed to be "welfare benefits." Although pension benefits under qualified plans are required to vest according to the schedules permitted by the Internal Revenue Code, welfare benefits do not have to vest. If the employer has taken the precautionary step of drafting the retiree health benefit plan in a manner that reserves the right to alter the plan, the employer will probably be allowed to change the plan at its discretion.

In arranging health coverage for retirees, it is important not to forget that Medicare coverage is determined on the basis of age or disability, not employment status. Although Social Security provides spousal benefits, Medicare does not. A spouse under age 65 of a Medicare beneficiary is not entitled to Medicare coverage merely because the beneficiary is covered, even though he or she may have been covered as a dependent under an employment-related health plan. Therefore, a person who retires early and who does not have retiree health benefits must find some other way of filling the "gap" between employer-provided health coverage during work life, and Medicare benefits.

Fortunately, the Health Insurance Portability and Accountability Act of 1996 (HIPAA) protects early retirees who have preexisting health conditions from being turned down for individual health coverage. This doesn't mean that the premium will be affordable—only that a preexisting condition limitation will not be applied.

COBRA Continuation Coverage

COBRA stands for Comprehensive Omnibus Budget Reconciliation Act of 1985,[8] a statute that seeks to prevent individuals who lose a job, or retire, from losing access to insurance (at least in the short run). In effect, a person who purchases continuation coverage takes over the obligation of paying the premium formerly shouldered by the employer. But instead of paying the insurer, the ex-employee pays the employer, who is not allowed to charge more than 102% of the actual premium. (The extra 2% is for administrative costs.) COBRA does not apply to companies with fewer than 20 employees. COBRA "qualifying events" include death or divorce of the employee, Medicare entitlement, layoff or termination, or the employer's bankruptcy.

In the retirement context, COBRA is especially important because the spouse and dependents of a former worker may have COBRA rights. Therefore, they can elect continued coverage under the employer-provided plan if the retiree is eligible for Medicare but the spouse and dependents are not. Individuals who are at risk of losing their health care coverage because of divorce from a person who has health coverage can also make a COBRA election.

Eligibility for continuation coverage can last for 18, 29, or 36 months, depending on the reason triggering entitlement to the coverage. Entitlement ends as soon as the person electing the coverage becomes eligible for coverage under another employer-provided plan. Typically, this happens when a younger person gets another job that provides health coverage. A 1998 Supreme Court decision, *Geissal v. Moore Medical Corp.,* 118 S.Ct. 1869 (1998) clarifies that COBRA coverage can be terminated only on the basis of coverage obtained *after* making the COBRA election, not coverage (e.g., spousal benefits) existing at the time of the COBRA election.

COBRA eligibility can also be cut off when the ex-employee has actually enrolled in Medicare (although not merely because he is Medicare-eligible.)

Insurance Availability

A mid-1998 General Accounting Office (GAO) report[9] assessed the availability of health coverage for the "near elderly" (i.e., persons over 55 but below Medicare eligibility age). Typically, this group is reducing its workforce participation and reporting declining health status over time. The GAO report's conclusion is that at present, the proportion of this group that is uninsured is comparable to (or even smaller than) the proportion of other age groups.

However, early retirees face challenges in finding affordable coverage, especially after their COBRA entitlement ends, and especially if they suffer from poor health. The percentage without insurance was higher in the age 62-64 subgroup than in younger subgroups. This makes sense, given the greater access of younger people to employer group health plans and COBRA continuation coverage. The higher the household income of the near-elderly person, the more likely that he would be insured by the employer. This was true in 85.7% of the families where income was $75,000 or over, but only 15.6% of those where income was under $10,000.

According to this report, over 60% of large employers offered retiree health coverage in the 1980s, but as of 1998, under 40% did so.[10] Thus, in the future, as new individuals enter the near elderly age group and approach retirement, they will be less likely to have access to retiree health coverage, and more likely to have to spend a significant portion of their income on paying for health insurance. The GAO estimates that in 1989, 76% of the near elderly were insured, either via an employer group health plan, retiree health benefits, or privately purchased insurance. However, by 1995 this percentage that had declined to 69%.

Availability of retiree health benefits to early retirees has been highly dependent on the industry. In 1997, for instance, 78% of government agencies provided retiree health benefits versus 57% in financial services, 47% in transportation, communication and utilities, 39% in manufacturing; 35% in services (the fastest-growing sector of the economy), and only 14% in wholesale/retail. Ironically, less than a quarter of health sector workers had access to retiree health benefits.

The Health Insurance Portability and Accessibility Act of 1996 (HIPAA) serves to protect eligible people against insurance coverage denials based on preexisting conditions. However, HIPAA applies only if the individual has at least 18 months of "creditable coverage" under an employer group health plan or other prior health plan, did not have a coverage gap exceeding 63 days, and has used up all COBRA entitlements. Furthermore, the fact that a person can purchase coverage doesn't mean that he can afford the coverage or can do so without severe financial stress. Even if the insurance premium is currently affordable, future increases may place it out of reach.

SUMMARY

For older clients who have not yet retired, it is important to offer guidance about the best time to retire in order to maximize the size of the pension and obtain optimal tax treatment. The client who has not yet retired may also have the option of taking a lump sum distribution instead of an annuity, and then transferring the lump sum, purchasing an annuity, entering a continuing care retirement community or otherwise using it to further an elder plan.

Early retirees should be sure to consider their COBRA options for continued acute health insurance coverage, because they typically will not be Medicare-eligible until age 65. All retirees should be aware that their former employer probably has the legal right to reduce or terminate retiree health benefits, so plans should be made for alternative coverage.

Once retired, older clients need advice about the best deployment of their pensions, as well as how to use income to secure the appropriate housing and health care.

CHAPTER FOOTNOTES

1. "What is Your Savings Personality?" Issue Brief No. 200 (August, 1998), Employee Benefits Research Institute. See http://www.ebri.org/ibex/ib200.htm and http://www.ebri.org/serv/Personality.htm.

2. See, e.g., Ellen E. Schultz and Elizabeth MacDonald,"Employers Win Big With a Pension Shift; Employees Often Lose," *Wall Street Journal* December 4, 1998, p. A1; Ellen E. Schultz, "Ins and Outs of 'Cash Balance' Plan," *Wall Street Journal* December 4, 1998, p. C1; Ellen E. Schultz, "Some Workers Facing Pension Hit," *Wall Street Journal* December 18, 1998, p. C1; Ellen E. Schultz, "Some Pension Funds Look Like 401(k)'s, But They Sure Don't Behave Like Them," "Cash Balance Plans' Key: Interest Rates," *Wall Street Journal* December 31, 1998, p. C1 and C19; "'Cash' Pensions Trigger Protest of New Allies," *Wall Street Journal* January 21, 1999 p. C1; and "Older Workers Fight 'Cash Balance' Plans," *Wall Street Journal* February 11, 1999, p. C1.

3. See *Hughes Aircraft Company v. Jacobson*, 119 S.Ct. 755 (1999). See also, David Cay Johnston, "Ruling Favors Employers on Pension Gains," *New York Times*, January 26, 1999, p. C1.

4. See Carole Ann King, "Women Face Financial Crisis in Retirement," *National Underwriter*, Life and Health/Financial Services Edition, November 9, 1998, p. 31.

5. For discussions of 401(k) issues, see, e.g., Ellen E. Schultz, "Warning: Be Wary of Retirement Plan Cash Out," *Wall Street Journal,* December 4, 1997 p. C1; "The 401(k) Loan: Let Borrowers Beware," *Wall Street Journal,* January 16, 1998, p. C1; "Playing Safely with 'Matches' In Your 401(k)," *Wall Street Journal,* May 1, 1998, p. C1; Vanessa O'Connell and Pui-Wing Tam, "Employer Stock May be Risky for Nest Eggs," *Wall Street Journal,* February 11, 1998 p. C1; Virginia Munger Kahn, "There's Strength in Diversity: Mixing 401(k) Funds to Help Reduce Risk," *New York Times* January 11, 1998 Business page 45; Sidebar, "Trends in 401(k)'s: How Does Your Plan Compare?" *New York Times,* November 23, 1997, Business page 6.

6. Employees who started receiving minimum distributions under the pre-SBJPA '96 rules, but who remain employed, may be able to cease distributions and restart them after they retire. See Notice 97-75, 1997-51 IRB 18.

7. See "Retiree Health Insurance: Erosion in Retiree Health Benefits Offered by Large Employers," GAO/T-HEHS-98-110 (March 10, 1998).

8. The latest COBRA regulations are contained in an IRS Final Rule published in 64 Federal Register 5160 (February 3, 1999).

9. "Private Health Insurance: Declining Employer Coverage May Affect Access for 55- to 64-Year Olds," GAO/HEHS-98-133 (June 1, 1998).

10. For a discussion of the declining availability of retiree health coverage, see "Retiree Health Insurance: Erosion in Retiree Health Benefits Offered by Large Employers," GAO/T-HEHS-98-110 (March 10, 1998).

Chapter 9

SOCIAL SECURITY

The Old Age, Survivors, and Disability Insurance (OASDI) program is Title II of the federal Social Security Act. As its name suggests, it provides benefits for persons who are totally disabled and unable to work, but its major function is providing retirement benefits to retired workers and benefits to survivors of retired workers.

The OASDI system is funded by taxes imposed on self-employed persons, and on employers and employees. For 1999, this FICA (Federal Insurance Contribution Act) tax is imposed on earnings up to $72,600. The tax rate is 7.65%, each, for employer and employee, or 15.3% for the self-employed, made up of a 6.2% FICA tax and an additional Medicare tax of 1.45%. The Medicare tax is imposed on all earnings, without limit. It does not phase-out as the FICA tax does.

The Social Security system is a fundamental part of the economic landscape, especially for senior citizens. According to the Social Security Administration, in December 1998, 44.2 million of the total United States population of 271 million received Social Security benefits. About two-thirds of those receiving benefits (62%) were retired workers, 7% were the spouses and children of retirees, and 16% were survivors of deceased workers.[1] The average individual received a benefit of $953 a month; the average retiree couple received $1430 a month.

SOCIAL SECURITY RETIREMENT BENEFITS

Traditionally, the Social Security Normal Retirement Age (NRA) was set at 65, which is also the conventional level for pension eligibility. However, one step being taken to preserve the soundness of the Social Security system is a gradual increase in the NRA. By 2027, the NRA will have increased to 67. For most members of the Baby Boom generation, it will be 66.

Under the Social Security system, workers can receive a full benefit if they retire at their NRA. The benefit is actuarially reduced if they retire early (i.e., between the ages of 62 and normal retirement age), and actuarially increased if they retire late. Late retirement is much more of a gamble: it is easier to determine the number of additional checks that will be received between actual retirement and the NRA than to determine how long the person will survive after late retirement.

The 1999 cost-of-living adjustment (COLA) was only 1.3.%. The average monthly Social Security benefit for all workers in 1999 is estimated to be $780 a month versus $1,310 for a senior-citizen couple, both of whom receive Social Security benefits, or $749 for a widowed senior citizen. The maximum Social Security benefit for a worker retiring at age 65 in 1999 is $1,373 a month. (This is much higher than the average because the maximum benefit is received by those individuals who paid the maximum FICA tax each year because they earned significantly more than the average worker.)

A particular individual's Social Security benefit, based on his or her earnings record, equals his or her Primary Insurance Amount (PIA). (Derivative benefits paid to spouses, ex-spouses, etc., are also set as a percentage of PIA — in this case, the PIA of the worker whose earnings record the benefits derive.)

Generally, the PIA is calculated by indexing the worker's Social Security earnings (after 1950), determining Average Indexed Monthly Earnings (AIME), and applying the appropriate formula to the AIME to determine the PIA. Broadly speaking, indexing involves a comparison between actual FICA earnings and average national earnings. Because FICA earnings are used, earnings above the FICA maximum do not count for this purpose. The indexing computation also involves using the "indexing averaging wage" for each year after 1950 up to, but not including, the "indexing year" (i.e., the second year before the worker reaches age 62, or dies, or becomes disabled before age 62). Thus, the benefits of persons reaching age 62 in 1999 are calculated using the 1997 indexing average wage (which is $27,426.00).

The actual benefit is calculated with AIME and "bend points"– i.e., for 1999, the PIA equals 90% of the first $505 of the person's AIME, plus 32% of AIME between $505 and $3,043, plus 15% of any AIME in excess of $3,043.

Also for 1999, an elderly person who earns income *and* collects Social Security benefits will be penalized $1 in benefits for every $2 in earnings above $9,600 a year if he or she is younger than age 65, or $1 in benefits for every $3 in earnings above $15,500 a year if he or she has reached age 65 but has not yet reached age 70. After an individual's seventieth birthday, he or she can earn any amount without reduction in his or her Social Security benefit.

The Senior Citizens' Right to Work Act of 1996 (P.L. 104-121) calls for significant increases in the amount that senior citizens can earn without losing Social Security benefits. For the year 2000, persons over 65 but under 70 will be able to earn $17,000 a year without loss of benefits; the figure is $25,000 for 2001, and $30,000 for 2002.

The first year subsequent to retirement is a "grace year," during which additional earnings are permitted without penalty during any month the individual does not (1) earn more than $1,292 (age 65 - 69) or $800 (under age 65) as an employee, or (2) render substantial services in self-employment.

DERIVATIVE BENEFITS

For unmarried people, benefit eligibility is a fairly simple matter — the calculations are made based on the earnings record. However, the majority of workers are married and, thus, matters become much more complicated. A variety of "derivative benefits" for family members can be paid based on a worker's earnings record. The major ones are:

- Spouse. In a two-earner couple, a husband or wife is entitled to a benefit as a retired worker, or as a spouse, but is not entitled to both benefits. If the spousal retirement benefit is higher than the spouse's own retirement benefit, then the spouse may receive a combination of benefits equalling the higher spousal benefit.

- Divorced spouse

- Surviving spouse

- Surviving divorced spouse

Benefits can also be paid to the children of disabled or deceased workers; the dependent, surviving parents (age 62 or older) of a deceased worker are also eligible for survivor's benefits. Generally, a person receives either a derivative benefit or a benefit based on his or her own earnings record, whichever is higher, but cannot receive the full amount of both benefits.

To qualify for derivative benefits, the spouse of a worker must be married to a retired or disabled worker already receiving benefits, and must be at least 62 years old. The divorced spouse of a retired or disabled worker can receive derivative benefits based on that worker's earnings record as long as he or she is at least 62 years old, the marriage lasted at least 10 years, and the divorced spouse is not married at the time of the benefit application. (If the divorced spouse married and divorced someone else after the divorce from the worker, that marriage will not bar the receipt of benefits based on the first spouse's earnings record.) The benefit to a divorced spouse can be paid even if the worker spouse has not yet begun to receive benefits.

The benefit for a spouse or divorced spouse is 50% of the worker's PIA. These derivative benefits are reduced if the worker's own benefit is reduced because of retirement before the normal age, excess earnings, or if the spouse or divorced spouse chooses to receive benefits before his or her own normal retirement age.

The benefit for a surviving spouse or surviving divorced spouse is 100% of the deceased worker's benefit. It can be paid to a surviving spouse or surviving divorced spouse who has reached age 60 (or has reached age 50 and is disabled), and is not married. However, remarriage after the survivor's benefit begins does not always terminate benefit eligibility.

Derivative benefits are limited by a "maximum family benefit" that applies to all earnings based on a particular person's earnings record. For 1999, the family maximum is 150% of the first $645 of the worker's PIA, plus 272% of PIA between $645 and $931, plus 134% of PIA between $931 and $1214, plus 175% of PIA in excess of $1214.

TAXATION OF SOCIAL SECURITY BENEFITS

Low-income Social Security recipients do not have to pay income tax on their benefits. However, for individuals or married couples whose total income ("modified adjusted gross income") plus one-half of the Social Security benefit exceeds the "base amount" ($25,000 for single persons or married persons filing separately; $32,000 for married couples filing a joint return), then between 50% and 85% of the benefit will constitute taxable income. Total income includes certain tax preference items, such as municipal bond interest, that generally escape taxation.

Starting February 1, 1999, senior citizens were given the option of voluntary income tax withholding on their Social Security benefits. This can provide convenience to individuals subject to taxation on the benefit, and who would otherwise have to make quarterly estimated tax payments (or would have to increase their current estimated tax payments) to compensate.

LONG-RANGE PROSPECTS FOR THE SYSTEM

The Social Security system does not operate like a private pension system — although individuals can receive information about the size of their Social Security "account," the account is a purely hypothetical entity. The Social Security system does not accumulate the FICA taxes paid by each person and his or her employer, investing the funds until the individual begins to collect benefits. Instead, current taxes paid by current employees are used to pay benefits to current retirees and disabled individuals.

By the way, the Social Security Administration issues its predictions in three versions, optimistic, pessimistic, and neither optimistic nor pessimistic. However, their viewpoint is the opposite of most people's viewpoints. Their optimistic estimate, for instance, predicts shorter life spans and more deaths. It is optimistic only in the sense of reducing the cost of providing Social Security benefits, not in the sense of improving most people's individual situations.

The strength of the economy in recent years allowed the Social Security Administration to revise its estimates in early 1999. The 1999 estimate was that the Social Security trust fund would stay solvent until 2034 (rather than 2032, as earlier predicted). See "Status of the Social Security and Medicare Programs," a summary of the 1999 Annual Reports issued by the Boards of Trustees of Social Security and Medicare and available on-line at *www.ssa.gov/OACT/TRUSM/trsummary.html*. However, even the most optimistic figures show that by that time, Social Security and Medicare will account for a huge portion of the federal budget.

The soundness of the system depends on many factors, including the "dependency ratio" (the number of active tax-paying workers to retirees and other non-taxpayers), and the size of the benefits payable to current retirees. Certain demographic facts create significant problems for Social Security retirement benefits (and Medicare, SSI, and disability benefits as well). The Baby Boom generation is very large, and includes many people who earned at the top of the FICA wage scale and, therefore, are entitled to the maximum Social Security benefit. Unfortunately the generation behind the Baby Boomers are fewer in number and declining fertility rates make it likely that the number of future cohorts will also be small (i.e., it is physically possible that an only child or an individual with one sibling will decide to have eight children, but it is unlikely as a social matter).

Congress has already taken steps to reform the system by increasing the Normal Retirement Age (NRA) to 67 (in 2027).[2] The Normal Retirement Age could be increased even further, but this is not politically popular. Social Security benefits could be reduced, in the interest of keeping the system solvent longer, but this would definitely be unpopular. An increase in the already heavy payroll taxes would probably be just as unpopular. (In fact, many low-income persons pay more in Social Security taxes than they do in income taxes.)

In the short run, the Social Security Administration could keep benefits going by borrowing from the private sector, but this would be an expensive proposition and would make the problem even worse in the long run. Alternatively, the computation of benefits could be changed so that the system would be less costly while still providing full benefits according to its own termsb by:

- adjusting the number of years of earnings used to calculate the PIA, increasing it from 35 to 38. (However, more men than women have 38 years of covered earnings experience, so this measure could have the effect of reducing women's Social Security benefits even lower (see below);
- reducing the automatic COLAs that are currently applied every year;
- making Medicare more like Medicaid by restricting benefits to persons with low income and assets, or by reducing benefits to the affluent elderly; or
- increasing the proportion of the Social Security benefit that is subject to income tax.

The Social Security Advisory Council has proposed three options: (1) the Maintain Benefits plan (MB); (2) the Individual Accounts plan (IA); and (3) the Personal Security Accounts plan (PSA).[3]

The MB plan is much like the present system, but bases the computation period for benefits on 38 years of earnings, not 35. The IA plan would operate much like a 401(k) plan. Workers would have to contribute 1.6% of taxable earnings to a government-maintained individual account. Each person would direct the investments in his or her account based on a limited number of investment options. This plan would also reduce the basic derivative benefit from 50% to 33% of the worker's basic benefit, would accelerate the legislated increases in normal retirement age, and would index it to keep pace with increases in longevity.

The PSA plan would scrap the existing system and create a new, two-tiered system. The Tier I benefit, set at 65% of the federal poverty line, would be available after 35 years of covered service. The Tier II benefit would be distributed from the 401(k)-type investment account, funded by diverting 5% of the worker's Social Security payroll tax into the account. The PSA would be administered by the private sector, not the government. Workers could take lump-sum payments from their accounts at retirement instead of collecting monthly benefits and, unlike pension lump-sum distributions, consent of the spouse would not be required. The PSA plan is the most radical, the riskiest for workers, and the one that opens up the most potential opportunities for the financial services sector.

The idea of investing Social Security funds in the stock market, where there is the potential for appreciation, is attractive to many people and is favored by many lawmakers. The Clinton administration is in favor of investing part of the Social Security reserves in the stock market; at press time the fate of the proposal was unresolved.[4] However, the 1998 stock market downturn is a painful reminder that whatever goes up at least has the potential to come down. Furthermore, in order to proceed with this proposal it would have to be determined who would administer the accounts, what fees would be due, and who could be blamed if something went wrong.

A simple answer would be to let each worker control the investment of his or her own account. However, that might put unsophisticated, low-income workers with little investment experience at risk. In addition, fees and charges would take a much bigger toll on small accounts than on big ones. Furthermore, many people's notions of fairness would be violated if two people with the same earnings record and family make-up received Social Security benefits that were very different.

There may also be some lessons to be learned from the British experience. Starting in 1988, the British government encouraged its citizens to opt out of their counterpart to our Social Security system and to invest instead in "personal pensions" that they could manage themselves. Financial services organizations benefited greatly from the new market, but in many instances they gave bad advice. Furthermore, high loads made the personal pensions compare badly to the corporate pensions they replaced. Employers usually matched some part of the employee contributions to the government system, but did not match the personal pensions. The financial services companies were ultimately forced to pay compensation — estimated in the range of $18 billion — for "misselling."[5]

Ironically, the financial status of the Social Security system would have been even worse off if the Department of the Treasury had done a better job of computerizing the system under which the Social Security Administration invests FICA and Medicare taxes to buy Treasury securities. At the end of 1998, the Treasury discovered that it had overpaid the interest to the Social Security and Medicare systems for 18 years. Each system received about $1.4 billion in unearned interest between 1988 and 1998, and would receive about another $3 billion excess interest on bonds already purchased. Treasury bonds purchased in 1999 and after will pay only the correct amount of interest, reducing the Social Security trust fund by $700 million to $1 billion a year.[6]

ISSUES FOR ELDERLY WOMEN

As noted throughout this book, women's greater longevity and the tendency of women to marry men older than themselves combine to make it likely that the average married woman will experience widowhood — perhaps a prolonged period of widowhood. The majority of married women today spend most of their adult lives in the work force, and most of them will be subject to FICA taxes. Unfortunately, the basic structure of Social Security has not changed since its inception (after the Great Depression) when only a minority of married women were employed outside the home. Consequently, they will be eligible to collect a retirement benefit based on their own earnings record, or based on 50% of their husband's earnings record — but not the full amount of both. The benefit paid to a surviving spouse is calculated on the deceased spouse's earnings record.

Women are also at a disadvantage with respect to private pensions due to: a pattern of working in lower-paid jobs; a higher probability of working at a company that does not provide a pension plan; and time spent out of the work force because of child rearing. Furthermore, on the average, women tend to be more afraid of financial risks than men are. In a pension plan that shifts investment risks to participants, a common pattern among women is that they tend to invest in low-risk — but also low-return — investment alternatives, and often end up with smaller pension entitlements as a result. The combination of little or no private pension entitlement, and lower Social Security benefits, can be extremely dangerous to the financial security of elderly women.

In practice, a low-income, two-earner household will receive less in Social Security benefits than a single-earner household earning the same amount. Figures from consulting firm William M. Mercer Inc.,[7] show that if a married couple earns $17,100 each, they will pay $2,120 a year in FICA taxes. The basic Social Security benefit for the couple would be $1,348 a month; if the husband dies first, the wife would be entitled to a surviving spouse benefit of $674 a month.

However, another couple, in which the husband earns $34,200 a year and the wife is not employed outside the home, would pay the same $2,120 in FICA taxes but nevertheless receive a combined monthly benefit of $1,623. Furthermore, the surviving wife would be entitled to $1,082 per month in surviving spouse benefits. In other words, the one-income couple would receive *more* in benefits despite paying the *same* amount of FICA tax to "buy" the benefits.

The scenario works out differently for high-income couples, especially if they earn enough for part of their compensation to be free of FICA tax because it exceeds the maximum threshold. Consider two couples with household income of $102,600 a year each. The single-earner couple would be responsible for $4,241 in FICA tax, and the combined retirement benefits for the couple would be $2,036 a month. The surviving wife could receive a $1,357 monthly benefit.

A dual-earner couple, each of whom earns $51,300 a year, would contribute $6,361 a year in FICA taxes to the system. They would receive a *higher* monthly benefit than the single-earner couple, $6,361 a year, but the surviving wife's widow's benefit would be *lower*, $1,258 versus $1,357 a month. Furthermore, the higher monthly benefit would not be an accurate representation of their greater tax burden, because they would pay 50% more FICA tax but receive only 24% more in each monthly check. The disproportion is even greater because most people are FICA-paying workers for more years than they are benefit-receiving retirees.

CHAPTER FOOTNOTES

1. These Social Security Act figures are quoted in David E. Rosenbaum, "Social Security: The Basics, With a Tally Sheet," *New York Times*, January 28, 1999, p. A21.

2. For information on Social Security reform, see GAO/T-HEHS-98-43, "Social Security Reform: Demographic Trends Underlie Long-Term Financing Shortage" (November 20, 1997); GAO/T-HEHS-98-95, "Social Security: Restoring Long-Term Solvency Will Require Difficult Choices" (February 2, 1998); GAO/T-HEHS-98-207, "Social Security Reform: Raising Retirement Ages Improves Program Solvency But May Cause Hardship for Some" (July 15, 1998); GAO/OCG-99-20, "Major Management Challenges and Program Risks: Social Security Administration" (January 1, 1999); GAO/T-HEHS-99-52, "Social Security Reform: Implications for Women" (February 3, 1999); GAO/T-HEHS-99-94, "Social Security: Criteria for Evaluating Social Security Reform Proposals" (March 25, 1999); Christina Duff and Laurie McGinley, "Economy Gives Social Security a Reprieve," *Wall Street Journal*, April 29, 1998, p. A2; Bob Davis, "After Election Triumph, Clinton Turns Attention to Social Security Reform as Legacy Polisher," *Wall Street Journal*, November 6, 1998, p. A16; Jacob M. Schlesinger, "Clinton Social Security Plan Faces Critics," *Wall Street Journal*, February 10, 1999, p. A2; Richard W. Stevenson, "Social Security Is Issue, But Solution is Elusive," *New York Times*, November 11, 1998, p. A22; Jacob M. Schlesinger, "Economy Lifts Medicare, Social Security Solvency," *Wall Street Journal*, March 31, 1999, p. A2; David E. Rosenbaum, "Longer Solvency for Medicare and Social Security," *New York Times*, March 31, 1999, p. A22; Michael M. Weinstein, "No Comfort in New Solvency Figures," *New York Times*, April 1, 1999, p. A22. For a reminder that, no matter how serious the system's problems, it has done a great deal for America's elderly, see "Social Security Found to Save Third of Elderly From Poverty," *New York Times*, April 9, 1999, p. A16. Laura Castaneda's "Prices that Don't Fit the Profile," *New York Times*, November 8, 1998, p. 10, deals with a related issue: the price index that the Bureau of Labor Statistics creates to track the expenses of the elderly, and that is also used by the Social Security Administration to calculate COLAs. Advocates for the elderly point out that the index understates inflation in prescription drug costs — a major budget item for the elderly.

3. See GAO/T-HEHS-97-112, "Social Security Reform: Implications for the Financial Well-Being of Women" (April 10, 1997), for full details.

4. See Diana B. Henriques, "Social Security Investment Plan Raises a Debate," *New York Times*, January 24, 1999, p. A16.

5. Sara Calian and Steve Stecklow, "Social Security Switch in U.K. is Disastrous; A Caution to the U.S.?" *Wall Street Journal*, August 10, 1998, p. A1.

6. David Wessell, "Treasury Interest-Calculation Mistake Has Benefited Social Security for Years," *Wall Street Journal*, December 21, 1998 p. A4.

7. Quoted in Alice Lipowicz, "Social Security's Dirty Secret: Little Benefit for Some Women," *Crain's New York Business*, September 28, 1998, p. 38. See also GAO/T-HEHS-97-112 and GAO/T-HEHS-99-52, above, and Anna M. Rappaport, "Retirement Security for Women Needs Work," *National Underwriter*, Life and Health/Financial Services Edition, September 28, 1998, p. 8.

Chapter 10

INDIVIDUAL RETIREMENT ACCOUNTS (IRAs)

As Chapter 8 shows, there has been a revolution in the labor law and tax rules affecting qualified plans. Equally major changes have occurred in the rules governing Individual Retirement Accounts (IRAs).

Individual Retirement Accounts (IRAs) were originally created by Congress so self-employed people, and people whose employers didn't have a pension plan, could save for retirement. Today, eligibility is much broader. Anyone under age 70½ and who earns income can have an IRA, and can deposit up to $2,000 a year (or the amount of earned income, if it is less than $2,000). Married couples can deposit up to $4,000 a year, even if one of them works and one of them is a homemaker or retiree. (The rules refer to a "non-working spouse," but there is no requirement that the individual not have held paid employment in the past.)

However, not everyone can DEDUCT the full amount of the IRA contribution. Depending on income level and participation in an employer-sponsored plan, the deduction may be limited or unavailable. Contributing to an IRA can be financially worthwhile even if the deduction is small, or if no deduction is allowed, because of the potential for tax-free appreciation, perhaps over many years. Multiple IRA accounts are permitted (although adding more accounts does not increase the potential deduction; it must be allocated among all accounts), so the client can have accounts with different investment objectives and choose one or more accounts to which to contribute each year, based on a judgment about which will perform best under current and predictable future scenarios. That is, in a year when growth stocks are doing well, the client may place the entire $2,000 (or $4,000 for a married couple) in a growth stock fund. Conversely, a "contrarian" client might figure that if bonds are doing poorly in a particular year, they are a bargain and the IRA should be invested in a bond fund in the happy anticipation of future appreciation.

IRA contributions can be made at any time during the calendar year, and until April 15 of the following year, so individuals making contributions after January 1 and before April 15 should indicate for which year they are being made.

ROTH AND OTHER SPECIAL IRAs

The conventional IRA works well for its designed function: allowing non-affluent persons to accumulate a meaningful sum of money for retirement by making steady, affordable contributions, often receiving a deduction from current income tax. However, as discussed below, conventional IRAs are not a very effective estate planning tool, because tax penalties are imposed if the account is not substantially drawn down during the owner's life.

The "back-loaded," "Roth," or "non-deductible" IRA, enacted as part of the Taxpayer Relief Act of 1997, is basically designed for people who don't need another tax deduction, but who want to leave a bigger estate. Congress has authorized "SIMPLE IRAs" for use in small-firm pension plans; Roth IRAs might have been nicknamed "complex IRAs" because of the potential problems they can generate. Nevertheless, they are an exceptional tool when used correctly. The Website http://www.rothira.com is a very good resource about the use of Roth IRAs, including the subtlest tax and estate planning implications.

Non-deductible contributions can be made to a Roth IRA, up to a maximum of $2,000 per person per year, minus amounts contributed to all other IRAs. The permissible contribution amount is reduced if the taxpayer's AGI is over $95,000 ($150,000 for a married couple filing a joint return). Taxpayers with AGI over $110,000/$160,000 respectively are not permitted to make Roth IRA contributions. Amounts can be withdrawn tax-free by any person over age 59½ after a five-year period that begins with the first year the person contributed to any Roth IRA. (If a premature withdrawal is made, there is no income tax or penalty on the original amount contributed to fund the IRA, only on its appreciation in value. Furthermore, the calculation is done on a FIFO basis—i.e., it is assumed that the original deposits are withdrawn before the appreciation, even though the tax bill would be higher if the assumption were reversed.) Some states have adopted legislation that is similar to the federal Roth IRA legislation, but others have not. Clients should consult their tax advisor regarding the state-tax impact of funding a Roth account or converting funds from conventional to Roth IRAs.

Funds can also be accumulated in a Roth IRA to become part of the estate, because minimum withdrawals are not required during lifetime; the entire account can be accumulated until the death of the account holder.

The IRS has published official forms that can be used to set up a Roth IRA in the form of a trust account (Form 5305-R) or a custodial account (Form 5305-RA). Form 5305-RB is the annuity counterpart, endorsed to an insurance company annuity contract.

Other IRA Forms

An Education IRA is not really an IRA because it's not a retirement account. In an Education IRA, the taxpayer can make a non-deductible contribution of up to $500 per year per child, then take the money out tax-free to pay higher education expenses. A Medical Savings Account works like an IRA, but is combined with a high-deductible health insurance policy. Funds from the MSA are used to pay medical bills, not retirement costs. A SIMPLE IRA is a pension plan created by a small employer wherein the employer sets up IRA accounts for employees and contributes to them.

IRA TAXATION

The basic rule is quite simple: each year, the account owner can withdraw any amount from the account, up to 100% of the account, with no upper limit. However, anything withdrawn from a conventional IRA account is taxed as ordinary income, not capital gains. If the account has always been maintained as a conventional IRA, with fully-deductible contributions, there is no need to calculate an exclusion ratio, because no part of the account constitutes a tax-free return of capital.

However, now that there are other options (such as non-deductible contributions; Roth IRAs; rollovers from qualified plans; and transfers from conventional to Roth IRAs), these more complex situations may require exclusion-ratio calculations. Even if the individual continues to work past age 70½, contributions to a conventional IRA may not be made after this date (and, in fact, withdrawals must begin—even if the individual is still working), but Roth contributions can be made at any age.

In most circumstances, withdrawals are considered premature and subject to a penalty of 10% of the premature withdrawal amount (which is also taxed as ordinary income) if they occur before the account owner reaches age 59½ or becomes disabled. However, penalty-free withdrawals are permitted if the money is withdrawn in a lifetime stream of payments. Penalty-free withdrawals are also permitted:

- in a lifetime amount up to $10,000 for a first-time home buyer's expenses of acquiring or fixing up a home (technically speaking, it is possible to be a first-time home buyer more than once, as long as the individual has had no ownership in a principal residence during the two-year period ending on the date of the home purchase; IRA funds can also be used penalty-free to assist a close family member who is a first-time home buyer), and

- for the account owner's higher education expenses, or such expenses of a spouse, child, or grandchild.

Although removing excessively large amounts from a conventional IRA does not carry a tax penalty (other than the obligation to pay income tax), FAILURE to withdraw enough is penalized, and so is failure to begin payments on the Required Beginning Date (RBD). The RBD is April 1 of the year after the year in which the account owner reaches age 70½. The minimum required distribution (MRD) is a function of the size of the account and the account owner's actuarially predictable life expectancy. If the actual amount withdrawn from the account in any year after the RBD is less than the MRD, a penalty is imposed equal to 50% of the difference between the MRD and the actual withdrawal, in addition to income tax on the actual withdrawal.

If the account owner does not designate a beneficiary, only his or her life expectancy is used in the actuarial calculation. Designating a beneficiary is therefore a way to "stretch" the IRA account. If the beneficiary is the spouse, then calculations are based upon the joint life expectancy of the couple. If the beneficiary is a non-spouse, calculations are made using the account holder and beneficiary's actual joint life expectancy if the beneficiary is not more than ten years younger than the account holder. If the non-spouse beneficiary is more than ten years younger than the account holder, calculations are made as if the beneficiary were only ten years younger than the account owner. Therefore, it is not possible to achieve long-range deferral by selecting a grandchild or even great-grandchild as beneficiary. The designation must be made no later than April 1 of the year following the year in which the individual reaches age 70½. Failure to designate means that tax calculations must involve only the lifetime of the owner.[2]

It is permissible to name a trust or charitable organization as beneficiary, and it may make sense to do so (to coordinate with the estate plan), but it is not a beneficial income tax strategy, because trusts and organizations are not deemed to have a life expectancy. Therefore, the MRD is calculated based only on the life expectancy of the human account holder. (The relative importance of income tax versus estate tax depends on several factors. Income tax has to be paid every year; estate tax comes due some time in the future. However, if the estate is large, estate tax rates are much higher than income tax rates. So the question becomes whether it makes sense to save money on each year's tax bill, or making sure that the eventual estate tax will be avoided or reduced.)

The Internal Revenue Code (IRC) permits annual "recalculation," in a counter-intuitive fashion. You might think that the older a person gets, the more likely that he or she will die in the following year—and therefore, recalculation should reduce the life expectancy and increase the MRD. In fact, it works just the other way. The IRC assumes that surviving another year is proof of toughness and predictable INCREASED lifespan, so the recalculation actually reduces the MRD. However, if the recalculation method of determining the MRD is elected, the life expectancy used to calculate the MRD is reduced to zero in the year of death.

The tax picture for Roth IRAs is much simpler. There is no RBD or MRD during the account holder's lifetime. (MRD does apply upon the death of the account holder.) As long as the funds remain within the Roth IRA for at least five years, they can be withdrawn tax-free for qualified distributions (i.e., attainment of age 59½, on account of death or disability and qualified first-time home purchase). It's within the account holder's discretion to retain part or all of the balance within the account, for later consumption or for inheritance.

However, if funds are taken out of a Roth IRA, the question then becomes whether or not they qualify for tax-free status. Code Section 408A(d)(4)(B) contains the "ordering rules" for analyzing the funds in a Roth account. The withdrawals are analyzed as if they come from non-rollover contributions first (i.e., the non-deductible contributions used to fund the Roth account in the first place), then from conversions from conventional IRAs (starting with taxable amounts), then non-taxable conversions, and finally from the appreciation in value of the Roth account. If there was more than one conversion of the same kind (taxable or non-taxable), the assumption is that the first one in is the first one out. All of the taxpayer's Roth IRAs, if he or she has more than one, are aggregated for this purpose.

ROLLOVERS AND CONDUIT IRAs

Individuals and married taxpayers filing jointly with AGI under under $100,000 can transfer (convert) funds from a conventional to a Roth IRA, at which point the account is subject to the Roth rules. Funds that are converted are treated as taxable income for the year of the conversion. There was a special rule for conversions which occurred in 1998—individuals could spread out the tax on the conversion over a four-year period. Congress did not make the rule available for later years.[3] Even in 1998, when the tax advantage was available, conversions to Roth IRAs were fairly uncommon. Investment companies found that only about 11-15% of eligible persons converted any IRA funds to Roth form in 1998, and the amounts involved were usually small.[4]

A conduit IRA is used to provide relief from the basic rule that all pension funds are taxable in the year of receipt. The general rule could create a serious problem for a person who changes jobs but is not yet eligible to participate in the new job's pension plan (and therefore cannot have the vested pension benefits from the first job rolled over to the second job's plan). The pension funds can be placed into a conduit IRA, then rolled over into the second qualified plan. There is no income tax as long as the individual never receives the funds directly (they are always in the hands of a trustee or custodian)—or even if he or she does receive the funds, but deposits them with a trustee in 60 days or less, and the conduit IRA did not receive any other contributions nor issued any distributions prior to being rolled into the second job's plan. However, if the individual receives the funds to be deposited into a conduit IRA, there is a mandatory 20% withholding on the amount distributed which must be replaced by the individual within 60 days in order to avoid the IRS having deemed the withheld amount to be a distribution.

ESTATE PLANNING WITH IRAs

For many years, IRA estate planning was a contradiction in terms. The tax laws were drafted to make it likely that the account would be depleted or greatly reduced in size during the owner's lifetime. However, Congress has gradually accepted the validity of using the IRA, especially the Roth IRA, as a planning device. Clients making an elder plan should decide what their objective is for their IRA: do they plan to use it during life ("consumption objective") or save it to become part of the estate transmitted to the spouse and other heirs ("estate planning objective"). Of course, it may be impossible to maintain a pure estate planning objective if, for instance, health expenditures become very heavy.

A person with a consumption objective has little planning to do. Each year, he or she simply decides how much to withdraw, bearing in mind that withdrawals from a conventional IRA will be generally taxed as ordinary income, and making sure that the account (in conjunction with other sources of income and assets) will not be depleted during his or her lifetime.

The estate planning objective takes more work. The older client should assess whether any funds should be moved from a conventional to a Roth IRA, bearing the tax consequences in mind. For funds remaining in the conventional IRA, the client should take only the MRD each year. He or she should be certain to name a beneficiary, so that the MRD can be calculated using two lifespans (if the beneficiary is the spouse) or the owner's life expectancy and the life expectancy of a person ten years younger. A natural person, not a trust or charity, should be selected as beneficiary. Recalculation should be done every year—all in order to maximize the amount remaining in the account when the account holder dies. See the Estate Planning chapter for more about estate planning aspects of the conventional IRA.

Inherited Roth IRAs

When the named beneficiary inherits a Roth IRA, he or she will be able to withdraw earnings from the account free of income tax only if the funds have spent the necessary five years in the account. This is true even if the original owner died before the five years have elapsed. However, the heir is entitled to take advantage of any part of the five-year period that passed while the original owner was still alive.[5]

There is an additional tax benefit if the designated beneficiary is the account holder's surviving spouse. The surviving spouse can choose to treat the inherited Roth IRA as his or her own account, and then the five-year period during which funds must remain in the account to be withdrawn tax-free ends on the fifth anniversary for the decedent's IRA or the spouse's own Roth IRA—whichever comes first.

Tax and estate planning expert Noel C. Ice points out that Code Section 408A doesn't say in so many words that a spouse who inherits a conventional IRA can convert it to a Roth IRA, but it should be possible to do so (if necessary, by rolling over the funds to a conventional IRA, then to the Roth, or by treating the IRA as the survivor's own account). However, the surviving spouse is the only person allowed to roll over an inherited IRA, so presumably a son, daughter, or other relative or friend who inherits an IRA would not be able to do this.

MULTIPLE IRAs

In some instances, a person will have two or more IRAs: perhaps several conventional IRAs with different investment styles; or, after 1997, both conventional and Roth IRAs. The owner of multiple IRAs subject to MRD requirements can take the full MRD from one of the accounts, leaving the others intact, or allocate the MRD among accounts in any desired proportion. On the practical level, it makes sense to withdraw from the IRA that has the worst investment performance, while keeping better-performing accounts intact. However, for this purpose, conventional IRAs can only be aggregated with other conventional IRAs and the same with Roth IRAs.

Roth Conversions and Reconversions

Obviously, it was impossible to use Roth IRAs before they were authorized by the Taxpayer Relief Act of 1997. Thus, taxpayers now face another choice: taking funds out of a conventional deductible IRA and placing them in a Roth. All funds transferred from a conventional to a Roth IRA are deemed taxable income to the account holder, and all such income is taxed in the year of the conversion. (There was a special transition rule, for 1998 only, permitting taxation over a four-year period, but Congress declined to extend the rule.)

Furthermore, taxpayers with AGI over $100,000 (single filers and married filers filing a joint return) are not allowed to convert conventional IRA funds to Roth funds. (Married taxpayers filing separate returns are not allowed to convert a traditional IRA to a Roth IRA.) However, a person frustrated by this provision may have some control over his or her income for the year of the desired conversion.[6]

He or she might switch some investments into low-paying growth stocks, for instance; it might be possible to arrange for payments to be made in installments instead of as a lump sum in the year of conversion. This could also be a factor in deciding whether or not to take a lump-sum pension payout. It could also be a good time to weed losers out of the portfolio, thus generating tax losses that reduce taxable income. However, it could be an argument against profit-taking if high appreciation could foreclose a Roth conversion. An older person who wants to start a small business or consulting practice after retiring from a corporate post might purchase business equipment in the year of the desired conversion: for 1999, up to $19,000 worth of business equipment can be expensed if an election is made.

Theoretically, Roth conversions can only be made from conventional IRAs, not from qualified plans, but in practical terms, funds can be rolled over from a qualified plan to a conventional IRA and then converted to a Roth (minus any required MRDs to be made during the year of the conversion). Remember that rolling over funds from a qualified plan to a conventional IRA defers taxation; taxes are due on the amount converted to a Roth IRA.

The taxpayers may then decide that the conversion was imprudent, and re-convert (i.e., roll some funds back into a conventional IRA). Re-conversion triggers certain tax issues. As a general rule, if a taxpayer who has not yet reached age 59½ (the minimum age at which all IRA withdrawals are free from the premature withdrawal penalty) shifts funds from a conventional to a Roth IRA, the premature withdrawal penalty will not be imposed on the conversion.

For amounts converted in 1998 that are subject to the four-year income spread, income inclusion is accelerated for any amounts withdrawn during the four-year period of 1998 through 2001. Under this rule, a taxpayer who withdraws converted amounts prior to the last year of the spread will be required to include in AGI the amount otherwise includable under the four-year spread, plus the lesser of (1) the taxable amount of the withdrawal, or (2) the remaining taxable amount of the conversion.[7] This rule does not require the inclusion in AGI of any amount to the extent it exceeds the total amount of income to be included in the four-year period.

The mathematics of deciding whether to convert conventional to Roth accounts (or how much of the accumulated IRA balance should be converted) are quite sophisticated, and involve some scenarios that are beyond the scope of this book, such as projections of the client's future lifestyle and income tax rate. The topic is discussed on the Website http://www.rothira.com, especially by Peter James Lingane ("Should You Convert to a Roth IRA? It Depends on Your Circumstances," and *Forbes* Magazine's "Optimum Roth IRA Conversion" calculator.)

Some sophisticated taxpayers converted and re-converted several times between conventional and Roth accounts, attempting to "lock in" a lower tax value and decrease the tax bill by timing conversions based on reductions and increases in market value (they would move funds from conventional to Roth when the values were at their low ebb, then move them back as market values increased.)

In November, 1998, the IRS issued an interim ruling on reconversions imposing tax penalties on "excess reconversions" occurring after November 1, 1998.[8] (Earlier transactions are exempt from the rule.) A reconversion is "excess" if the taxpayer transfers funds from a conventional IRA, to a Roth IRA, then back to the conventional IRA. The taxpayer is allowed one penalty-free reconversion during calendar 1999, whether or not there was also a reconversion during 1998. Additional Roth rules were issued in early 1999. The IRS issued a lengthy Final Regulation dealing with Roth IRAs, and especially with recharacterization of IRA contributions, in February of 1999.[9] IRS Announcement 99-18 explains how to fill out Form 8606 to reflect conversions and recharacterizations of Roth IRAs, and how to calculate the 10% penalty tax when a non-disabled person takes a Roth IRA distribution before age 59½.

Note that a person who converts funds from conventional to Roth accounts, but who continues to make Roth contributions, should segregate the converted funds into a separate account. The separate account should be left untouched for at least five years; distributions during such period are subject to the premature withdrawal penalty (even though such distributions may not be includable in income).

Nor should taxpayers forget to increase their withholding or estimated tax payments for the year of a taxable conversion.

IRA INVESTMENT CHOICES

There are arguments both pro and con as to whether already tax-exempt investments should be included in tax-deferred retirement accounts. If they're the best bottom-line values, they should be included; otherwise, their counterparts that would be taxable outside the retirement context are preferable. If you have separate growth and income-oriented investments, and are satisfied with the performance of each, it might make sense to put the income-oriented investments into tax-deferred retirement accounts, while retaining the low-income growth investments outside the IRA accounts. This is because investment income goes "on top" of the taxpayer's other income, and is taxed at his or her highest marginal rate.

Wall Street Journal writer Vanessa O'Connell raises another issue: the "tax bomb" mutual fund that trades stocks both frequently and successfully. The "successful" part is great, but the downside is investors' exposure to large capital gains distributions from the fund. In a taxable account, this could be annoying, but the problem doesn't arise in a tax-free account. She also points out that a low-load or low-fee account is much more important in an IRA than in an ordinary investment account, because fees take a heavier toll on an IRA (where the maximum contribution is only $2,000 per person per year) than an investment account (where the impact of the fees is spread out over annual investments that may be much greater than $2,000).[10]

If the individual does not have enough money to take full advantage of all the tax-deferred investment options available (i.e., conventional and Roth IRAs; annuities; and a work-related 401(k) plan), it then becomes necessary to balance the advantages of each and select one or make an allocation among them.[11]

According to T. Rowe Price's calculations, a person who opens an IRA account at age 45 and makes the maximum contribution each year until 65, earning 7% a year, will have an account worth over $80,000 (for the Roth IRA) and over $100,000 (for the conventional IRA); the difference comes from the assumption that the conventional IRA contribution will be tax-deductible.

If the individual is in the 28% federal bracket and 6.85% state bracket both before and after retirement, he or she will be better off with the Roth IRA (assuming that he or she uses the account for current income instead of accumulating it), because annual after-tax income from the account at ages 65-85 will be $7,216 a year for the Roth, versus $6,405 for the conventional IRA (remember, income from the conventional IRA is subject to income taxation.) If the tax bracket drops from a combined 34.85% before retirement to a combined 20.9% after retirement (and much retirement planning strategy assumes a lower post-retirement bracket), then the Roth will yield $7,216 a year—slightly less than the $7,433 from the conventional account.

The Roth IRA was so attractive that some corporate compensation planners felt compelled to increase employer matches, or otherwise make the 401(k) seem more attractive. Contributions to 401(k) plans, like conventional IRA contributions, are made with pre-tax dollars. Roth IRA contributions are made with after-tax dollars. However, 401(k) plans offer the potential for an employer match whereas employees must fund their IRA contributions themselves. So the basic strategy is to fund the 401(k) first, to the extent that the employer match is maximized. After that, the best choice is probably a conventional IRA if the idea is to have more current income after retirement (especially if the individual's tax bracket will drop after retirement) or a Roth IRA if the objective is estate planning.

CHAPTER FOOTNOTES

1. See Ellen E. Schultz, "Tax Advantages of Roth IRAs Top Annuities," *Wall Street Journal*, October 16, 1997, p. C1.

2. Lynn Asinof, "IRA Holders of a Certain Age Face a Deadline," *Wall Street Journal*, March 26, 1998, p. C15.

3. The IRS Restructuring and Reform Act of 1998 provides that the 10% penalty on early withdrawals from an IRA is also imposed on amounts converted from a conventional to a Roth IRA, then withdrawn in less than five years. If the person who made the conversion dies before the four years elapse, and the beneficiary of the Roth IRA is not the surviving spouse, the amounts not yet recognized in income must be included on the final income tax return for the deceased account holder. See Sidney Kess, "Technical Corrections Bill for Taxpayer Relief," *New York Law Journal*, October 20, 1997, p. 3 and Bryan Schmitt, "New Rules Clarify Roth IRA Choices," *Best's Review* Life/Health Edition, October, 1998 p. 89.

4. M. Christian Murray, "Conversions to Roth IRAs Fell Short in '98," *National Underwriter*, Life and Health/Financial Services Edition, January 25, 1999, p. 4.

5. Reg. § 1.408A-6, Q&A 7.

6. Such strategies are discussed in Karen Hube and Bridget O'Brien, "Roth IRAs Prompt the Wealthy to 'Earn' Less," *Wall Street Journal*, October 30, 1998, p. C1.

7. Reg. § 1.408A-6, Q&A 6.

8. Notice 98-50, 1998-44 IRB 10. See Karen Hube, "IRS Rule to Close Loophole in Roth IRAs," *Wall Street Journal*, October 21, 1998, p. C15.

9. Reg. §§ 1.408A-1 through 1.408A-9.

10. Vanessa O'Connell, "Strategies to Try During Roth IRA Rush," *Wall Street Journal*, February 26, 1998, p. C1.

11. The New York Times' Website includes a calculator for allocating funds between IRA and 401(k) accounts: http://www.nytimes.com/taxes. See Virginia Munger Kahn, "Roth I.R.A.'s Giving 401(k)'s a Run for the (Retirement) Money," *New York Times*, March 1, 1998, p. Business 21.

Chapter 11

SPECIAL PORTFOLIO ISSUES FOR THE OLDER INVESTOR

Investment planning is crucial to retirement and post-retirement planning for many reasons. In general, Social Security benefits (even if they continue to be paid as scheduled) are a fairly minor factor in post-retirement security for most people. Once a person retires and chooses an option for payment of qualified plan benefits, there is not much the person can do to change or control the adequacy or inadequacy of the pension income. But, as long as the person retains contractual capacity and is interested in doing so, he can respond to market trends and changes in personal needs and preferences by changing his investments. This chapter deals with general investment issues for the senior citizen. Chapter 12 focuses on annuities, a complex type of investment that can perform many functions in the elder plan.

Traditional thinking calls for a shift from growth-oriented assets (with concomitant risk) to income-producing assets for older investors. One simple rule of thumb is to decrease the proportion of equities in the portfolio and increase the proportion of bonds and other income instruments every five or 10 years. The shift from growth to income is, by and large, a sound strategy, but it is not the complete answer. Remember, it is very likely that a person who retires at 65 will still be alive 20 years later, and it is not at all impossible that he or she will be alive *30* years later. This is a fairly long-range planning horizon, and a growth component is important[1].

Traditional thinking also assumes that having more income is better than having less. Yet, if the older person is a current or potential Medicaid beneficiary, having less income is better because it decreases the spend-down obligation. (See Chapter 6.) Even if Medicaid is not a factor, the older person may be unable to handle funds prudently because of medical or psychiatric factors. Having a small income that one can handle as one likes can be important to self-esteem, whereas having a large income would be counterproductive. Much of this chapter is concerned with the advantages of annuity investments for middle-aged and older investors.

In the 1980's, retirees with fixed incomes often suffered as inflation ran rampant. Inflation is one of the factors that triggered the transition from defined benefit to defined contribution plans. Defined contribution plans are more market-sensitive than defined benefit plans, so they offer the potential for increasing income during periods of high inflation (which is often identified with a booming stock market).

It is hard to think of the decade of disco music and Qiana shirts as a golden era, but it did have one characteristic that is a legitimate source of nostalgia. Risk-averse investors could earn double-digit returns on safe money market funds and CDs. Today, the returns from comparably safe investments are vanishingly small. By the late 1990's, retirees were in a paradoxical situation: insert extra space inflation risk was low, but investment risk was fairly high.

The bull market reigned supreme for almost 10 years until a break in the market occurred in August, 1998. Although the markets quickly recovered, there is no doubt that investors' anxiety levels increased — especially older investors, who relied on their portfolios for a large portion of their income. Consequently, probably the best thing a planner can do for older clients is to stress diversification and tailor the portfolio to the client's risk tolerance.

DIRECTIONS FOR THE OLDER INVESTOR

Although each client (of any age) must be approached as an individual, there are some patterns that are characteristic of senior citizen investors:

- They are usually intolerant of risk, which is only logical since they do not have much time to make up for mistakes, and they rely on portfolio income for a substantial part of their living and health care expenses.

- They tend to be income-oriented, rather than growth-oriented.

- They are very interested in accumulating an estate, and also extremely interested in avoiding federal estate tax liability.

A good planner will help clients assemble a portfolio that meets their needs for lifetime and estate objectives, at a tolerable level of risk, and to make sure that they understand that stock prices do not inevitably go up.

Interestingly, it may be necessary to steer male and female clients in different directions. In many instances, older male investors may be too willing to undertake unnecessary risks. Alternatively, older female investors may be too risk-intolerant, loading up their portfolios with fixed-income investments that fall behind inflation, thus depriving themselves of critically needed growth that would promote real financial security.[2]

A good planner will also help clients avoid some of the scams that plague all investors, but particularly older investors — whether the con artists operate in cyberspace or in the real world. Elders who are afraid their money will run out (whether or not this fear is well-grounded) are easy prey for get-rich-quick schemes. Lonely, isolated senior citizens are vulnerable to financial elder abuse committed by people who seem to be their friends and appear to genuinely care about them.

INVESTMENT CHOICES FOR THE OLDER INVESTOR

The number of components of the portfolio, the degree of risk in the portfolio, and the amount of time that can reasonably be spent on monitoring the portfolio all depend on the client's preferences, capacity for risk, and the size of the amount under investment. The conventional wisdom is that risk and return move in tandem: the investor endures greater risk in the hope of securing greater return. This is sometimes known as a choice between "eating well" and "sleeping well." Portfolios are usually built based on a pyramid, starting with the safest options, then adding more diversification and risk once it is assured that the individual will have adequate income for lifetime needs, and the surviving spouse (if any) will be provided for.

Therefore, investments work in conjunction with other financial assets. The larger the income deriving from the individual's pension and Social Security, the less current investment income is required for daily needs, and the more likely that the individual can concentrate on growth and creating an estate. (However, personal preferences may call for adding extra income for a more luxurious lifestyle, or there may be heavy costs associated with health and custodial needs.)

Although the markets offer a baffling variety of investment options, most of them are unsuitable for senior citizen clients of low-to-moderate means. Wealthy and very affluent older clients should have a correspondingly larger planning team, including investment professionals — although it is important for someone (e.g., a family member or fiduciary) to keep an eye on the investment professionals, with respect to both integrity and performance.

Broadly speaking, investments are selected for their growth potential (i.e., the belief that they can be sold at a higher price than they were purchased for), their income potential (i.e., interest, dividends, or other payments made with respect to the investment), or for both reasons.

For example, a person may purchase a coupon bond, intending to hold it to maturity (at which time the face value will be returned), while also receiving regular interest payments. However, the owner also has the option of selling the bond if the price of the bond has risen so much that selling it has become attractive, or he simply needs additional funds. Some investors like preferred stock because it combines the liquidity of common stock (i.e., the ability to be sold at any time) with the potential for price appreciation, and the opportunity for income in the form of dividends, which must be paid (at a fixed rate) before any dividends can be paid on the company's common stock.

Most older investors will choose some combination of these reasonably safe, conventional investments:

- *Government Securities*. Perhaps the safest investments are direct federal government obligations, such as Treasury bonds and notes. (The security is a "note" if its maturity date is from one year to ten years; "bonds" have maturities in excess of ten years.[3]) These obligations are backed by the entire financial and taxing power of the United States government. Notably, there are many other kinds of securities issued by federal agencies that are *not* direct obligations of the federal government, including housing securities issued by the Government National Mortgage Association, the Federal National Mortgage Association, and the

Federal Home Loan Mortgage Corporation. These securities are known as "Ginnie Maes," "Fannie Maes," and "Freddie Macs," respectively. Ginnie Maes are the safest of these securities because they are backed by the "full faith and credit" of the United States; the other two types merely have an implicit federal guarantee.

- *Corporate and Municipal Bonds.* Bonds can be issued by private-sector corporations or by government entities and agencies. Municipal bonds ("munis") are issued by states, cities, municipalities, and their agencies. The safety of these bonds depends on the issuer's credit, whether good or bad. Traditionally, municipal bonds were a favorite choice of conservative older investors, because of their tax-exempt status. However, not all municipal bond interest is free of tax consequences. Thus, it is important to ascertain this status in advance. Some municipal bonds are insured by third-party guarantors, but this guarantee means only as much as the financial soundness of the guaranteeing organization.

- *Coupon and "Zero-coupon" Bonds.* A conventional "coupon" bond makes regular (e.g., quarterly or semi-annual) payments of interest at a stated rate. However, a "zero-coupon" bond is sold at a deep discount (i.e., a reduction in price from face value), and does not make interest payments. Zero-coupon bonds work well for an individual who wants to make a small investment in order to get a larger amount at a scheduled future date. The downside is that zero-coupon bond prices fluctuate more than coupon bond prices. Thus, if an individual desires to sell the bond before maturity, significant losses are possible. "Original issue discount" (OID) is a tax concept which means that the owner of the bond has to pay taxes each year on the interest that was *not paid* on the zero-coupon bond, but that was *accrued* (i.e., accumulated but not paid). See IRC Code Secs. 1272 and 1273. (However, OID on tax-exempt bonds is not taxed.) In effect, the owner of the bond has to pay federal income tax each year on the accrual (accumulation) even though he does not receive cash income from the bond.

- *Mutual Funds.* A mutual fund assembles a portfolio of stocks, bonds, and/or other securities, then sells shares in this portfolio to the public. One advantage of a mutual fund is that it provides diversification and professional management. Sometimes, however, professional managers do not produce returns higher than well-publicized measures of the combined performance of certain groups of stocks (i.e., indexes) — hence, the popularity of index funds that invest in *all* of the securities covered by a particular index (such as the Dow Jones Industrial Average or the Standard & Poor's 500) and, naturally, achieve the same results as the index.

There are a multitude of mutual funds in existence today. Some of them are identified by their objective: aggressive growth; high growth; growth; growth and income; balanced growth; high income; income; tax-exempt income. Others are identified by the sector in which they invest: technology stocks; health care stocks; international stocks; short-term bonds; etc.

- *Common and Preferred Stock*. Corporations issue various kinds of securities: common stock; preferred stock (which is "preferred" in the sense that it must pay dividends before the issuing company is allowed to pay dividends on its common stock); rights; warrants; and options. (Options are different ways to give someone the opportunity to speculate (or hedge) on price movements in the stock without actually purchasing the stock immediately).

- *Real Estate*. Most people have some degree of real estate investment in that they own a home. Many other kinds of real estate investment are possible, including: buying raw land and developing it, or holding it for sale to a developer; investing in commercial properties; buying real estate-oriented securities such as Ginnie Maes; investing in real estate limited partnerships; or investing in real estate investment trusts (REITs), or real estate mortgage investment conduits (REMICs). REITs and REMICs assemble portfolios of real property and mortgages, respectively — in effect, they resemble real estate mutual funds.

- *Precious Metals and Collectibles*. "Hard assets" include precious metals, artwork, and collectibles. These are not income-producing assets and, in fact, can cost money for conservation and security. The investor hopes to identify "bargains," then hold them for personal enjoyment with the ultimate goal of selling them at a profit. These are not very liquid investments — it is not always easy to find a buyer when one is wanted and sales are usually subject to high commissions. (Auction houses impose commissions on both buyers and sellers.)

Very Small Investor

A client who has only one major asset (e.g., a home), receives only a pension and Social Security, and has a small amount of money saved does not need, and would not benefit by, a complex investment plan. A better strategy would be to invest some or all of the savings in a commercial annuity, a charitable annuity (if the individual is religiously or charitably minded), or an income- or growth-and-income-oriented mutual fund with a good track record and low expenses.

Small Investor

A client with somewhat larger savings may benefit from investing in several (say, two to five) mutual funds. It often makes sense to select all of the funds from the same mutual "fund family" as long as it:

- has a good reputation and track record;
- offers a wide variety of funds satisfying various objectives;
- does not impose excessive fees, charges, and commissions; and
- provides useful disclosure information in easy-to-understand form.

The small investor should choose funds that provide a low-to-moderate risk level, and that offer genuine diversification in that they respond differently to different market conditions. If all the funds invest in similar securities with similar objectives, there is no point in having all of them. It makes far more sense to guard against a downturn in the *stock* market by investing in some *bonds*, or bond funds. Within the stock sector, investing in emerging growth stocks should be balanced with investing in higher-capitalization, more stable "blue chip" stocks.

In the past, small investors usually had some money market funds and/or bank CDs because of the safety and convenience of these investments for small portfolios. Unfortunately, under current conditions, their rate of return is low, so they would probably only be recommended to small investors who are extremely intolerant of risk.

Medium Investor

An individual with more funds to invest, and who has adequate insurance coverage (to protect the surviving spouse in case the investor dies at a time when the portfolio has a low value), would probably begin by creating a diversified mutual fund portfolio. He might want to add a commercial or private annuity to the portfolio (see Chapter 12).

With this basic program in place, the investor would probably want to add some investments in individual securities. He might buy Treasury bonds or notes, rather than just investing in bond funds. He might also invest in particular stocks, not just in stock funds. A mutual fund allows an investor who otherwise could afford to invest in only one or two stocks to invest in a broad portfolio of stocks. However, an investor who can afford to buy stock in a dozen or so companies may prefer simply to buy those stocks individually.

At this level, the investor (or advisor or fiduciary acting on the investor's behalf) will probably engage in more active trading. At lower levels of investment, it is probably not worthwhile to trade a lot because the fees, commissions, and taxes involved in selling 100 shares of stock at a profit of $2.00 a share tend to overwhelm the profits. However, if the profits are greater, or the number of shares involved significantly larger, active trading makes more sense.

It should be noted that municipal bond income is taken into account when computing income taxes on Social Security benefits (see Chapter 9), which may make municipal bonds somewhat less attractive than they would otherwise be to this group of investors.

The successful moderate investor may be at risk of having a federally taxable estate, especially if he owns a valuable home. Therefore, he should implement basic estate planning measures (see Chapter 13) such as a gifting program, credit shelter trust, and/or QTIP trust. It is possible that there will be no tax due on the first estate because of the marital deduction, but there will be a significant risk of a second estate tax problem.

Large Investor

As noted above, the large investor will probably have a multi-person team responsible for investment choices. (Sophisticated portfolio management techniques are beyond the scope of this book.) Certain high-risk/high-opportunity investments that might otherwise be suitable for large investors (such as options and futures) are probably unsuitable for older investors because of the possibility of having to turn the portfolio over to a fiduciary, at some point in the future.

A large investor will no doubt be in the top income tax bracket, so tax-exempt investments may gain in attractiveness. In this bracket, however, the impact of the alternative minimum tax (AMT) must be considered. Naturally, estate planning will be critical because it is extremely likely that there will be a taxable estate for both spouses unless planning steps are taken. A complex, multi-trust estate plan may be necessary, perhaps in conjunction with a giving program and significant charitable bequests (outright or in trust).

BOTTOM-LINE FACTORS

The initial choice of investments, particularly investments chosen to re-balance a portfolio or in response to changing market conditions, must take into account the impact of costs and fees on overall investment performance. For instance, a "full-load" mutual fund purchased through a broker will have an initial "load" (fee) that may be as high as 8%. A "low-load" fund purchased directly from a mutual fund family may impose an initial fee as low as ½ of 1%. (Although initially there was a sharp distinction between load and no-load funds, mutual funds have increased the amount, variety, and number of fees that they charge, so true no-load funds are rare.) Technically speaking, a "12b-1" fee is not a load, but the 12b-1 fee, imposed to cover a fund's marketing costs, functions about the same way from the customer's perspective.

Once an investment has been purchased, there may be ongoing fees for maintenance of the account. Certainly, when an investment that is a capital asset is sold at a profit, there will be capital gains tax liability — and, generally, there is no potential to "roll over" the gain and escape taxation by buying another security.

PRACTICE TIP: Many mutual funds offer the convenience of check redemption (i.e., the account owner can write checks on the account to any payee). But this is a taxable transaction, and the account owner will have to calculate the capital gain or loss on the transaction. This is not a simple matter if the $5,000 check to the home health care agency actually constitutes a redemption of 468.22 shares, 137 of which were purchased at $9 a share, and 77 of which were purchased at $12.13 a share.

Another convenience offered by many mutual fund families is "switching" between accounts (i.e., moving $10,000 from the Sunshine High-Income Fund to the Bits 'n' Bytes High Tech Fund). However, it is common for the fund family to impose fees on switches, or to limit the number of switches per year that can be performed without a fee. Make sure that your clients are aware of the cost of shifting assets within a fund family. Furthermore, these switches are also taxable events in that securities have been sold at either a profit or a loss.

Taxes and expenses are vital considerations in determining the final yield of an investment (i.e., the amount that is actually available for the client to spend, reinvest, or leave to heirs). A return that appears high may shrink a good deal when these factors are considered. If the choice is between a taxable and a tax-free investment, the calculation is simple: subtract fees and costs from the tax-free investment; subtract fees, costs, and income tax (at the marginal rate, i.e., the taxpayer's top tax bracket) from the taxable investment, and compare. If necessary, adjust the figures to correspond for differences in risk level.

On the other hand, clients should not worry too much about small differences in return. If one person invests $5,000 in a mutual fund that scores top performance for the quarter in its class, and someone else invests $5,000 in a comparable mutual fund that scores only average performance for the class, the two will probably end up with very similar returns. It probably would not make sense for the second investor to dump the disappointing fund and reinvest in the leader because next quarter the rankings may be reversed.

TAILORING THE PORTFOLIO OVER TIME

In many instances, persons who have retired recently are still active and vigorous, and they may take an especially strong interest in hands-on portfolio management. They may need some gentle guidance to avoid serious errors. Over time, it is typical (though not universal) for interest in active investing to decline. A shift from a portfolio that is primarily invested in individual stocks and bonds to one with a predominance of mutual funds might be appropriate.

The financial planner should also pay attention to changes in the client's level of activity, ability to communicate with others, or his interest in life in general. Negative changes should be discussed with other members of the planning team and/or members of the client's family to determine whether intervention is required, or if incapacity planning steps should be taken.

If the portfolio might have to be turned over to a fiduciary one day, bear in mind that the attorney-in-fact, guardian, or trustee is likely to be a family member, who in turn is unlikely to be a financial professional. For a smooth transition, the investment plan should be flexible, fairly simple, and so well documented that the fiduciary can pick up the reins immediately.

Although, as noted above, moving the entire portfolio into income investments is probably poor strategy, it is often a good idea to alter the equity-income balance of the portfolio as the client ages. A typical allocation at age 60 would be 60-70% stock and 30-40% bonds and other income instruments. Perhaps, at age 70, the same individual would prefer a 50-50% split, or even a predominance of income instruments.

It should also be noted that many individuals drop from a high to a lower tax bracket as they age, so taxable investments may become more attractive than tax-exempt investments. Also, municipal bond income may be a tax preference item for alternative minimum tax purposes, and in any event, it can result in taxability, or increased taxability, of Social Security benefits (see Chapter 9) — another factor that could argue in favor of holding more taxable investments.

If the stock market declines, or the older client is afraid that it might, then reducing the risk level of the portfolio might be a good idea. Once again, shifting from small-cap stocks to more stable, higher-yielding utility stocks could be called for. Alternatively, switching funds within a mutual fund family to more balanced, less risky funds, investing in bonds or bond funds rather than stocks, or even shifting part of the portfolio into money market funds or other cash equivalents could be the proper move. On the other hand, an older investor with a strong interest in enhancing the size of the estate to be transmitted to his heirs might view a time of market uncertainty as an excellent opportunity for bargain-hunting, trusting that the value of the stocks will increase in time (without generating significant taxable capital gains for the heirs due to the "step-up" in basis).[4]

The senior citizen's portfolio often requires wise investment of lump-sums, such as pension payouts, home sale gains, and life insurance proceeds. Sometimes the proceeds can simply be allocated in the same proportion as the rest of the portfolio. In other plans, purchase of an immediate annuity (see Chapter 12) can be an excellent way to generate needed income without generating a large amount of effort in managing the portfolio. In still other instances, lump-sums should become the subject of a giving program to reduce the potentially taxable estate, and/or as part of a Medicaid plan.

Last, but not least, there may be events beyond the investor's control that affect the investment plan. For instance, someone may buy bonds intending to hold them to maturity, but the issuer of the bond may exercise a right to "call" the bond (i.e., to repurchase it after a particular date at a stated price, or according to a price schedule set out in advance). And, of course, as soon as a bond matures, the owner will have to have a strategy for re-investing the principal from the initial investment.

INCOME TAX, INCLUDING CAPITAL GAINS TAX: INVESTMENTS

Dividends paid on corporate stock are ordinary income (see Code section 61(a)(7)). A dividend is a payment that is made to shareholders because of their stock ownership deriving from the corporation's current or accumulated earnings and profits. Distributions made by a corporation from sources other than earnings and profits are generally not taxed as dividends. Instead, they are first applied to reduce the owner's adjusted basis in the stock. Once adjusted basis reaches zero, any remaining distribution is taxed as gain, usually as a capital gain.

Amounts paid or credited to life insurance policyholders are not taxed as dividends if they serve as partial refunds of the insurance premium (see Code section 316(b)(1)). But dividends that exceed the consideration paid for the policy are taxable as dividends.

Throughout much of the history of United States taxation, capital gains (which are, broadly speaking, gains generated from sales of investment assets) have received preferential treatment. The theory is that the economy as a whole will benefit if people have an incentive not only to save instead of consuming, but to invest in securities rather than simply retaining all their savings in bank accounts. Interest earned on bank accounts, or on taxable bonds, is taxed at ordinary income rates and does not receive preferential treatment. However, there was a period of time when capital gains and ordinary income rates were identical, or at least not significantly different.

The Taxpayer Relief Act of 1997, as amended by the Internal Revenue Service Restructuring and Reform Act of 1998, dramatically altered the taxation of capital gains, generally in a downward direction favorable to most investors. Most long-term capital gains, generally those on capital assets held more than one year, are taxed at a maximum rate of 20%. That is only about half the top income tax bracket. Senior citizens who are asset-rich but have a fairly low income, and therefore are in the 15% income tax bracket, qualify for a lower capital gains rate of 10%.

A rate of 18% will be available for gains on assets that were purchased after December 31, 2000 and held for five years or more before the sale or exchange. An even lower rate of 8% applies after 1999 to property held more than five years before the sale or exchange and sold by an individual in the 15% income tax bracket.

The complex rules for capital gains transactions can require especially sophisticated record keeping to keep track of which shares and other assets were purchased or otherwise acquired (e.g., through reinvestment of dividends) at which time. There are also many situations in which it may be necessary to sell some assets to pay expenses, or it may be desirable to give or sell some assets for other purposes. In either case, a decision has to be made which assets should be sold or donated. If the senior citizen client will have to pay capital gains tax on the gain, then the best choice might be the assets that have appreciated the least. On the other hand, if the capital gain can escape taxation, then the better choice might be the asset that has appreciated the most. But for 2006 and later years, in the case of assets acquired after December 31, 2000, it might be worthwhile holding on to assets to take advantage of the very low rate.

Code section 1211 provides that capital losses are deductible in any year only to the extent of gains. The excess of the loss over the gain (net short-term or net long-term capital loss), can offset ordinary income on a dollar-for-dollar basis, up to $3,000 a year. (The limit is only $1,500 for married taxpayers filing separate returns.) Losses greater than the limit can be carried forward to later tax years

Interest from corporate bonds is taxed as ordinary income. Interest on municipal bonds, other than certain private-activity bonds or other atypical bonds, is tax-exempt under Code section 150. (See IRC Sec. 149 for classifications of municipal bonds that are not tax-exempt.) Interest paid on Treasury bonds is taxable for federal purposes, but exempt from state and local income taxes. Interest on United States Savings Bonds is taxable.

A "stripped" bond has been divided into an underlying right to have principal repaid and a series of interest coupons; the two are traded separately. Code section 1286 treats stripped bonds and coupons like zero-coupon bonds, and OID is taxed each year.

CAPITAL GAINS TAX: HOMES

The Taxpayer Relief Act of 1997 (TRA '97) replaced former Code section 121 (one-time capital gain exclusion for sale of a home after age 55) and Code section 1034 (rollover of gain when a more expensive home was purchased) with a single new provision, Code section 121. Under this provision, a person of any age generally can exclude up to $250,000 in home-sale capital gain from taxable income. A married home seller who files a joint return can exclude home-sale gain of up to $500,000.

To qualify for this tax break, the property must have been the principal residence of the owner for two of the five years preceding the sale, or one of the five years preceding the sale if the sale was occasioned by the owner's entering a nursing home. A 1998 amendment permits a partial exclusion from capital gains taxation if the home was owned for less than the two-out-of-five years required for a full exclusion.

INVESTMENT AND DISINVESTMENT PLANNING

Pre-retirement planning is largely concerned with accumulation of additional assets. The best case scenario is that investment income, in conjunction with Social Security benefits and the individual's pension, will be more than ample for a comfortable lifestyle, and the capital can also be kept intact for inheritance by the spouse, children, or other heirs. Unfortunately, many people fail or are unable to save enough to satisfy this scenario; or, they are excellent savers and investors, but encounter a high-cost health or other crisis. In that case, the question becomes how to plan for "disinvestment"—drawing down on the capital without completely exhausting the fund.

A simple rule of thumb is that the fund will never diminish if the principal sum remains invested and only the investment appreciation is withdrawn. One factor to keep in mind in choosing investments is how easy it is to set up a withdrawal schedule or to make withdrawals or redemptions as desired — including whether there are fees associated with the withdrawal.

T. Rowe Price Associates has constructed a matrix[5] based on two factors: (1) the number of years of anticipated retirement, and (2) and the composition of the portfolio. The theory is that the higher the percentage of stocks in the portfolio (which have the potential for growth and appreciation), and the lower the proportion of bonds (which provide a fixed income), the higher the percentage that can safely be withdrawn. Similarly, the shorter the expected duration of retirement, the more that can be withdrawn (because the fund has to last for fewer years).

According to this matrix, it is safe to withdraw 4.9% a year for a 30-year retirement with an 80% bond portfolio (the minimum listed on the table). It is safe to withdraw 12.7% of the fund if 10 years of retirement are expected (the maximum), and the portfolio is 70% stocks and 30% bonds. Furthermore, after the first year of retirement, the withdrawal can be increased by an amount that represents the inflation rate for the year.

Disinvestment planning can be yield-based or needs-based. The older investor can decide to sell securities and make withdrawals from savings and CD accounts based on a percentage of the yield for the year. Alternatively, the decision can be made by striking a balance between current spending needs and anticipated future spending needs. The former approach is more controlled. If the latter approach is taken, it might make sense to transfer some investment funds into an immediate annuity, so that there will be at least a predictable level of income (annuity payments plus Social Security benefits) that cannot be outlived.

The question of selecting assets for various purposes (to sell, donate, or transfer) has been mentioned here several times. When choosing assets for "disinvestment," it may be necessary to pay capital gains taxes on the withdrawals — in which case, it may be better (after 2006) to use assets purchased after 2000 and that have been held for five years because these have the lowest capital gains rate.

Otherwise, it may make sense to use investments that have not appreciated much, or that have even depreciated, because those assets will generate either small capital gains tax liability or, tax losses. If depreciated assets are liquidated, they may generate capital losses too large to be used in the current year, requiring a carry-over of the unused loss. In that scenario, it may make sense to restrict the amount of capital loss to the amount that can be currently deducted.

THE ROLE OF THE FIDUCIARY

The older client may have appointed an agent under a durable power of attorney who has full power over all of the older person's assets, or limited powers that include some degree of investment management. Perhaps the client has placed funds into a trust, and the trustee must find suitable investments. Or, a court may have appointed a guardian to manage the property of an incapacitated person.

What an agent, trustee, and guardian have in common is that they are all fiduciaries (i.e., they are all subject to a legal duty to safeguard someone else's property). Fiduciary authority can be created by contract (e.g., a durable power of attorney or trust instrument), or by court order (with respect to a guardianship).

Fiduciaries are required to act in the best interests of the principal. They are forbidden to engage in self-dealing (i.e., promoting their own interests at the expense of the principal). They are also required to act prudently, which involves taking care of the principal's funds (and, if possible, making the funds grow) while avoiding excessive risks that could reduce the principal's capital.

In many instances, the instrument appointing the fiduciary, when read in conjunction with state law, explains what is permissible and what is forbidden for fiduciary investments. In doubtful cases, it makes sense for the fiduciary to petition the court for authorization of a transaction that might give rise to liability.

Fiduciaries are required to balance the need to generate additional income and to create additional value against the obligation to invest prudently for the preservation of principal. The safety of the capital must be preserved. It is not enough to simply choose investments; the fiduciary must also monitor their performance, remove assets that have failed to perform at a satisfactory level, and substitute more appropriate investments when necessary.

The traditional approach to controlling investments by fiduciaries was to create a "legal list" of extremely safe investments, such as United States government obligations and first mortgages on valuable property. A few states still forbid fiduciaries to engage in any investment outside the "legal list." Other states use the "legal list" as a guideline, but permit other prudent investments.

The modern approach to trust investing is to discard the "legal list" entirely, but retain the duty of prudence. A fiduciary acts prudently by using the degree of attention, skill, and care that a reasonable person would use in investing his or her own money. In additional to legal list investments, government-related financing devices (such as Ginnie Maes), and state bonds on which there has been no recent history of default, will probably be deemed prudent. Municipal bonds are probably prudent, especially if they are insured by a third-party guarantor or adequately secured (such as by sufficient tax revenues). Blue-chip stocks and highly-rated corporate bonds are also probably prudent.

On the other hand, direct investment in real estate (as distinct from high-quality mortgages or mortgage pools) is probably not prudent unless the property is immediately salable and the fiduciary has the expertise to manage the property and place it on the market. Unsecured loans to corporations or individuals are probably not prudent. Nor are investing in business start-ups, or selling trust or guardianship property in exchange for an unsecured note instead of cash or a secured obligation considered prudent. Investing in high-tech stocks, other speculative stocks, options, futures and commodities are almost certainly imprudent.

The prudence of a investment transaction depends on factors such as:

- the research done by the fiduciary prior to investing;
- the rating assigned to the investment by recognized rating authorities;
- whether the fiduciary acted on advice from an attorney, broker, or other professional;
- whether the investment was part of an overall pattern of diversification (among prudent investments only, of course); or
- the fiduciary's attention to tax planning and cushioning the impact of inflation.

The fiduciary often has to balance several interests — not just the current trust beneficiary (who usually desires additional income) but also the trust remainderman (who will be harmed unless the principal is preserved and, preferably, augmented). In addition, a guardian may have to think about the ward's spouse or other dependents of the ward.

Guardianship law has not squarely confronted Medicaid planning. Under traditional principles, still adhered to by some probate judges in guardianship cases, the fiduciary's duty is to increase the ward's income, on the theory that more income is better than less income. Other judges will allow a guardian to carry on a ward's pre-existing pattern of benefiting relatives or charities, or maintaining a structured gifting program, but will not allow creation of a new pattern. The judicial treatment most favorable to the ward is the theory that the guardian can do anything that the ward could have done personally. Thus, the guardian can engage in tax-saving or Medicaid-oriented transactions if they would have been done by the ward before he became incapacitated, or if they are in the ward's best interests.

OLDER INVESTORS "ON-LINE"

Although some older people are afraid of, or distrustful of computers, others have embraced the technology enthusiastically. A surprising number of older people are now using the internet to gather investment information and to discuss it with other investors, as well as to buy securities directly. About seven million people over age 55 used the internet in 1998, and of this group, two-thirds are college graduates, one-third have an advanced degree, almost one-quarter have household income over $100,000, and more than one-quarter have a portfolio worth at least $250,000. Almost one-fifth not only get investment information through the internet, but are also active seekers of trading information[6]. (Note that including people aged 55-64 may distort the picture of senior citizens in general, because this younger group is typically healthier, more affluent, and more active.)

It is very common for recent retirees to take an extremely active interest in money management and investing. In a sense, they become full-time investors as a substitute for their prior careers. In a more negative sense, investing can become a substitute for gambling — another financially risky pastime that attracts a disproportionate number of senior citizens. Older people frequently need less sleep than they did in their younger days, so the ability to chat on an investment forum at 2:00 a.m. is valued by some senior citizens. The ability to trade at deeply discounted commissions is attractive to frugal older people.

Unfortunately, much of the "information" available on-line is naive, misguided, foolish — or outright fraudulent. Furthermore, individuals who are lonely, anxious about their financial future, or declining in capacity are particularly vulnerable to manipulation and are unduly willing to believe anything they read on a computer screen. An important part of incapacity planning is monitoring the older individual's transactions to see if they reflect declining capacity or victimization. If necessary, the amount of capital that the individual can manage directly should be reduced, or durable powers of attorney, trusts, and other management mechanisms should be brought into play.

CHAPTER FOOTNOTES

1. See Joseph D'Allegro, "Insurers Say Seniors Should Keep Some Risk in Their Investments," *National Underwriter*, Life & Health/Financial Services Edition, August 10, 1998, p. 7.

2. Judith Burns, "Gender Gap in Retirement Investments is Cited, With Women Too Conservative," *Wall Street Journal*, June 20, 1997, p. A5A.

3. Treasury securities are sold at regular auctions. Treasury securities are redeemable at maturity at face value. If the buyer's purchase price was below the face value, a refund will be granted to the purchaser for the difference between the purchase price and the face value. This amount will generally be taxed as original issue discount (OID). On the other hand, if the buyer's purchase price is higher than the face value (because Treasury securities were paying higher rates than the market rate for comparably safe securities), then the purchaser has paid a "premium," which can be amortized over the life of the security (reducing its basis by the amortized premium deducted each year).

4. Karen Hube, "Vulnerable Retirees Need to Maintain Their Cool," *Wall Street Journal*, August 31, 1998, p. C1.

5. Discussed in Jonathan Clements' article, "Squeezing the Right Amount From a Retirement Stash," *Wall Street Journal*, February 25, 1997, p. C1.

6. David Barboza, "On-Line Traders: Older, Wiser and Richer," *New York Times*, December 20, 1998, Section 3 (Business), p. 1.

Chapter 12

ANNUITIES

THE BASIC CONCEPT

The basic annuity concept is very simple. Someone who has a large sum of money, but who wants continuing income, transfers the funds to a commercial issuer (usually an insurance company) or a private person. The annuity issuer promises to provide a continuing stream of income payments. The payments can be promised for life, the joint lives of two people, a number of years, or a number of years with refund provisions if the annuitant dies before the term ends. The more payments that must be made based on the deposit of a sum of money, the smaller each individual payment will be.

There are many reasons why annuities are useful in the elder care financial plan. A person whose judgment is somewhat impaired might be capable of administering each month's income and paying bills, but incapable of managing large principal sums. Even a mentally sound person might concede limited investment expertise, so that professional management of an annuity could provide a larger monthly income and better lifestyle. Annuities receive quite favorable tax treatment. Persons in mid-life may achieve better total after-tax return by investing in annuities than in mutual funds.

In many ways, annuities and IRA accounts are similar; in fact, the taxation of distributions from IRAs depends on Internal Revenue Code section 72, the annuity section. An important difference is that no tax deduction is available for investing in annuities, while some taxpayers can deduct up to $2,000 per person (or $4,000 per married couple) per year for funding IRAs. (Contributions to Roth IRAs are not tax-deductible.)

A taxpayer who does not qualify for an IRA deduction, who has more than $2,000 per year to invest, who finds the tax savings attributable to a "mere" $2,000 deduction a trivial factor in planning or who has already made the maximum IRA contribution, may find an annuity an attractive investment option.

When capital gains and ordinary income tax rates were essentially the same, deferred annuities had a clear advantage over mutual funds and investments in individual securities: tax liability was also deferred for the annuities. Tax deferral works much like compound interest. Compound interest allows the investor to earn "interest on interest" while tax deferral allows the entire pre-tax amount, not just the reduced after-tax amount, to appreciate. Under current law, capital gains rates can be much lower than ordinary income rates, so some clients will be deterred from purchasing annuities by the requirement of paying tax, when it finally falls due, at ordinary income rates. The tax deferral and convenience of annuities must be balanced against their often-higher fee structure and reduced ability to be taxed at capital gains rates.

In most states, a person who engages in Medicaid planning is better off having additional income than having additional financial resources (e.g., bank accounts, investment real estate, or securities). Purchase of an annuity makes it possible to convert inconvenient resources into an income stream. (See Chapter 6 for a discussion of annuities in Medicaid planning.)

Unfortunately, in the future the amount of income produced by each $1,000 of annuity funds applied will decrease because companies will begin using the Annuity 2000 table adopted by the National Association of Insurance Commissioners (NAIC).[1] The new table reflects increased life expectancies and therefore reduces each annuity payment because of the prediction that more payments will have to be made.

CLASSIFYING ANNUITIES

A closer look at annuities shows that the simple basic concept supports many variations:

- When will the first annuity payment be made? If it is due as soon as the annuity is purchased, the annuity is immediate; if it is scheduled for the future (e.g., post-retirement), the annuity is deferred. Deferred annuities are divided into an accumulation period, during which appreciation is not taxed; and a payout period, when the payment stream begins (and a portion of each payment will become subject to income tax).

- What determines the span over which the issuer will make payments to the owner?[2] If it is a certain number of years, such as 10 or 20, it is a term certain annuity. (Payments are made to the designated beneficiaries if the annuitant dies before the end of the term.) If it is the lifetime of the annuitant it is a life annuity. If it is the lifetime of both the annuitant and a designated beneficiary (usually the spouse), it is a joint and survivor annuity. A further complication is that the benefit might be cut in half after the first death (joint and 50% survivor annuity), continue at the original level (joint and 100% survivor annuity), or fall anywhere in between.

- Although many annuities are purchased with a single lump-sum payment (i.e., are classified as single premium annuities), multiple premium annuities are possible. A scheduled premium multiple premium annuity contract includes a schedule of payments in specific amounts to be made by the annuity purchaser, whereas a flexible premium contract permits the purchaser to control the timing and amount of premium payments.

- Is the rate of return set in advance, responding to interest rates (fixed annuity) or subject to change based on market forces (variable annuity)? Many hybrid forms are possible. For instance, the rate may be guaranteed at its initial level for a certain period of time, then permitted to float.

- How much control does the purchaser have over the investment of the account? Typically, variable annuities permit the investor to select among several mutual fund-like accounts investing in different types of securities with different risk levels, as well as a fixed account with a guaranteed return. In contrast, the issuer manages the funds invested in fixed annuities.

- Is a charge imposed for surrendering the annuity? A frequent provision is a "back-end" charge that starts out fairly high, is reduced each year, and phases out after seven years. There may be other charges as well, such as an investment management fee.

- Is there an insurance element and, if so, what is its effective cost? Most annuities include a death benefit provision of some type. For example, there may be a guarantee that the account of a variable annuity will be re-valued to the minimum guaranteed amount if the market value of the account is lower than this amount should the account holder die during the accumulation phase.

- Who regulates it? Variable annuity products are considered securities, so the person selling them must have a securities license.

FACTORS IN THE ANNUITY PAYMENT

Usually, the size of each benefit payment under a fixed annuity will be the same, and will be determined at the time of the initial benefit payment, based on the earnings of the funds deposited in the account (minus the fees charged by the company issuing the annuity). Variable annuity payments can fluctuate with market factors, although there may be a guaranteed "floor" below which benefit payments will not fall.

The more payments the issuer has to make, naturally, the smaller each individual payment will be. The more risk the issuer takes, the smaller the payments will be. Therefore, payments will be smaller for a joint and survivor annuity than for a single-life annuity. In the same vein, payments will be smaller for a term certain (e.g., 10 or 20-year) annuity if payments will be made to a designated beneficiary after the initial owner's death than if the payments stop if the owner dies during the term and there is no refund feature.

A single person would be more likely to select a lifetime-only annuity than a married person concerned with the financial welfare of the surviving spouse. The married individual would be more likely to prefer a joint-and-survivor annuity (unless the other spouse is already amply provided for). Someone who is concerned about outliving other income sources would tend to prefer a life or joint and survivor payment, unless these payments are too small to meet the financial objective. In that case, it might make sense to assume the risk of outliving the income in order to make sure that current expenses can be paid for at least a few years.

ANNUITY FEES

Although the company issuing the annuity has the opportunity to benefit from the "float" on the invested funds, it also has expenses related to marketing and administering the annuity. Thus, fees of various kinds are imposed, depending on the annuity contract. The various fees reduce the amount that will eventually be available to the owner of the annuity (or his or her heirs). The longer the investment horizon, the greater the potential impact of fees.

A contract fee is a defined amount, either charged when the annuity is issued or billed to the annuity each year. A transaction fee is imposed on each transaction, such as additional premiums added to an account that permits additions. A percentage of premium charge is deducted from each premium and could be expressed as a sliding scale that diminishes over time, or is inversely proportional to the amount invested in the account.

Charges may be imposed for withdrawals (reducing the annuity balance) or surrenders (removing the entire balance and terminating the annuity). Typically, these charges begin at a fairly high level, to discourage premature depletion of the annuity, but phase down each year until they phase out-usually between the seventh and tenth year. Depending on the terms, the percentage could be calculated on the entire value of the contract, the premiums paid to purchase the contract, or the amount withdrawn.

Penalty-free withdrawals might be permitted in hardship situations, such as nursing home institutionalization or terminal illness. Or, the account might permit a certain number or dollar amount of withdrawals without charge, but impose a charge on additional withdrawals or withdrawals in excess of a particular percentage of account value. A "rolling" charge on a multiple-premium annuity applies to funds that can be traced to each premium, running from the date of deposit of the premium to the date of withdrawal or surrender.

It is conventional to waive the surrender charge when a death benefit is paid on an account that has not yet annuitized. In an annuity with a "bail-out" option, there is no surrender charge for surrendering a contract that fails to live up to its own stated minimum interest rate. If the annuity is structured to include a "market value adjustment," the cash surrender value may go up or down based on whether interest rates at the time of surrender are higher or lower than at the time of purchase. (This is intellectually similar to the rise or fall in the value of bonds, depending on whether their interest rate is higher or lower than prevailing market rates.) Recently, a group of variable annuities has been introduced that does not impose surrender charges on withdrawals.[3] This type of annuity might be attractive to cost-conscious customers who fear that they may need to take money out of their annuity accounts.

Although most annuities can be maintained as an investment for the rest of the owner's life, some annuity contracts stay in force only for a particular number of years (i.e., equity-indexed annuity contracts, discussed below). With this type of annuity, at the end of the term the contract expires unless, during the permitted "window," the owner takes steps to renew the contract or exchange it for another type of contract. Typically, surrender charges do not apply to annuities that expire by their own terms and are not renewed.

Another cost factor is the premium taxes imposed by some states on annuity accounts. These taxes may be deducted from each premium as it is paid to the issuer, at the time of withdrawal, once the account annuitizes, or when death benefits are paid.

THE ANNUITY MARKET

In 1997, sales of variable annuities were $84.3 billion. In that year, about $34 billion in traditional fixed annuities were sold.[4] Equity indexed annuities, a new wrinkle in fixed annuities, were introduced in 1995. Sales of this new type of annuity doubled between 1995 and 1996 and again between 1996 and 1997, reaching $3 billion in 1997.[5]

The marketplace has certainly changed. In 1985, the Life Insurance Marketing Research Association (LIMRA) found the annuity market to be $28.9 billion, with about 82% fixed annuities and 18% variable annuities. By 1992, the market was much larger, at $73.7 billion, but the fixed annuity share had dropped to 58.3%. In 1997, the market was a huge $121.6 billion but the balance had shifted: more than two-thirds of annuities were variable and less than one-third were fixed annuities.[6]

According to the Fisher Annuity Index[7], in September of 1998, 944 fixed annuities were available from 129 companies with interest rates ranging from 4.45% to 7.24%. For CD-type annuities, as of September, 1998, the average rate for a one-year guarantee period was 4.35%; for a four-year guarantee, it was 4.41%; and for a 10-year period, it was 5.09%. As of November, 1998, the number of annuities had declined slightly, to 973 while the number of issuers was still 129. The annuity range of interest rates went down, to 4.18% to 7.08%; CD-type annuities averaged 4.1% for a one-year guarantee period; 3.89% for a four-year guarantee; and 4.98% for a ten-year guarantee.[8]

As of September 30, 1998, the leading investment objectives for variable annuities were growth and income (26.6%) and fixed interest/general account (25.4%). Growth was the objective of 14.5% of accounts, versus miscellaneous equity (13.9%) and balanced asset allocation (10.0%).[9]

Variable annuity results varied quite strongly by sector: at the end of 1997, for instance, the one-year total return for various investment styles of investment annuity varied from 0.60% for funds invested in international bonds to 23.17% for growth-and-income investments. However, international bonds performed much better in the test with three-year annualized return (an average of 6.68%) or five-year annualized return (5.15%).

Over the three-year period, the growth and income sector led once again (25.35% a year), followed closely by U.S. diversified equity funds (23.44%) and growth funds (25.35%). Three-year performance was much better than five-year performance. Over a five-year haul, the annualized return for the top-performing sector, growth and income, was 17.75%, followed once again by U.S. diversified equity (16.38%), growth (15.79%) and aggressive growth (15.40%).[10] But then, these results are quite typical of investments as a whole. Although well-chosen growth-oriented products usually do well there is no guarantee that they will do equally well in every year or that the relative position of various investment styles will not change.

DEPLOYING A LUMP SUM

There are many contexts in which an older person comes into possession of a lump sum but is unable or unwilling either to manage the money personally or turn over management to a broker or other financial adviser. From the older person's view, it is possible that this adviser might misappropriate funds or make honest but misguided choices. One example of a lump sum that an older person might come into is if, after due consideration of Medicaid consequences, the older person sells the family home and moves to other accommodations. In most cases, no capital gains tax will be due on the sale, so the entire amount can be invested. Lump sums may also be encountered as a result of a pension payout, an inheritance, or as life insurance death benefits for which settlement options are not elected.

If the goal is to arrange a secure lifetime income stream, a single premium immediate annuity is a good choice. *Best's Review* found that, as of June 1, 1998, a 65-year-old male could get payments of anywhere from $779.23 to $840.00 a month by investing $100,000 in one of the top-10 ranked annuities. For women, the top-10 annuities paid between $733.27 and $771.00.[11] (The difference is due to women's longer life expectancy.) It should be noted that, although June 1998 was the height of a long-range bull market, it was also a time of low interest rates, and thus the median monthly payment for a lifetime-only immediate annuity was much lower in June 1998 than it was in June 1988: $732/month versus $1,032/month; the median fell 6% ($777 to $732) between June 1997 and June 1998.

As of June 1, 1998, a 70-year-old male investing $100,000 in a non-qualified immediate annuity might get anywhere from $761 to $935 a month while his female counterpart might get anywhere from $663 to $831. At 75, the corresponding range would be $856 to $$1,115 for men, $777 to $964 for women.

A person coming into possession of a lump sum but who will not need additional income until a later time might prefer a single premium deferred annuity (SPDA). A five-year survey[12] of 134 SPDAs offered by 85 insurers showed that guaranteed interest rates have stayed in the 3 to 4% range during this time frame.

TYPES OF ANNUITIES

Fixed Annuities

The National Association of Insurance Commissioners (NAIC) defines a fixed deferred annuity as one that earns interest during the accumulation period at a set rate or based on a methodology set out in the annuity contract and subject to an interest-rate floor.[13]

Fixed annuities have an important role in elder care planning that may not even be noticed by the planning client. They are an important tool used by employers to fund pension plans.[14] Plan investment managers are fiduciaries, constrained to secure the best investment returns consistent with a very low acceptance of risk. Generally speaking, fixed annuities do not fluctuate in response to market forces and so offer predictability. They can also be "laddered," i.e., different maturities can be combined in a single plan in order to lock in rates for various durations.

Another important role is as a mechanism for Individual Retirement Annuities (IRAs) into which pension funds are rolled over. Generally, more than 90% of fixed annuity contracts accept IRA rollovers.

Several interest rates are used with respect to fixed deferred annuities. The current interest rate is the rate credited to a contract at a particular time, subject to a guarantee that it will be maintained until a stipulated date. Some issuers offer an initial rate that is a "bonus" rate, i.e., more favorable than the renewal rate that will take over a defined time after purchase. The renewal rate is often indexed, i.e., calculated based on an objective factor such as prime rates. It is not necessarily true that a single interest rate will apply to the entire contract. The contract may specify adjustments to the interest rate for each premium payment or for time periods during which premiums are paid.

Equity Indexed Annuities

The equity indexed annuity[15] is a counterpart to index funds that try to reduce risk by duplicating the performance of the entire market or an entire sector of the market. About 40 companies currently sell equity indexed annuities.[16] This type of annuity is generally not considered to be a security. Therefore, an equity indexed annuity can be sold by persons who do not have a securities license and buyers do not have to be given the full range of securities disclosures before they purchase. In mid-1998, about 60 equity indexed annuity products were available.

The difference between a variable annuity and an equity indexed annuity is the way it responds to market changes. The investor in a variable annuity divides his or her investment among several accounts and is permitted to switch several times a year if his or her investment preferences change. Equity indexed annuity investments are controlled by the issuer who guarantees a floor interest rate (typically, 3%) but also promises to return a specified percentage of the gain in the chosen index (e.g., S&P 500) to investors. The percentage, such as 70%, is called the participation rate and can be fixed for the entire term of the annuity contract or changeable at stated intervals. The calculation could be based on simple or compound interest. The contract might also include a cap amount that limits the upside potential. Usually, the computation does not include dividends on the stocks comprising the index. Yet another approach is to compute the change in the relevant index then subtract an administrative fee before crediting the investor's account.

Equity indexed annuities use several methods to adjust account values, including ratcheting (also called annual reset), high-water-mark, and point-to-point. The annuity is enhanced each year of an annual reset based on changes in the value of the index at the start and end of the contract year. High-water-mark adjustments are based on changes in index value during the term, usually as of anniversary dates of purchase of the annuity, measured by the difference between the highest value of the index during the term and the initial value. Point-to-point adjustments are made based on the ending and beginning values of the relevant index.

As a general rule, the annual reset generates the lowest participation rate and is the most likely to be subject to a cap on upside appreciation. But it might offer the best results during a period of significant fluctuations in the index. Furthermore, interest is credited each year whereas interest is only credited at the end of the term using high-water-mark or point-to-point methodologies. Thus, surrender of the annuity in mid-term could result in loss of interest for part of the term.

Interest is credited to annuity accounts at the end of a specified term, which can be anywhere from one to ten years, but usually is either six or seven years. A variation is to make calculations based on a series of consecutive terms. At the end of each term, there is a window period when withdrawals will be permitted without penalty.

An equity indexed annuity could be a good choice for an individual who wants the steady income of a fixed annuity, but also believes that the market as a whole will go up, (thus influencing the index) but prefers to invest in the market as a whole, not individual securities. But, as the discussion above shows, these are complex products, with the eventual return responsive both to the design of the individual annuity and to outside market factors. For instance, between March 31, 1997 and March 31, 1998, the S&P 500 went up 45.52%. The average equity indexed annuity went up 38.69%—a slightly better performance than the average mutual fund that invested in large-cap stocks, which went up 38.46%. However, after the 1998 market break, many issuers had to cut their participation rates significantly. Some rebounded, but some did not.[17]

There are significant differences among equity indexed annuities. It's simplistic to choose merely on the basis of participation rate because that is not the only determinant of the actual value of the annuity to its owner. Furthermore, even if the owner fully intends to maintain the annuity and avoid withdrawals or surrenders this objective may be frustrated by a sudden need for cash.

Variable Annuities

The variable annuity, unlike the fixed annuity, is a security product so only persons holding a securities license can sell it. During the accumulation period, the premium (net of charges) is invested in accordance with the account owner's directions. Several choices, including a guaranteed account, are offered. The payments from a matured variable annuity might be either fixed (as defined by the contract at the outset) or variable (responding to market conditions at the time of annuitization).

The entire balance of the variable annuity can be withdrawn in a lump sum or annuitized using one of the typically available settlement options. Some contracts allow "commutation," or surrender of the contract in exchange for the present value of the expected future payment stream. If the owner of a straight single-life annuity dies before his or her predicted life expectancy in effect part of the value of the account will be forfeited, because the insurer has no obligation to make any payments to the heirs of the deceased owner.[18]

STRATEGIES FOR THE DEATH BENEFIT

One approach to life insurance planning is simply for financial advisers to assist their elder clients in selecting an appropriate life insurance program. Then, the elder clients can keep their investment decisions separate from their insurance decisions. However, savvy clients often like combination products, especially if there is a tax advantage to be gained. Before mid-1998, some claimed that the variable annuity death benefit was essentially valueless because the stock market would never decline enough to force the value of variable annuity accounts below the death benefit. The events of that year proved them wrong, as did earlier unpleasantness in 1997.

A strategy that can work if the stock market declines is to withdraw funds from the variable annuity account, leaving in enough to keep the account open. The death benefit is defined as at least the principal minus withdrawals, so this strategy operates as a form of unofficial life insurance.[19]

Throughout the variable annuity industry, the average "mortality and expense risk" (M&E) fee is about 1.25% of assets per year. However, some companies offer both a basic death benefit and an optional, higher-cost enhanced benefit. A rising-floor death benefit recalculates the value of the death benefit regularly (it could be anywhere from annually to every six years). A stepped-up benefit readjusts the death benefit to equal the market value of the annuity account, rather than the initial investment. The death benefit might even be generously defined as the highest of the current contract value or the value of the contract as of any anniversary of the purchase.[20]

Some advisers suggest that it makes sense to divide a large variable annuity investment between two or more accounts with differing risk profiles. That way, if one account (usually the riskier one) drops in value, the death benefit can be used to make up for the loss. The overall result, in the somewhat unlikely case that the account holder dies before the accounts recover value, can be better than if there were only one account, which lost less and therefore got a smaller death benefit.[21]

ANNUITY OR ?

Clearly, then, a commercial annuity bears a striking resemblance to an Individual Retirement Account (IRA), but it also resembles a mutual fund or Certificate of Deposit (CD). What determines which should be selected when an older client wants to make an investment?

- *Size of investment*: Contributions to an IRA account are limited to $2,000 per person per year and a penalty tax is imposed on excess contributions. Persons who invest in annuities, CDs, or mutual funds are not constrained by such a limit and can invest on any schedule.

- *Possible tax deduction*: Depending on the client's income and compensation situation, part or all of the maximum $2,000 annual contribution to a conventional IRA may be deductible for income tax purposes. Roth IRA contributions, annuity contributions, and funds used to purchase mutual fund shares are not deductible.

- *Tax on accumulation*: Funds within an IRA (conventional or Roth) or annuity account accumulate on a tax deferred basis, but mutual fund shareholders are taxed each year on distributions from the account. (Distributions from the account are not necessarily the same amount as the appreciation in the account's value). Some of the mutual fund distributions will be taxable at ordinary income rates, others at capital gains rates. Naturally, the taxpayer's income tax bracket will determine the value of the distinction between capital gain and ordinary income taxation.

- *Tax accounting*: Even a premature withdrawal from a Roth IRA is treated as if it were made first as a non-taxable return of capital and only subsequently from income. Thus, there is no income tax or premature withdrawal penalty on a premature withdrawal that does not exceed the actual contributions made by the taxpayer. But annuity withdrawals are taxed as if the taxable appreciation was withdrawn first and the premature withdrawal penalty applies to the portion of the withdrawal that is taxable.[22]

- *Liquidity limitations*: A penalty income tax is imposed on withdrawals from an IRA account or annuity before the owner reaches age 59½ (unless he or she is disabled, or other special conditions apply). There is no penalty when mutual fund owners withdraw funds from the account (i.e., sell some of their shares), but they do have to pay income tax (usually at capital gains rates) on any profits earned by selling shares. In addition, many annuities impose surrender charges on withdrawals at least until the funds have remained in the account for seven to ten years.

- *Mandatory withdrawals*: A penalty tax is also imposed on conventional IRAs if the owner fails to withdraw the mandated minimum amount each year. There is no minimum required withdrawal from Roth IRAs, mutual fund accounts, or annuities. It is perfectly permissible for the owner of the account to permit most or all of it to accumulate for inheritance by his or her heirs.

- *Tax on distributions*: In general, the amounts withdrawn from a conventional IRA account represent ordinary income. Withdrawals from a Roth account are generally tax-free as long as the funds remained in the account for at least five years. Mutual fund distributions are taxed as either capital gains or ordinary income depending on the nature of the transaction at the level of the mutual fund. Annuity payments are part tax-free return of capital and part ordinary income. Even though some of the annuity income stream comes from capital transactions, the annuity owner is not allowed to take advantage of capital gains tax rates on such payments.

- *Tax on switches*: Internal Revenue Code section 1035 permits certain tax-free exchanges of insurance products (including annuities). However, a person who switches between mutual funds (even mutual funds in the same family) will be taxed on any profits on the sale of one fund and cannot "roll over" the gains to the second fund.

- *Fees and costs*: Variable annuities have an insurance aspect which is absent from mutual funds. The average expense ratio for variable annuities was 2.02% in 1987 versus 1.3% for mutual funds. Both types of investment have some kind of investment and management fee. Some mutual funds have up-front loads (not present in variable annuities) but most variable annuities have surrender charges which are less common in mutual funds.[23]

- *Estate inclusion or exclusion*: Under appropriate circumstances the designated beneficiary of a deceased person's IRA can defer taxation of the inheritance.[24] There are no corresponding provisions for mutual funds or annuities. If the account owner has "annuitized" for life there will be nothing to go into the estate, i.e., nothing subject to estate taxation but also no benefit to heirs. Under Internal Revenue Code section 2039, the present value of any amount payable to heirs under a joint-and-survivor annuity or under a term-certain is included in the taxable estate of the deceased account owner.

- *Security*: Which investment is most likely to make payments as promised? What is the availability of government or other safety mechanisms if the issuer fails?

- *Personal preference*: Which investment makes the client feel most secure? For instance, even though the death benefit feature of annuities is seldom triggered, it provides comfort to many older investors who are afraid that, at the time of their death, the value of their annuity may have declined beneath its initial value.

Probably, the older client should begin by investing in the appropriate housing. This may be a free-standing home, a retirement community or a continuing care retirement community (CCRC) unit, or some other living arrangement that suits the client's financial profile, tax bracket, Medicaid plan, and estate plan. Next, the older client should address any security needs by having a sensible portfolio of life and health insurance (including long-term care insurance, if desired and affordable).

Afterward, the first move is probably using highly tax-favored mechanisms such as 401(k) plans and IRAs and then investing. A deferred annuity can be an especially compelling investment because of its potential to defer taxation on appreciation. An immediate annuity can be an appropriate investment for a retiree whose main interest is in a continuing income stream that does not require active investment monitoring.

DOUBLE DEFERRAL: PROS AND CONS

About half of variable annuities are sold for use in IRAs or corporate retirement plans. The other half are sold as alternatives to investments in mutual funds and individual securities. One viewpoint is that annuities are a poor choice to fund retirement accounts that are already tax-deferred, especially if the annuity will be surrendered quickly enough to be subject to a heavy surrender charge.

The opposite viewpoint is that annuities are an insurance product as well as an investment product and the availability of a death benefit offers some hedge against market risk, in that it provides security for the account holder's heirs even if the investor dies when the market value of the annuity is at a low ebb. Further, it may be easier and less costly to shift between annuity subaccounts than to sell mutual fund shares and re-invest in another mutual fund. Market factors are also crucial: at a particular point in time a fixed annuity may simply offer a higher rate of interest than the taxable mutual fund that might be selected instead.[25]

JUMBO SHRIMP

An annuity that isn't annuitized, like a jumbo shrimp, may seem like a contradiction in terms. Yet the majority of annuity purchasers withdraw the funds from their accounts in one or more installments, rather than leaving the funds in place to create an income stream. In fact, in any given year, only about one percent of annuity owners actually begin to receive payments.[26]

Why? It could be because they believed that a variable annuity offered a better return than a comparable mutual fund or individual security but they now want to withdraw funds to re-invest in a more favorable opportunity or that they need the money for some other reason. Yet again, they could be concerned that they will die after a straight life annuity goes into pay status but before they have recovered the full amount deposited with the result that their heirs will not receive anything deriving from the annuity investment. They might discover that, because they live in a Medicaid "cap" state, additional income from the annuity is perilous to their Medicaid plan. They could dislike the fact that, once they select an annuitization option, they will not be able to alter it to respond to market conditions or changing needs but will simply receive the benefit as stipulated.[27]

In the short run, annuity investors may also be able to benefit from the antiquated mortality tables used to calculate annuity payments. Many investors have a predicted life expectancy greater than the figure from the mortality table and thus will receive more payments. This is a short-run play, because the insurance industry is moving toward adoption of more realistic life expectancies.

Insurers are responding to the reluctance to annuitize by offering more flexible options. There is a trend among an increasing number of companies to allow the chance to "commute" (take the remaining funds in a lump sum), for instance. Or, the insurer may allow a lump sum withdrawal of part of the sum, with the rest converted into a payment stream.

INCOME TAXATION OF ANNUITIES

As noted above, Internal Revenue Code section 72 governs annuity income taxation.[28] Annuity taxation starts with a simple principle. The investor gets back his or her capital tax-free, but must pay income tax on the portion of the payment that represents investment income built up before the annuity entered pay status. But since the tax code is involved, the simple rule soon gathers complexity.

It should be noted that, for income tax purposes, annuities are either qualified or nonqualified. Nonqualified annuities are purchased with after-tax dollars and therefore, as mentioned above, the portion of each payment attributable to principal is received tax-free. In contrast, the entire payment from a qualified annuity, including the part that can be traced back to the initial investment, is taxable. Qualified annuities, which generally are used to fund qualified retirement plans, are subject to limitations on the amount that can be invested initially and specify the age at which withdrawals must begin.

The central concept in nonqualified annuity taxation is "investment in the contract." The net cost of the annuity includes everything the annuity owner paid for the contract minus any non-taxable amounts received under the contract before the annuity starting date or date of first payment.[29] This net cost is the maximum that can be recovered without paying tax. Once the entire net cost is recovered, the whole annuity payment (not just part of it) will be subject to income tax.

Refunds

The refund concept doesn't apply to a life annuity or a joint life annuity, but a term annuity (e.g., payments for 10 or 20 years) may include a refund feature in case the annuitant dies before the term ends. The net cost of such annuities has to be reduced to account for the value of the refund feature. (Generally, as the net cost goes down, the amount that might be taxable goes up.) In some instances, the value of the refund feature is considered to be zero, so there will be no effect on the taxation of the annuity benefits. In other situations, the refund feature does have a value for tax purposes. The value depends on IRS actuarial tables (see Publication 939 for details).

Expected Return

Once the net cost of the annuity is known, the next hurdle is calculating the expected return which is the total payments that can be expected based on the terms of the annuity contract. For a fixed period annuity (for a term of years), the expected return is simply the number of fixed payments times the amount of each payment. For example, a ten-year annuity paying $500 a month would have an expected return of $600,000 (120 x $500).

The expected return for a single life annuity is the amount of the annual payment multiplied by a "multiple" found in the IRS actuarial tables. For example, the multiple for a man whose annuity starting date is closer to his 66th birthday than to his 65th or 67th birthday is 19.2. In other words, it is expected that payments will be made for 19.2 years, so the expected return is 19.2 times the payments for one year.[30]

The IRS defines "temporary life annuities" as those where payments are made for life or until a specified period ends, whichever is shorter. The IRS has male and female actuarial tables for this situation.

For joint and 100% survivor annuities (i.e., the payment is not reduced after the first death), expected return is based on the combined life expectancies of the two annuitants. Adjustments are required if the annuity is reduced. In that case, expected return is calculated separately, based on payments that will be received during the joint life expectancies of both plus reduced payments that will be received during the predicted period of survival.

Income Tax Calculation

An exclusion percentage is determined by dividing the investment in the contract (as adjusted for refund features) by the expected return. This percentage of every regular payment is tax-free. The rest of each payment is taxable. If the payment level subsequently increases, the entire increase is taxable.

However, once the entire net cost of the annuity (for this purpose, calculated without a reduction for any refund feature) has been recovered, typically, because the annuitant has exceeded his or her predicted life expectancy, then all further annuity payments are taxed as ordinary income.

On the other hand, if the annuitant dies prematurely, so that some of the net cost remains unrecovered at death, the "leftover" net cost can be claimed as a deduction on the annuitant's final tax return.

Income Taxation of Variable Annuities

The income tax issues are even more complex for variable annuities because there is no certainty about the size of each payment. One thing is clear: any withdrawals made before the annuity starting date are fully taxable as ordinary income (up to the amount of gain in the contract). In other words, even though the annuity is an investment, withdrawals are not taxed at capital gains rates.

The basic method described above is used to calculate the exclusion percentage for the annuity. However, since the investment nature of the variable annuity means that each benefit payment will not necessarily be the same amount, the exclusion percentage is calculated by dividing the investment in the contract by the number of years over which the annuity benefits will be paid.

It is also possible that, in a time of low returns on the variable annuity, payments for a particular year could be lower than the amount that could be received free of income tax. In this situation, the tax-free portion of future payments can be re-calculated to make up for the shortfall.[31]

Transfer of Annuities

Like other investment assets, an annuity can be given away, sold, or exchanged. As a general rule, the sale of an annuity results in ordinary income, not capital gains, taxation to the seller. The amount of taxable income is equal to the sale price less the net premium cost of the annuity.

However, there is no gain or loss on the exchange of one annuity for another annuity with the same annuitant. Nor is gain or loss taxable if the reason for the exchange is the insolvency of the company that issued the annuity.

ESTATE TAXATION OF ANNUITIES

The estate tax implications of single life annuities are simple: there aren't any. The annuity ends at the annuitant's death, so there is nothing to be included or taxed in the estate.

However, Internal Revenue Code section 2039 does create estate tax consequences for joint and survivor annuities. The estate of the first annuitant to die may have to include the value of the benefit that the survivor will receive. Section 2039 also requires estate inclusion in some cases when the decedent died before the first annuity payment, but there was a guarantee feature to prevent the decedent's interest from being entirely extinguished.

The value of the survivor's interest that is included in the decedent's estate depends on whether the annuity is pension-related or was purchased as an investment. For investment annuities, the value equals what it would cost the surviving annuitant to buy a comparable annuity as of the date of the decedent's death. For other annuities, such as pensions paid in joint and survivor form, the valuation depends on the present value of the survivor's right to annuity income.

CHAPTER FOOTNOTES

1. Sandra K. Meltzer, "On Ramp: Annuity 2000 Mortality Table," *National Underwriter*, Life and Health/Financial Services edition, December 14, 1998, p. 14.

2. This discussion assumes that the owner of the account is the annuitant — the person who receives annuity payments — but other scenarios are possible: someone could purchase an annuity that makes payments to or for the benefit of someone else (such as the purchaser's spouse or child); or the account could be surrendered before annuity payments begin.

3. Linda Koco, "No-Surrender-Fee VAs Hit the Street," *National Underwriter*, Life and Health/Financial Services edition, December 28, 1998, p. 13.

4. Although fixed annuities suffered because of generally low interest rates paid to investors, Jack Marrion points out that fixed annuities can be a better choice than certificates of deposit, when their rates are comparable, because of the tax deferral, guaranteed minimum rate, and lifetime income features of fixed annuities: "Some Fixed Annuities Still Competitive," *National Underwriter*, Life and Health/Financial Services edition, January 18, 1999, p. 20. This article also discusses equity indexed annuities and their reset features. For more about equity indexed annuities, see Michael Ebmeier, "Some Next-Gen EIAs Offer Multiple Options," *National Underwriter*, Life and Health/Financial Services edition, January 18, 1999, p. 5.

5. These figures come from Ron Panko, "Stock Performer," *Best's Review*, Life/Health edition, August 1998, p. 63. For sales of nonqualified variable annuities in 1996 and 1997, and analysis of the size of nonqualified variable annuity contracts and their age profile (about 30 percent of contracts in force were owned by senior citizens, and slightly over one-quarter of new contracts were purchased by senior citizens), see "Variable Gains" (no by-line), *Best's Review*, Life/Health edition, January 1999, p. 67.

6. LIMRA figures are quoted in Linda Corman, "Fixed Annuities: New Twists and Old Gnarls," *New York Times*, March 1, 1998, p. BU6. Also see Variable Annuity Research and Data Service figures, quoted in Joseph B. Treaster, "The Money Keeps Rolling in for Variable Annuities," *New York Times*, January 11, 1998, p. BU 62, showing the size of the variable annuity market fairly steady at below $10 billion a year from 1986-1989; strong growth in 1990 and 1991, reaching $20 billion a year in 1991, explosive growth in 1992 ($30 billion) and 1993 (close to $50 billion), followed by slow growth in 1994 (reaching $50 billion) but decline in 1995 (back down below $50 billion), and another banner year in 1996 (over $70 billion) with estimated 1997 sales of $85 billion.

7. See *National Underwriter* , Life and Health/Financial Services edition, September 28, 1998, p. 12.

8. *National Underwriter*, Life and Health/Financial Services edition, November 16, 1998, p. 26.

9. See Rick Carey, "9-Month VA Sales Total $75.7 Billion," *National Underwriter* , Life and Health/Financial Services edition, November 20, 1998, p. 4. This article notes that year-to-date sales as of the third quarter of 1998 were 17.5 percent higher than year-to-date sales as of the third quarter of 1997, and sales in the third quarter alone were 10.5 percent higher than sales for the third quarter of 1997.

10. Figures come from Morningstar Inc., quoted in Bridget O'Brien, "Annuity Countertrend: Investors Can Choose Their Own Features," *Wall Street Journal*, January 8, 1998, p. R10.

11. "Start It Up" (staff-written article) *Best's Review*, Life/Health edition, August 1998, p. 77.

12. Kim Kelleher, "Taking a Closer Look," *Best's Review*, Life/Health edition, December 1998, p. 89.

13. The NAIC issues a *Buyer's Guide to Fixed Deferred Annuities*. The text is available at http://www.naic.org/drafts/misc/byguid8.

14. See Jeremy Alexander, "Fixed Annuities Play Major Role in Pensions," *National Underwriter*, Life and Health/Financial Services edition, September 28, 1998, p. 21.

15. Bridget O'Brien and Leslie Scism, "Equity-Indexed Annuities Score Big Hit, But They Put a Big Price on Protection," *Wall Street Journal*, May 30, 1997, p. C1; Ron Panko, "Stock Performer," *Best's Review*, Life/Health Edition, August 1998, p. 63.

16. The NAIC has issued a consumer guide to equity-indexed annuities; it forms an appendix to the *Buyer's Guide to Fixed Deferred Annuities*. See http://www.naic.org/lnews/releases/equityan.htm.

17. Bridget O'Brien, "Annuity Designed to Battle Volatility is Also Hurt By It," *Wall Street Journal*, December 7, 1998, p. C1.

18. See Bridget O'Brien, "Bet Your Life: How to Weigh Payout Choices," *Wall Street Journal*, June 16, 1997, p. C1.

19. Ellen E. Schultz, "Stock Loss in Variable Annuity Can Be Used to Lift Insurance," *Wall Street Journal*, November 11, 1997, p. C1. Wall Street Journal writer Ellen Schultz gives the example of a variable annuity account initially funded with $100,000, but whose value has declined to $75,000. Withdrawal of $74,000 from the account would be treated as a non-taxable return of capital (although the impact of surrender charges would have to be considered); the benefit paid to the heirs of the account holder would be $26,000 if he or she died with the $1,000 account still open.

20. Bridget O'Brien, "Annuities Firms Market the Death Benefit," *Wall Street Journal*, July 14, 1997, p. C1.

21. Ellen E. Schultz, "Variable-Annuity Tip Finds Two Better Than One," *Wall Street Journal*, September 26, 1987, p. C1.

22. Ellen E. Schultz makes this point in "Tax Advantages of Roth IRA Top Annuities," *Wall Street Journal*, October 16, 1997, p. C1. Her conclusion is that Roth IRAs offer a better tax "play" to eligible taxpayers than annuities do.

23. The figures come from the National Association of Variable Annuities; see Bridget O'Brien, "Annuities Sellers Facing Pressure to Reduce Fees," *Wall Street Journal*, August 18, 1997, p. C1 and Vanessa O'Connell, "Commissions Hunting: Look to `M&E' Fees," *Wall Street Journal*, March 30, 1998, p. C22. Also note that about 10 annuity issuers (including financial giants such as Fidelity, John Hancock, and Vanguard Group) make their products available directly to the public, with no middleman and thus no commission, but they have attracted only about four percent of the variable annuity market, probably because this complex product requires personal explanation from a professional who can use the potential buyer's own financial figures in projections. See James S. Hirsch, "Direct-Marketed Variable Annuities Are Proving to be Tough Sell," *Wall Street Journal*, May 18, 1998, p. C1.

24. Prop. Reg. §1.401-(a)(9)-1.

25. Compare Danny Fisher, "Why Put IRA Money Into a Fixed Annuity?" and David Shapiro, "Annuity Vs. Mutual Fund: Fairer Comparisons," *National Underwriter*, Life and Health/Financial Services edition, August 3, 1998, p. 21 with Ellen E. Schultz and Bridget O'Brien, "Annuity Buyers May be Overdosing on Tax Deferral," *Wall Street Journal* , July 28, 1997, p. C1.

26. See Elizabeth MacDonald, "Annuity Firms Seek to Update Mortality Data," *Wall Street Journal*, May 4, 1998, p. C1.

27. Karen Hube's "Annuity Companies Pitch 'Annuitization' to Recover Their Appeal," *Wall Street Journal*, June 8, 1998, p. C1 addresses these issues.

28. Excellent guidance about applying the rules in various situations can be found in IRS Publications 939 (General Rule for Pensions and Annuity) and 575 (Taxation of Nonperiodic Payments).

29. The annuity starting date is the first day of the first period in which an amount is received as an annuity.

30. See Reg. §1.72-9, Table V.

31. IRS Publication 575, p. 14.

Chapter 13

SPECIAL ESTATE PLANNING ISSUES FOR THE OLDER CLIENT

Although certain basic estate planning concepts are applicable to all, there are also special issues that should be taken into account when elderly persons make an initial estate plan or modify an existing plan. Paradoxically, it can be hard to find the right moment to discuss estate planning with clients. To young, active clients, the entire subject seems impossibly remote (although it is often possible to get clients to understand the importance of maintaining adequate life insurance to protect growing families). To older clients, on the contrary, the subject may seem all too relevant and thus too threatening, with planning put off to "some other time."

Unfortunately, however, "some other time" might never arrive. Even if the older person is still alive, the person must have mental capacity to be allowed to make a will, set up a trust, or modify existing legal instruments and beneficiary designations. Some of these tasks can be performed by an attorney-in-fact (person authorized by a power of attorney, see page 273) or a guardian, but in most states making a will is considered inherently personal, so guardians are limited in their estate planning powers. It may be impossible to create a necessary document, or to update a document that no longer reflects current statutes.

How does elder estate planning differ from estate planning in general? In general, most estate planning clients are married, and taking care of the spouse is a very important planning objective. Yet, in the elder care context, a high concentration of widowed and never-married clients is found. In most estate plans, increasing the amount of funds available to the surviving spouse helps the surviving spouse. But if the survivor is elderly, reducing the available funds might be better—if the survivor is incapacitated and unable to handle money, and especially if the survivor has already made or might make a Medicaid application in the future.

Because federal law allows an unlimited marital deduction, estate tax on the estate of the first spouse to die can be eliminated completely by leaving the whole estate to the spouse. This simple approach (sometimes called an "I Love You Will") doesn't always work in the long run. Apart from Medicaid and capacity questions, it can create a "second estate problem." If the widow or widower dies without having remarried, the estate may be quite large (especially if the inherited assets have appreciated significantly), but there is no marital deduction available. The overall tax bill may be larger than if the survivor had received a smaller sum; or if other planning devices (such as the credit shelter trust; see page 247) had been used wisely to plan the first estate.

The older client's estate plan has to strike a delicate balance. There must be funds for current and continuing needs, especially medical and care needs. However, if a Medicaid plan is underway, it will be necessary to divest assets that are "excess" in the Medicaid context. This can also work well with the estate plan, where the objective is to reduce the estate, preferably below the taxable level. But in most instances, receiving Medicaid benefits will subject the estate to claims by the Medicaid agency after the recipient of benefits dies (see page 141)—so a decision will have to made whether receiving Medicaid benefits is more worthwhile than transmitting assets to future generations.

BASIC ESTATE PLANNING OBJECTIVES

An estate plan is a way to transmit wealth to other people, and across generations, in accordance with the client's wishes—while reducing the amount of taxes that must be paid (both during life and on the estate itself). The typical estate plan uses a will to govern transmission of assets at the testator's (will creator's) death. Many estate plans use trusts, both for tax reasons and for convenient long-term management of assets. Life insurance makes it possible to create an "instant estate" for a person who has family responsibilities but few financial assets. Even affluent people benefit by the use of life insurance, because it receives favorable tax consideration. Combining devices (e.g., life insurance trusts) often enhances the power of each separate planning device.

This chapter refers to the "potentially taxable estate," because in the real world the vast majority of estates are not subject to federal estate tax—because they're too small; because of the marital deduction; because of charitable and other deductions. An important theme of estate planning is using giving programs and other devices to reduce the estate below the federally taxable level—without creating further tax problems later.

An additional problem arises for estates larger than $1 million (or $2 million, for a married couple, each of whom is entitled to an exclusion of $1 million; the $1 million is indexed for inflation after 1998): a separate Generation-Skipping Transfer Tax (GSTT) is imposed on certain gifts and other transfers made to a grandchild or person of the grandchild's generation, but not on transfers to persons of the transferor's own generation or one generation younger.

PRACTICE TIP: Although these issues are beyond the scope of this book, both trusts and estates are potential payors of income tax. Most trusts are "grantor trusts," whose income will be taxed to the grantor (even if someone else receives the income). However, some trusts must pay tax on their own income, and the income tax rules for trusts are less generous than those available to individuals. Under some circumstances, the beneficiary rather than the grantor or the trust is taxed. Allowing a trust to "accumulate" income (save it up from one year to the next) can add useful flexibility for meeting beneficiaries' needs—but greatly multiplies the trust's accounting problems! Invasions of principal also create problems in allocating between principal and income.

Simple estates are frequently settled in the year of the decedent's death; but a more complex estate may linger on for one or even more years. As it generates income on the decedent's assets, it has the potential to become a taxpayer.

If a person owns real estate in more than one state, probate is required not only in the state of domicile, but in each state where real property was owned. This requirement of "ancillary probate" can often be avoided by putting ownership of the out-of-state real property into a trust.

State Death Taxes

Although this discussion revolves around federal estate tax, it should be noted that most of the states impose their own estate taxes. If an older person is contemplating a move to another state, one factor in choosing a new home is whether it is a high- or low-tax state—

definitely including its estate tax. The majority of the states have what is called a "sponge tax," i.e., their tax is defined as the maximum amount that can be used as a state death tax credit against federal estate taxation. IRC §2011(a) contains the formula for crediting state death taxes against the federal tax obligation; all states collect at least this amount.

A few states have "inheritance" taxes (imposed on the heirs, for the privilege of inheriting) rather than or in addition to "estate" taxes (imposed on the estate itself, for the privilege of passing along assets).

State death taxes are imposed by the state that was the decedent's "domicile" at the time of death, so disputes can arise about people who had more than one home or apartment. A person has only one domicile, no matter how many residences the person has. Domicile is a fairly complex concept, involving not just the intent to reside in one state rather than another, but the strength of the connection with the state (including where bank accounts were maintained, which state issued the driver's license, and where the person was registered to vote).

TRA '97'S HERITAGE

For a decade, from 1987 to 1997, federal estate tax law remained fairly inactive, and there was one thing that could always be relied on: an estate under $600,000 would be exempt from federal taxation because the $192,800 unified credit (see below) would shelter any estate up to that size. With proper planning measures, much larger estates could escape taxation.

The Taxpayer Relief Act of 1997 was extremely beneficial to owners of mid-sized estates because it set up a schedule for phasing in much larger amounts that would automatically be safe from estate taxation. Note that, although many members of Congress support lowering the estate tax rates, they remain the same (ranging from a minimum of 37% to 55%). What has changed is the size of the estate that can escape estate taxation.

Technically speaking, TRA '97 enacted a schedule for phasing in significant increases in the "unified credit." Under present-day law, estate taxes and gift taxes are supposed to work together. If a person dies without having made any nonexempt lifetime gifts, the entire estate qualifies for the unified credit. On the other hand, nonexempt lifetime gifts reduce the unified credit; if the entire credit is used up, gift taxes have to be paid during life. (Most gifts to spouses and most gifts to charities are exempt from gift tax. There is also an annual exclusion of $10,000, as adjusted for inflation, per donee. If a married person's spouse agrees to join in the gift, the annual exclusion goes up to $20,000 per donee (with inflation adjustments). By the way, gift tax liability has to be used to reduce the unified credit. The taxpayer doesn't have the option of paying gift tax immediately in cash in order to preserve the unified credit for later use.

People usually focus, not on the unified credit itself, but the amount of money that can be sheltered from estate and gift taxation by applying the unified credit. These are the figures for the years 1999-2006 (by which time the full unified credit should be phased in):

Year	Unified Credit	Max. Amount Protected
1999	$211,300	$650,000
2000-2001	$220,550	$675,000
2002-2003	$229,800	$700,000
2004	$287,300	$850,000
2005	$326,300	$950,000
2006	$345,800	$1,000,000

THE GROSS ESTATE

The first step in calculating estate tax is determining the "gross estate"; then various deductions are allowed. If the remaining estate is large enough to be taxable, then the applicable tax rate is applied:

$500,000-750,000	$155,800, plus 37% over $500
750,000-1,000,000	$248,300 + 39% over 750
1,000,000-1,250,000	$345,800 + 41%
1,2500,000-1,500,000	$448,300 + 43%
1,500,000-2,000,000	$555,800 + 45%
2,000,000-2,500,000	$780,800 + 49%
2,500,000-3,000,000	$1,025,800 + 53%
Over 3,000,000	$1,290,800 + 55%

Not that it probably matters in most practices, but the availability of the lower estate tax brackets phases out above $10 million, so that an estate of about $17 million would all be taxed at approximately the 55% rate.

Any tax calculated from the table is then reduced by various credits (including the unified credit referred to above).

The problem is that, for tax purposes, the gross estate excludes some important items that would, according to common sense, seem to belong in the estate; yet it includes some equally important items that would seem not to belong there, such as some items that were given away. Furthermore, the "probate" estate—the amount that is subject to the jurisdiction of a probate court—is different from either the gross or the taxable estate. Joint property is excluded from the probate estate, but part or all of it (depending on the circumstances) might have to be included in the gross estate.

The Internal Revenue Code provides, in sections noted here, that the following items must be included in the gross estate:

- Property in which the decedent had an interest at the time of death, such as unpaid salary and bonuses, dividends on stock the decedent owned at the time of death, the decedent's business interests in partnerships and closely-held corporations (§2033)

- Transfers of insurance made less than three years before death (§2035)

- Transfers with a retained life estate (§2036)

- Transfers to someone else, on condition that the transferee survive the transferor, if there is a meaningful chance that the property will revert to the transferor—what counts is the likelihood at the moment before death (§2037)

- Revocable transfers during life, such as "living trusts" (§2038). This section also requires that, if a parent or grandparent sets up a Uniform Gifts to Minors Act or Uniform Transfer to Minors Act account for a child or grandchild, and serves as custodian of the account, the property will be included in the donor/custodian's estate if he dies while the child is still a minor.

- Certain joint and survivor annuities (§2039); see page 268 for more about this.

- Jointly owned property (§2040)

- General powers of appointment (§2041)

- Life insurance proceeds (§2042)

For estate tax purposes, the gross estate is reduced by creditors' claims against the estate; funeral and estate administration expenses; charitable bequests; and the marital deduction. State and foreign death taxes paid act as a credit: that is, within limitations, each dollar paid to another jurisdiction reduces the federal estate tax liability by one dollar.

THE MARITAL DEDUCTION AND THE SECOND ESTATE PROBLEM

Any married person can leave his entire estate to his spouse, and there will be no gift tax on interspousal gifts, and no estate tax on the spouse's inheritance—even if the gift or inheritance is in the millions or tens of millions of dollars. But it would be short-sighted to plan a very large estate using nothing but the marital deduction. After all, sooner or later the surviving spouse will die. In some cases, the surviving spouse will have remarried, and will be able to repeat the process—but often, the survivor will die unmarried.

Depending on the size of the estate, the survivor's needs, the investment climate, and how well the inheritance was invested, the estate may have fallen below the taxable threshold—or may be much larger, as a result of good investment choices. At this point, then, there may not only be a taxable estate, but one that is large enough to be taxed in the highest (55%) estate tax bracket, not just the lowest (37%) bracket. True, the estate tax has been deferred (one reason that the estate could grow), but now it's time to pay the price.

To avoid this second estate problem, the bequest to the surviving spouse can be limited; gifts to charities can be used to reduce the estate; a lifetime giving program can get assets (especially appreciated assets) out of the estate; or a credit shelter trust (see below) can be created. If the second estate is likely to be fairly small, the surviving spouse might choose to enter a retirement home or Continuing Care Retirement Community (see page 281); if a substantial entrance fee is required for admission, but this fee does not create an equity interest in a particular residential unit, the funds can be effectively removed from the potentially taxable estate.

Many couples engage in “estate splitting”: that is, because it’s impossible to tell which will die first, they use interspousal gifts (which are free from gift tax) to divide their assets more or less equally. That way, there will be two estates of roughly equal size (preferably each small enough to escape taxation), not one large and one small estate.

Another approach to the second estate problem is to use second-to-die insurance (see page 28) to provide funds to pay the taxes, without reducing the bequests. This approach solves the problem of having to predict which spouse will die first, because the insurance becomes payable when both spouses have died, in whichever order.

THE RIGHT OF ELECTION

The basic rule of estate planning is that people can do anything they want with their property. There are also some basic exceptions to the basic rule: joint property passes automatically to the other joint tenants, not by will. It’s legal to disinherit your children, but there are limitations on disinheriting a spouse. The “right of election” is a surviving spouse’s right to challenge a deceased spouse’s will that leaves nothing, or less than a statutory share (usually one-third to one-half of the estate[1]) to the survivor. The result of the challenge is automatic: the probate court is obligated to give the statutory share to the surviving spouse, at the expense of the estate plan set out in the will. It has nothing to do with the surviving spouse’s needs, financial condition, or even ability to manage money.

In general, the right of election belongs to the surviving spouse. The surviving spouse can decide to exercise it or forego it (if, for instance, the couple’s children need the money more; or the survivor anticipates a significant second-estate problem if the right is exercised). A pre-nuptial or post-nuptial agreement can be used to surrender the right to exercise the right of election in the future. For our purposes, there is an important exception to the rule: making a Medicaid application involves a commitment to exercise the right of election, even if exercising the right and inheriting the funds means loss of Medicaid benefits. (See page 161 for more about this issue.)

CREDIT SHELTER/BYPASS TRUSTS

The credit shelter trust (also called the bypass trust) is one of the bedrock estate planning tools; in fact, many smaller estates can be handled very adequately merely by drafting simple wills for each spouse, planning for incapacity, creating a credit shelter trust, and leaving all assets over and above the credit shelter trust to the spouse. (Some plans also leave the credit shelter trust to the spouse[2].)

Until 1997, it was simplicity itself to define the optimum size of the credit shelter trust: $600,000, the largest estate that would automatically be exempt from estate taxation. Today, the optimum amount is found in the table on page 243: the maximum amount that can be sheltered by the current level of unified credit. Any kind of trust can be used as a bypass trust; unlike the QTIP trust discussed on page 254 below, there is no requirement that the surviving spouse receive all (or, indeed, any) of the trust income.

To see how the bypass trust works, consider a fairly small taxable estate. When the first spouse dies, the estate is divided into two parts: a credit shelter trust and either another trust or outright inheritances. There's no tax on the credit shelter trust, because it is protected by the unified credit. Also, amounts passing to the surviving spouse are free of estate tax.

Assume that the surviving spouse inherits the credit shelter trust, and keeps it more or less intact (but withdraws enough so that it never gets larger than the amount that can be sheltered by the prevailing unified credit), leaving it to a son or daughter. When the second spouse dies, the credit shelter trust is still free of estate tax; only the balance of the estate might be taxable.

ESTATE PLANNING FOR RETIREMENT BENEFITS

In many instances, senior citizens will already be getting retirement benefits when they make or revise a will. In the simplest case, it's not necessary to make an estate plan for pension benefits received after retiring from a job, because the benefits are received in joint and survivor annuity form, and payments continue after the death of the retiree (to the surviving spouse) or surviving spouse (to the retiree). But many other, more complex, situations occur, especially in connection with pensions received in lump-sum form, IRAs and other self-funded plans, and nonqualified benefits. Furthermore, it is quite legitimate for clients to differ in their objectives for their retirement funds. Some want to consume the funds for current needs; others want to accumulate them to become part of the estate.

If an employee dies before the first pension payment is made, the plan must do one of two things: either distribute the employee's whole interest in the plan within five years after the employee's death; or make the first payment within one year, and continue the payments over the lifetime of the designated beneficiary.

The basic pension payment form for married persons is the "joint and survivor annuity": i.e., payments are made as long as either spouse is alive. IRC §2039 provides that, when the first spouse dies, the decedent's estate includes the present value of the survivor annuity payments that will be made to the other spouse. However, the amount passing to the surviving spouse generally qualifies for the marital deduction.

It sometimes make sense for the nonemployee spouse to agree to payments being made only for the first life. This increases the amount of income available during the first spouse's life (because the fewer the payments the employer expects to make, the larger each payment will be) and could reduce second death estate tax consequences (because there are no survivor benefits paid to the surviving spouse)—but, of course, should only be elected if the survivor can be expected to have adequate funds after the first spouse's death. Sometimes life insurance is purchased with the increased payments received during the first spouse's life, and the life insurance proceeds could be made available to the surviving spouse if desired.

Choice of Beneficiary

Before the Taxpayer Relief Act of 1997, married people with large pension benefits had a real incentive to choose their spouse as beneficiary of pension plan death benefits, because the 15% excise tax on excess accumulations was imposed unless virtually all of the assets remaining in the plan at the employee spouse's death went to the survivor. Today, the excise tax has been repealed, so in certain estate plans, it makes sense to select a nonspouse beneficiary (e.g., a child or grandchild, a charity, the decedent's own estate, or a trust).

Once again, this should not be done if the surviving spouse will genuinely need the money. Even if the survivor can spare the funds, there are real tax advantages to naming the surviving spouse as beneficiary. Death benefits that go to the surviving spouse qualify for the marital deduction in the first spouse's estate (although they might create a second-estate problem). The surviving spouse (but no other beneficiary) is allowed to take lump-sum death benefits and roll them over into an IRA, thus escaping taxation.

Making an irrevocable beneficiary designation is considered a taxable gift (and of a future, not a present interest, so the annual exclusion is unavailable). Interspousal gifts are free from gift tax. However, if there is a subsequent divorce, and the person is no longer a spouse, an irrevocable designation will remain intact.

As noted above, payments of the "qualified preretirement survivor annuity"(QPSA) required when an employee dies before receiving a pension can be made over the "lifetime" of the beneficiary. Under earlier rules, a revocable trust was deemed not to have a life expectancy, and therefore the entire pension would have to be distributed over five years. But IRS proposed regulations provide that if a trust is named as beneficiary, the pension can be paid out over the life of the beneficiaries of the trust. It's OK to name a revocable trust as beneficiary of the QPSA, as long as the trust is drafted to become irrevocable when its grantor dies. The IRS and the pension plan must be given copies of the trust document, or at least a complete and accurate list of trust beneficiaries; and, after the employee dies, the executor of the employee's estate must give the pension plan a final list of the trust beneficiaries no later than nine months after the death.

Planning For and With IRAs

When the owner of a conventional IRA dies, the account is supposed to be distributed to the designated beneficiary over the life expectancy of the beneficiary starting no later than December 31 of the year after the year of the decedent's death. The beneficiary, including a surviving spouse beneficiary, has to pay income tax on distributions of the inherited amount; however, a surviving spouse beneficiary can defer taxation by rolling over the money to an IRA or spousal IRA. (Of course, as soon as the funds are withdrawn, they are subject to ordinary IRA taxation rules.[3])

If there's a lot of money involved, or the surviving spouse wants to benefit several children or grandchildren, the money could be rolled over into several IRAs. The surviving spouse names a child or grandchild as beneficiary of the IRA into which the inherited IRA was rolled over (or names one as beneficiary of each of multiple IRAs). To get maximum deferral, the required minimum distribution can be calculated based on the lives of the surviving spouse and the beneficiary (but the required minimum distribution and the deferral is limited as if the beneficiary were only ten years younger than the surviving spouse, no matter what their actual ages are). If one IRA has multiple beneficiaries, the required minimum distribution must be calculated using the life expectancy of the oldest beneficiary and the ten-year rule still applies.

Further deferral is permitted, based on the true life expectancies of the surviving spouse and such spouse's designated beneficiaries, minus the number of years that the surviving spouse survived the original account holder.

EXAMPLE: Marie Schechter inherits her husband Thomas' IRA; she rolls the money into her own IRA and names her son Lawrence as beneficiary. According to official IRS tables, the joint life expectancy of Marie and Lawrence is 38 years. Marie dies fifteen years after Thomas, and Lawrence inherits the IRA. If he wants maximum deferral, he can calculate the required minimum distribution on this "doubly inherited" IRA over 23 years: the 38 years of joint life expectancy, minus Marie's actual 15 year survival.

The Roth ("back-loaded") IRA is an estate planning tool much superior to the conventional IRA. Although creating and funding such an account does not give rise to a tax deduction (see page 186), contributions can be made after age 70½ and there is no requirement of minimum distributions while the IRA owner is alive, so any part of the Roth account (including all of it) can be kept intact during the owner's lifetime with the explicit objective of transmitting it as part of the estate. The Roth account can also be preserved during the life of a surviving spouse who treats the IRA as the spouse's own. When a child or grandchild inherits a Roth IRA, withdrawals are required; however, the child or grandchild doesn't have to pay income tax on the funds removed from the inherited Roth IRA.

Naming a charity as beneficiary of a conventional IRA is not helpful from an income tax standpoint (because it doesn't have a life expectancy, it can't be used in the "stretch out" calculation described on page 347) but can yield good estate tax results. The charity gets pre-tax dollars, not the after-tax dollars that would be used to fund an ordinary bequest.

Nonqualified Benefits

A company gets tax benefits by maintaining "qualified" pension and welfare benefit plans for its workers, but at a heavy price. The plan must benefit all eligible workers, without discrimination in favor of the highly-compensated, and contributions generally must be made each year, even if the company needs the money for other things. Therefore, some companies do not provide qualified plans; or they supplement the qualified plans with plans that offer generous benefits to top management. Such "nonqualified" plans are perfectly legal, but do not provide the company with as many tax benefits.

Some nonqualified plans either guarantee a certain number of payments (even if the highly-compensated executive has died in the interim) or provide for payments to survivors. Deferred compensation that is paid after the executive's death generally becomes part of the gross estate. Not only do these payments have estate tax implications, they are also Income in Respect of a Decedent which must be included in income by the person receiving such payments. (The person who inherits these funds is entitled to an income tax deduction equal to any extra estate tax generated by the inclusion of the funds in the estate.)

TRUSTS IN ESTATE PLANNING

A trust is an arrangement under which the owner of money, securities, or other property (usually, but not always, income-producing property) transfers ownership and control of the property to a trust[4]. The original owner of the property is known as the grantor, creator, or settlor of the trust. The principal or corpus of the trust is the total sum of the trust's assets and accumulated income. The trust is managed by one or more trustees; sometimes the grantor is the trustee, or one of the trustees. Inter vivos ("living") trusts are created by contracts; testamentary trusts are created by wills.

The terms of the trust generally call for the trust to exist for a certain number of years, or for a person's lifetime or the joint lifetime of more than one person. During this trust term, income is paid to beneficiaries named in the trust (or described as a class, such as "all my grandchildren then living"). Or, the trustee can be given the discretion to accumulate the income instead of distributing it, or to distribute the income among a class of beneficiaries as the trustee sees fit. (This last variation is known as a spray or sprinkle trust.)

The trustee may also have discretion to invade the principal of the trust—to distribute part of the corpus. Often, discretion is limited by an "ascertainable standard" such as the health and support needs of the beneficiary (because this keeps certain amounts out of the estate that would otherwise be included). But see page 146 for Medicaid problems with ascertainable standard language in trusts. Finally, when the term of the trust ends, the remaining corpus (plus any accumulated income that was not distributed) goes to the remainderperson(s) named in the trust.

As a general rule, the more control the grantor has over the trust after its establishment, the more likely the trustee is to be liable for income tax on the income the trust earns, and the more likely the trust is to be included in the trustee's estate. It is also possible that the trust itself will be taxed on trust income, or that the beneficiary will be taxed. The "kiddie tax" requirements reduce the value of income-shifting within the family by providing that the unearned income of a minor under 14 is taxed at the parent's highest tax rate.

If the trust is revocable, the grantor retains the power to terminate the trust, alter its terms, or get back part of the corpus. The grantor of an irrevocable trust surrenders these powers (although even then, there may be a legal mechanism for ending the trust or revising its terms).

In practical terms, very small trusts usually don't work, because the legal fees for setting up the trust, the problems of transferring assets into the trust, and the continuing costs of management outweigh the benefits.

Trusts are discussed at many places in this book: in incapacity planning, and as a Medicaid planning tool (see page 117), for instance. See the chapter on the family home (page 144) for a discussion of PRTs and QPRTs—trusts that take title to homesteads and vacation homes. The Life Insurance chapter considers the advantages of placing policies into an ILIT: an Irrevocable Life Insurance Trust. But perhaps the classic use of trusts is as an estate planning tool. Revocable trusts are included in the estate, because of the grantor's degree of control over the corpus; but, under the right circumstances, irrevocable trusts can be used to get funds out of the estate.

Living Trusts and Probate Planning

Revocable living trusts are extremely popular, and are the subject of many books and planning seminars. To the elder planning team, living trusts are a valuable adjunct to the incapacity plan, with the caveat that living trust corpus remains available for Medicaid purposes. To the estate planner, living trusts are a useful though perhaps over-hyped device for avoiding probate, with the caveat that living trust corpus becomes part of the potentially taxable estate.

The probate process can be prolonged and expensive, and in rare instances the fact that a will is a public document can lead to disclosure of embarrassing facts. Therefore, a living trust can be a useful part of the plan for a large estate to minimize these problems. Probate fees usually increase with the size of the estate, so reducing the size of a large probate estate can be productive. However, the estate would have to be pretty large—setting up and maintaining a trust costs money. Furthermore, in larger estates, federal estate tax is a more important factor than probate costs.

Even people who decide against living trusts can take steps to cope with probate problems. Life insurance can be used to provide liquidity until the estate is settled. Each spouse should maintain a separate bank account with enough funds for several months' living expenses (because joint accounts are often frozen during the probate period). The actual court fees for probate are a given, but overall expenses can be reduced by making sure that all relevant records are easy to find, so that expensive attorney time is not consumed in detective work.

Assets that pass outside the probate process are sometimes called "will substitutes." They include jointly held real estate; joint bank or brokerage accounts; IRAs and pension plans where a beneficiary has been named; and bank accounts in trust for a named beneficiary. Ownership is automatically transferred to the other joint owner or the named beneficiary when the joint owner/account holder dies. These will substitutes should not be forgotten when the estate plan is made (they can determine if the provision for the surviving spouse is adequate, for example)—but it's important not to try to dispose of them by will, because the disposition will probably be ineffective, and a time-consuming, expensive lawsuit will probably be needed to settle the issue.

Qualified Terminable Interest Property (QTIP)

Amounts left outright to the surviving spouse do not become part of the deceased spouse's gross estate for federal estate tax purposes, because they qualify for the marital deduction. However, there are many possible legal forms other than outright ownership, including life estates and various kinds of trusts. For estate tax purposes, a QTIP is qualified terminable interest property—less than outright transmission of ownership that still qualifies for the marital deduction.

Although some other variations are possible, the basic QTIP is a trust that benefits the surviving spouse. During the surviving spouse's lifetime, the spouse must receive all the income from the trust (nobody else can get any of it, and the income can't be accumulated—it has to be distributed). At least one income payment must be made every year; usually quarterly payments are made.

The Code's QTIP provisions require all the income of the trust to go to the surviving spouse, but don't say anything about principal, so a trust can be a valid QTIP whether or not the surviving spouse[5] and/or the trustee is given the power to invade the principal. Another possibility is to make the decedent spouse's IRA payable to a QTIP trust for the surviving spouse, with the provision that the surviving spouse gets either all the income of the trust, or the minimum distribution required from the IRA, whichever is larger. This is a valid QTIP, because the survivor gets at least all the income from the trust, and possibly more[6].

When the surviving spouse dies, the corpus of the QTIP trust passes to whomever the deceased spouse designated—not according to the will or directions of the surviving spouse. However, because the trust was excluded from the estate of the first spouse to die, it must be included in the estate of the survivor. (In other words, QTIP trusts don't solve the second-estate problem.)

There can be many reasons for leaving a spouse less than an outright interest in money or property. In the elder planning context, it's important to note that the survivor's capacity may be limited or diminishing. The spouse may be able to handle income responsibly, but not to make decisions about investing large sums of capital. However, the IRS has ruled that a trust is not a QTIP, and not eligible for the marital deduction, if the trust calls for reduction or cessation of income when the surviving spouse becomes incapacitated[7]. (Nor can a QTIP stop income if the surviving spouse remarries; the spouse has to get trust income for life.)

QTIPs work well in general where the spouse who owns property wants the eventual ownership to pass to someone else (such as to his children). This is an especially strong rationale in the case of divorced and remarried persons who want to provide lifetime income for the current spouse, while making sure that the property eventually passes to the children of the first marriage. Also, the surviving spouse may receive Medicaid benefits, or be contemplating a Medicaid application—with the result that additional income is less detrimental to the plan than additional assets.

Although the trust is drafted while the grantor spouse is still alive, technically the trust doesn't become a QTIP until the executor of the grantor's estate makes an irrevocable election, on the federal estate tax return (IRS Form 706), to treat part or all of the trust as a QTIP.

A partial QTIP election might be better than a full one, if the surviving spouse is in poor health and might die soon, creating a second estate problem if the spouse is likely to die soon. In that circumstance, a smaller estate—and thus a nontaxable estate or one subject to lower estate taxes—would be preferable. If this is done, invasions of principal for the benefit of the surviving spouse can be charged to the QTIP trust, not the nonQTIP trust—with the result that the survivor's eventual taxable estate will be reduced.

Split-Interest Charitable Trusts (CLATs, CLUTs, CRATs and CRUTs)

Outright charitable giving can be very satisfying, and generous givers can get the satisfaction of being thanked in person, being elected to prestigious Boards of Directors, participating in gala social events, and the like. Lifetime gifts (with some limits) generally qualify for an income tax deduction. If the taxpayer contributes appreciated property to the charity (rather than selling the appreciated property and donating part or all of the proceeds), it will generally not be necessary to pay capital gains tax on the appreciation.

Furthermore, the income-tax charitable deduction is generally measured by the fair market value of the asset, not the donor's basis—so a large amount of otherwise taxable income can be offset by the deduction[8]. All outright gifts to public charities are exempt from gift tax, no matter how large the gift. However, sometimes it is inadvisable to make very large lifetime gifts, because it is quite possible that the funds will be needed, e.g., for long-term custodial care.

By the same token, outright bequests to charity qualify for the estate tax charitable deduction, and can eliminate estate tax by reducing the size of the estate below the potentially taxable level. (This can be an especially productive avenue for single people, who cannot take advantage of the marital deduction, and may not have close family members they particularly want to benefit.) But very large bequests may imperil the financial security of survivors.

One incentive for people to give more to charity is giving them a way to benefit the charity while still retaining personal or family financial benefits—and, in fact, that's exactly why the Internal Revenue Code includes provisions for irrevocable "split-interest" trusts, such as Charitable Lead Trusts and Charitable Remainder Trusts.

These arrangements are split-interest because the charity derives payments from the trust property for a defined term, at which time it reverts to the grantor or the beneficiary selected by the grantor (charitable lead trusts[9]), or they make payments to the grantor (or beneficiary selected by the grantor) for life or for a term of years, at which time the remainder passes to the charity (charitable remainder trusts). For instance, an older individual who has plenty of assets (including illiquid or highly appreciated assets that would generate an immense tax liability if sold) but requires more income and is charitably inclined might place some assets into a charitable remainder trust, and benefit by the additional income.

Split-interest trusts are classified into several categories; the most common are annuity trusts and unitrusts. The difference between them is the way that they define the payout that must be made to the beneficiary.

In an annuity trust, the beneficiary is entitled to a set percentage of the initial value of the corpus of the trust, paid every year: e.g., 6% of a trust set up with $100,000. The percentage does not change based on the actual current value of the trust or its investment success, with the result that it may be necessary to dip into capital to satisfy the payment obligation (and, if this happens often enough, the remainder may end up with a good deal less than the grantor originally intended). On the other hand, if the trust's rate of appreciation is greater than the payment obligation, the trust will grow in size, and the remainder will be larger than originally intended. Nor will the beneficiary get greater payments because of the trust's greater income; it's a risk the grantor takes.

In contrast, the payout under a unitrust does fluctuate; it is defined as a set percentage of the current value of the trust when the payout is made (e.g., 6% of whatever the trust is worth on a particular date of the year). As a practical matter, then, a CRUT should be funded with publicly traded securities or other assets that are easy to value. Under a CRAT, the beneficiary knows exactly what the payment will be; a CRUT beneficiary's payment is uncertain.

Another difference is that unitrusts can be drafted to accept additional deposits after the trust is first set up. This can be a worthwhile drafting technique for the next few years, as the estate tax unified credit exclusion continues to phase upwards until it reaches the $1 million level. That is, the trust can be set up with a present value amount for noncharitable beneficiaries that does not exceed the maximum credit shelter amount, then additional funds can be deposited to keep the trust at a level equal to the maximum credit shelter. (In other words, the charitable trust is used as a credit shelter trust; this strategy won't work in a plan where there already is a credit shelter trust.)

The term of a charitable remainder trust can be a term of years (but not over 20 years) or the life or lives of the annuitant(s). Although most charitable remainder trusts are inter vivos trusts (because the grantor wants to get personal benefits!), it is possible to set up a CRT by will, benefiting one's spouse or other heirs.

The choice between a CRAT and a CRUT, for a person already determined to set up a charitable trust, depends on the grantor's projections for future inflation and future appreciation in the value of the trust assets. The unitrust would probably work better for someone who is willing to accept some uncertainty and anticipates inflation- or appreciation-related increase in the value of the fund, or for someone who wants to continue adding to the credit shelter amount in the trust until 2006. Naturally, the selection of an irrevocable trust must be made after serious thought, because there is no possibility of dissolving the trust or increasing the payout percentage.

The grantor has discretion to determine the annuity amount or percentage, but the Internal Revenue Code sets a minimum and maximum range that is permitted. The minimum percentage payment under either a CRAT or CRUT is 5% a year of the initial corpus, or of the current value of the corpus, respectively. As a result of the Taxpayer Relief Act of 1997, for trusts either created or added to after July 28, 1997, a trust can qualify as a CRAT or CRUT only if the charity's remainder is worth at least 10% of the trust value, and the annual payout to the beneficiary must be no more than 50% of the trust value. (Special transition provisions are available for people who were mentally incapacitated on July 28, 1997 and therefore unable to amend their trusts to conform to the new requirements.)

In the gift tax context, the gift to the charity in a CRAT or a CRUT is not the entire corpus of a charitable remainder trust—only the present value of the charity's remainder.

If the grantor is also the beneficiary of the annuity or unitrust, initially the trust assets will be included in the grantor's estate (because of the retained life estate). An estate tax charitable deduction will be available for the actuarial value of the interest passing to charity.

Charities are allowed to maintain "pooled income funds"—in effect, big trusts made up of contributions from individuals who can't or don't want to contribute enough to set up their own trusts. Pooled income funds can provide a stream of payments (based on the fund's income), much like charitable remainder trusts.

Trusts as IRA Beneficiaries

See page 249 above for basic estate planning strategies with IRAs. As seen many times in this book, estate planning strategies can often be combined, sometimes creating significant leverage. This is also true of naming a trust as the beneficiary of an IRA. The trust must be created before it can be named as beneficiary—and before the account holder reaches 70½. The trust must be irrevocable, or become irrevocable no later than when the IRA account holder dies. The IRA custodian or trustee must be given a copy of the trust or a list of the beneficiaries and their rights under the trust. As long as these requirements are satisfied, many kinds of trusts can become IRA beneficiaries, including QTIP trusts and by-pass trusts.

A revocable living trust could be created, to be divided into two irrevocable trusts on the account holder's death, at which time the maximum amount that can be sheltered by the then-current unified credit is deposited into one trust and the rest is distributed into the other trust, which is a QTIP[10].

Another option is to name the spouse as the primary IRA beneficiary, but make a trust the contingent beneficiary. This often makes sense in a small estate, where it's possible but not certain that there will be enough nonretirement assets to fully fund a credit shelter trust. When the IRA owner dies, the question then becomes whether the credit shelter trust will be fully funded; if not, the surviving spouse can disclaim part of the IRA, which then goes into a trust which becomes a credit shelter trust.

Alaska-Type Trusts

A spendthrift trust is one which prevents the creditors of the beneficiary from getting access to the trust corpus. The creditors can claim each income payment as it is made, but they can't unlock the principal. Traditionally, it has been held that no one can set up a spendthrift trust for his own benefit, only for the benefit of someone else (usually a sibling, child, or grandchild who is financially irresponsible or suffers from a disability). However, in the late 1990s, Alaska pioneered a new type of trust, and several other states (Delaware, South Dakota) have adopted similar provisions.

These trusts are unusual in two ways. First, they allow self-settled spendthrift trusts, so the trusts can be protected against creditors—including former spouses after a divorce. So far, the courts have not ruled on the Medicaid implications of these trusts, but they may work in that context. Second, they eliminate the "rule against perpetuities": most noncharitable trusts have to end within three or four generations[11]; these trusts can go on much longer, allowing family wealth to accumulate without estate taxation.

Creditors' rights are very significant to estate planning. A transfer to a trust is incomplete (and therefore has no gift tax consequences) as long as the grantor's creditors can reach the entire corpus of the trust. The downside is that the entire trust corpus must be included in the estate of the grantor. If a trust, such as an Alaska-type trust, is exempt from creditor claims, it may escape inclusion in the estate under this rationale[12].

The Alaska Trust concept has not yet been court tested, and the IRS hasn't weighed in with its own policy for handling these trusts, so they should be used with caution, and only after professional advice.

Warning: Abusive Trusts

IRS Notice 97-24, 1997-1 CB 409, targets several kinds of abusive trust that, the agency warns, can lead to civil or even criminal penalties:

- Business trusts used to claim items that are actually nondeductible personal expenses as business deductions
- Equipment or service trusts that generate inflated deductions for the use of items whose ownership has not really changed hands
- Family residence trusts that inflate so-called rental expenses
- Purported charitable trusts that actually pay the grantor's own expenses rather than providing real charitable benefits to deserving recipients
- "Final" trusts involving expatriation to foreign tax havens.

Clients should also be wary of abusive "common-law business organizations" or "contractual business organizations" that are marketed on claims that they escape ordinary business taxes and permit deduction of business expenses[13].

LIFE INTERESTS, REMAINDERS, LEASE-BACKS, AND OTHER INTRAFAMILY TRANSACTIONS

The ownership of an asset can be divided among several people at the same time—or split among several people at different times. The simplest example is the gift or sale of a remainder subject to a life estate. That is, the original owner of property transfers the ownership, but retains the right to use the asset for the rest of his life. The typical case is giving ownership of the family home to a child, while retaining the right to live in the house for life. This technique might be used if the asset is expected to continue appreciating in value; the purpose is to remove the appreciation from the estate.

In this instance, the owner gives away the remainder (the right to inherit the property after the life estate ends), and keeps the life estate. Therefore, there has been a gift to the remainderman, and the gift tax on the gift will reduce the unified credit available when the donor eventually dies. (See page 243, above, for more about the unified credit.)

The value of the gift is the present value of the remainder interest, which is actuarially determined based on the donor's life expectancy (using IRS tables. Present value is less than the full value, because of the "time value of money"—the right to get $1 five years from now is worth less than $1. In other words, the gift can be made at a discount—and a lot of taxes can be saved by getting the remainder out of the estate if the property appreciates significantly after the gift.

Sometimes it makes sense for ownership of a senior citizen's asset (such as a home: see page 140) to be transferred, while the senior citizen continues to make use of the asset. While it's true that outright gifts can remove assets from the potentially taxable estate, they can also be taxable events in and of themselves, or transfers that are inconsistent with a Medicaid plan. In that case, it may make sense to sell the asset to children or other potential heirs, but lease it back from them; or to make a gift, but make the gift subject to a lease-back. (Gift tax is not due until a gift is completed—until there are no strings attached to it.) Frequently, such transactions are structured as installment sales, because the younger generation often lacks funds to make an outright, lump-sum purchase. An installment sale can be attractive to a senior citizen who wants more current income, but wants to divest assets from the estate.

In some instances, intrafamily loans make sense, such as when the younger-generation member needs money to buy a home, pay medical bills, or pay tuition bills for children. But for the transaction to be treated as a loan, rather than as a gift, the parent must have a rational expectation of repayment; there must be signed notes; it helps if there is a set payment schedule—which the younger generation member actually adheres to—and if the agreement calls for market-rate interest, which is actually paid[14]. The lender should report interest as income; in fact, making a no-interest or below-market-rate loan actually constitutes a gift of the interest that was foregone.

Self-Canceling Installment Notes (SCINs)

The self-canceling installment note (SCIN) is another intrafamily financial planning option. The usual structure is an installment sale by parents to children, with the additional feature that the note representing the transaction includes the provision that it will be canceled if the seller-parent dies before all the payments have been completed. The asset is removed from the parent's estate; the child gets possession of the asset—although with the somewhat ambivalent factor that the child can get the asset at a discount if and only if the parent dies before the installment payments have been completed. (The odds are that the payments made during the seller's lifetime will end up in the seller's estate—unless they are spent; and if the asset has appreciated, the parent will have to pay capital gains tax on the profit, unless the SCIN involves a family home for which capital gains can be excluded.)

The desired estate planning result will be obtained only if the SCIN is a legitimate transaction, so the IRS will require that the buyer pay somewhat above the normal market price for the asset, because the self-canceling feature is an additional benefit that is worth money. The transaction will be disregarded if the SCIN's term is longer than the seller-parent's life expectancy, or if the seller was terminally ill at the time of the transaction.

SPECIAL PROVISIONS FOR SMALL BUSINESS AND FAMILY FARMS

Estate planning for family businesses and family-owned farms can be difficult for many reasons. Stock in most large corporations is liquid and freely traded: that is, at any time, you can find a buyer, and there are standard, published prices for the shares. Neither of these is generally true for closely-held businesses. In many cases, it takes a long time to find someone who wants to buy the shares; there may be no market at all. This would not be a tragedy if the intention is to keep ownership in the family, and if there are younger-generation family members interested in and qualified to keep it running. However, without good estate planning, a deceased business owner may have an estate large enough to be taxable, but without enough nonbusiness assets to pay the estate taxes without depriving the survivors of funds they need to live on.

The Internal Revenue Code includes some relief provisions, and the rest of the problem can be solved by good planning. For one thing, the value of the estate could drop between the date of death and the date administration of the estate is completed, leaving a large estate tax liability and little money to pay it with. The executor of an estate can make an election (but can't change back, after the election is made) to value the estate as of an "alternate valuation date," six months after the date of death—but only if the effect of the election is to lower the value of the estate and therefore the potential estate tax.

Illiquid estates can also elect to pay their estate tax in installments, so that they avoid the need to sell farm land or closely-held securities to pay the taxes. IRC §6166 allows the estate to pay only the interest on the estate taxes for four years and nine months after the decedent's death, and to stretch out payments of the actual taxes over a ten-year period on the portion of the estate tax attributable to interests in a closely-held business (the value of the interests must exceed 35% of the adjusted gross estate). Installment payment can be used in conjunction with the Qualified Family-Owned Business Interest provisions discussed below. Installment payment relief is not automatic; the executor has to apply for it. If the IRS turns down the application, the estate can use the IRS' own internal appeal procedure, or go to Tax Court and ask for a court order authorizing installment payments. (It isn't necessary to pay the full estate tax first, then get a refund.)

Furthermore, §6166 allows estates to pay interest on the tax at very low interest rates: 2% for the first $1 million as indexed of value over and above the amount sheltered by the unified credit, and only 45% of the IRS' normal interest rate on underpayments for the balance. However, the executor can no longer claim an income tax or estate tax deduction for payment of interest under §6166.

Perhaps paradoxically, the IRS and the courts recognize several reasons to discount the value of a gift or bequest of closely-held business stock: blockage and minority interest and lack of marketability. The paradox comes from the fact that a blockage discount is available when the block of stock transmitted is so large that its disposition will distort the stock price. The minority interest discount is available for transmission of a block of stock that is so small that its recipient will not be able to influence corporate policy. In other words, a discount is available based either on the transmission of a very large or a very small percentage of corporate shares. Although the facts of each case are different, a 30-35% discount is usually recognized for the combined factors of minority interest and limited marketability. The estate claims a valuation for its assets and, if challenged, has to be able to back up its valuation methods.

Estate Freezes and Chapter 14

The "estate freeze" was a traditional planning technique. In its simplest form, a business owner who wanted to retire would recapitalize the corporation. The owner would get preferred stock; the people who were supposed to inherit the business would get common stock. The corporation would then possibly declare generous dividends, providing retirement income for the initial owner. Meanwhile, the appreciation in the value of the company would go to the younger generation and would be removed from the estate of the older generation member.

Chapter 14 of the Internal Revenue Code (§§2701-2704) limits this device by providing, first of all, that the preferred interest must yield dividends or interest proportionate to its value based on current market rates. If it doesn't, then the value of the preferred interest retained by the parent is deemed to be $0; in other words, a taxable gift of the entire transferred interest has been made, not just a gift of common stock valued at the parent's original interest minus the parent's retained interest.

Many businesses use buy-sell agreements not only to handle the practical task of making a transition to a new generation of owners, but to establish the value of the stock for gift and estate tax purposes. IRC §2703(a) says that an agreement can establish tax value only if it is a bona fide agreement, with terms comparable to those that would be negotiated in an arm's length transaction—not just a device for transferring property within a family.

Qualified Family-Owned Business Interest (QFOBI)

The Taxpayer Relief Act of 1997 added provisions dealing with qualified family-owned business interests (QFOBIs). For this purpose, a "family" business generally is a business that is at least 50% owned by a person; the spouse or an ancestor of the person; and lineal descendants of either the person, or the spouse or a parent of the person (including spouses of such lineal descendants). However, if the person's family owned at least 30% of the business, a family business also includes a business owned by two families if the families' combined interests is at least 70% (90% in the case of three families).

The next hurdle is whether the decedent's estate qualifies for the QFOBI deduction (a maximum of $675,000 is deductible); this requires that 50% or more of the adjusted gross estate consist of QFOBIs that pass to qualified heirs—pretty much defined as family members who are U.S. citizens and who materially participate in the business, plus employees with more than 10 years' service. The adjusted gross estate is the gross estate adjusted to deal with some business interests already removed from the gross estate via gifts to family members. The tax advantages have to be recaptured if the company moves out of the United States or the qualified heir stops materially participating in the business[15].

Real Estate Valuation

How much is farmland, or land used in a family business worth—what it can bring in based on the family's use of it, or a higher theoretical valuation if the land were developed? IRC §2032A allows valuation based on actual use (however, the maximum reduction in value is limited to $750,000 as indexed), not potential development, as long as the property was used for five of the eight years before the decedent's death as either a family farm or in a trade or business carried on by the decedent or his family. The property must have been left to a family member who will carry on the family business or farm. Tax benefits are generally recaptured if the property is no longer family operated.

GIVING PROGRAMS

If the older client is in reasonable health, and there is some prospect of estate taxation but the estate is not in the multimillion dollar league, a structured giving program can be an excellent estate plan, or an excellent tool within a larger estate plan. Properly planned gifts can reduce the estate below the taxable level, or at least reduce the tax cost of a large estate.

Don't forget that these gifts constitute transfers for Medicaid purposes. Therefore, unless there are ample funds and insurance to pay for care, and the client is unwilling or unable to make an effective Medicaid plan, consider doing a "half-a-loaf" plan (give half, retain the other half to pay privately for care while waiting for Medicaid benefits). Because Medicaid doesn't have to conform to tax rules, you can't assert a charitable deduction or annual exclusion when applying for benefits.

Some gifts are subject to gift tax, thus reducing the amount of unified credit available when an individual dies; other gifts are exempt. All gifts between spouses are generally free of gift tax. A person can give $10,000 per year per donee (adjusted for inflation) free of gift tax, or $20,000 per year per donee (as adjusted) if the giver's spouse agrees to join in the gift. This is a purely formal requirement—it's OK for all the funds for a split gift to come from one spouse.

The annual exclusion expires each year—it is not permitted, say, to give $5,000 to a particular donee in one year, then give $15,000 the next year to make up for the unused annual exclusion in the earlier year. There is no legal requirement that gifts be made consistently from year to year or even that gifts be repeated: it's up to the donor to decide when and to whom gifts are made. To qualify for the gift tax annual exclusion, the gift must be made to a person, not an institution; and the gift must be of a "present interest," not a right to receive something in the future.

EXAMPLE: Stephen Bannion's assets are currently worth about $800,000; his wife Marta's assets are currently worth about $500,000. Therefore, it is possible (although not certain) that one or both of them will have a taxable estate. It depends on when they die, how much they spend in the interim, and whether their assets appreciate or depreciate. One simple step they can take is for Stephen to make gifts of about $150,000 to Marta. The interspousal gift is free of gift tax, and equalizes the two estates at about $650,000 each, reducing the implications of the uncertainty as to which will die first because each now has a nontaxable estate—although the survivor may very well have a second estate problem. If they also agree to "gift-split" each year, they can reduce the estate by, for instance, giving $20,000 each year to each of their three children, giving them the potential to get $60,000 out of the estate each year. They can also make gifts to their grandchildren, to other relatives, and to friends, as well as charitable gifts.

Benefiting Children and Grandchildren

In most (though not all) cases, the focus of a married person's financial and estate plan is taking care of the surviving spouse; benefits to children and grandchildren are subsidiary. However, if it's clear that the surviving spouse will be taken care of, or if the financial needs of the younger generations are especially great, or if a giving program is in order, then children and grandchildren become natural recipients.

There are obvious problems with making large cash gifts to minors. Even if they are in fact very responsible people, and won't squander the money on motorcycles (or worse), they have legal disabilities that limit the extent to which they are allowed to handle funds. The states have coped with this problem by adopting various versions of the Uniform Gifts to Minors Act (UGMA) and Uniform Transfers to Minors Act (UTMA). Although they have technical differences, the acts share a common purpose: creating a simple, inexpensive way to make gifts to minors.

The money or property is placed into a special custodianship account; an adult, usually the parent[16], serves as custodian. As soon as the minor reaches adulthood (usually age 18, but age 21 in some states; state law may also give the donor the election of keeping the account intact until the child reaches 21), the funds belong absolutely to the minor.

PLANNING TIP: This can be a problem if the donor would prefer to impose tighter control—many grandparents are unhappy about the prospect of a possibly immature 18- or even 21-year-old getting a large sum of money and spending it on a motorcycle—or worse. For large sums of money, the answer is to establish a trust, which can keep the funds tied up long after the minor reaches adulthood, and can impose other conditions. However, where small sums are involved, or where even a comparatively large sum is used to benefit several grandchildren, then UGMA/UTMA, with all its flaws, is probably a better choice than a trust.

UGMA/UTMA gifts qualify for the gift tax annual exclusion, even though they may seem like future interests in that the child doesn't get access to the funds until attaining majority.

Another special gift tax rule says that there is no gift tax on an expenditure of any size used to pay directly for someone else's education or health care expenses. (Payment must be made directly to the education institution or care provider, not given to the student or patient who then uses it for the appropriate purpose.) There's no limitation on the number of people whose expenses can be paid. Nor does the money have to flow down to a younger generation: it works just as well for adult children who pay doctors, nursing homes, and others who provide care to their elderly parents.

Yet another special gift tax rule applies to the "2503(c) trust" (2503(c) is the governing Internal Revenue Code section). A 2503(c) trust provides that both principal and income of the trust can be used for the minor's benefit; once the minor reaches age 21, the remaining corpus goes to the minor. A permissible alternative, if it is not desirable to give control of the entire trust to a 21-year-old, is to give the minor a 30-60 day period after reaching age 21 during which the former minor can make withdrawals; the amount not withdrawn can be kept in trust for several more years. The Code requires the trust to provide that, if the beneficiary dies before reaching 21, the trust's assets must be distributed to the estate of the minor.

Valuing Gifts

Valuation is not a problem for cash or for readily marketable securities, but can be extremely contentious for other assets (for instance, real estate, artworks or shares in a closely held business). A charitable gift of over $10,000 in close corporation stock, or over $5,000 of other property for which current price quotes are not readily available requires an appraisal by a professional. The donor must complete IRS Form 8283 (Noncash Charitable Contributions) and attach it to the income tax return on which the charitable deduction is claimed. For artworks worth $20,000 or more, a copy of the actual appraisal itself must be attached to the Form 8283.

PRACTICE TIP: The donor should retain color photos or slides of the artwork in case the IRS wants to see them—but the photos or slides need not be included with the tax return.

The Tax Reform Act of 1997 encourages filing of a gift tax return reporting gifts, even if no gift tax is due. For gifts made after August 5, 1997, the IRS cannot challenge the value of any gift for estate tax purposes once the gift tax statute of limitation has expired if the donor has shown the gift on a gift tax return, or disclosed it on a statement to the government.

JOINT PROPERTY IN THE ESTATE

As noted above, jointly owned property with rights of survivorship doesn't become part of the probate estate, but that doesn't mean that it escapes estate taxation. For federal estate tax purposes, the most important question is generally whether joint property is owned by a married couple, or by anyone else (e.g., brothers and sisters who inherit shares in family real estate).

For married couples, 50% of the value of joint property is included in the estate of the first spouse to die. This rule is applied no matter which spouse actually bought the property, or whether one spouse contributed all the money to buy the property. The 50% included should qualify for the marital deduction.

Then, when the survivor dies (unless the survivor has disposed of the property in the interim), 100% of the value of the property is included in the survivor's estate. This is one reason why the "second estate" problem can be so acute. The surviving spouse does gets a stepped-up basis in the inherited joint property.

For joint property owned by anyone other than a married couple[17], inclusion in the estate generally depends on who paid for the property. The entire value of the property is included in the estate of the first joint tenant to die—except to the extent that the survivor(s) can prove that the survivor(s) paid part of the purchase price. Then, part or all of the value of the property is potentially included in the estate of the surviving joint tenant(s) when each one dies. In other words, joint property is potentially subject to multiple estate taxation.

However, if joint owners acquired the jointly owned property by gift or inheritance, at the first owner's death the property is treated as if each had contributed a proportionate part of the purchase price.

STRATEGIES FOR APPRECIATED AND DEPRECIATED ASSETS

Generally, $1 in cash or a cash equivalent is worth $1; but for most other investments, at any given time they may be either appreciated (worth more than their adjusted basis) or depreciated (worth less than their adjusted basis). The tax consequences of this fact can affect not only how many shares of stock or a mutual fund, how many bonds, how much real estate a person will buy, sell, or exchange; when the person will transact; but also which assets will be selected for sale or exchange, which will be retained, and which will be placed into trust or donated to charity. Furthermore, the older person may have a clear intention to benefit a relative or friend, while being uncertain about whether to make a lifetime gift or leave a bequest.

There are obvious practical differences between a lifetime gift and a bequest. Lifetime gifts immediately become unavailable to the donor. Funds intended to be bequeathed can still be used by the potential testator if the testator needs them (or if feelings about the potential donee change!). Lifetime gifts can be given when the donor can be thanked personally; bequests are colored by the sadness of a loved one's death. However, many affluent older people have a significant concern with estate planning. Properly handled lifetime gifts can remove assets from the potentially taxable estate, whereas most bequests (other than those to spouses or charities) cannot be carried out until the estate's debts are paid and its estate tax liability settled.

The basis of a lifetime gift is a carryover basis: that is, the donee has the same basis as the donor—the donor's purchase price for the asset, with whatever adjustments are permitted. The basis of an inheritance is generally referred to as a "stepped-up" basis, i.e., the basis measured as of the date of death or the alternate valuation date, if the estate has elected to use that. However, although it is usually true that value increases over time, it is not inevitable. Real estate values can decline; stock prices certainly can decline. In such a situation, the basis could actually be stepped down, not up.

Therefore, the basis of a lifetime gift is known in advance (as is the timing of its receipt), whereas the basis of an inheritance is uncertain and its timing is uncertain and generally not under the testator's control. One simple answer is to give or devise appreciated assets, but to sell depreciated assets (using the tax losses to offset other income), then give or leave the proceeds of the sale.

PLANNING TIP: A similar analysis should be used if the older person has to make a significant expenditure. In that case, it's probably best to use savings or cash equivalents first, because there are no capital gains implications. But if assets have to be sold, then it's probably best to sell depreciated assets and spend the proceeds (using the tax loss to offset other income).

It's probably better to sell assets whose capital gains will be tax-free (e.g., home sale proceeds up to $250,000, or $500,000 for a married couple) instead of fully taxable capital gains; and it's probably better to have taxable capital gains than a corresponding amount of taxable ordinary income, because capital gains rates are lower. On the other hand, if the sale can be postponed for a few years, extra low capital gain rates are scheduled to phase in in the year 2006 for assets purchased after 2000 and held for five years or more—another factor in deciding which assets to keep and which to sell.

Tax factors aren't everything, of course. In practical terms, it may be better to keep living in the family home than to sell it, even if there is no capital gains tax to be paid. Some assets are highly liquid, and can be disposed of at any time with low brokerage and other fees; other assets are illiquid, and even the process of disposition is costly. If a person needs money in a hurry, the person can't rely on illiquid assets, so the person has to use cash, cash equivalents, and freely tradable securities as a source of funds.

The recipient's tax concerns are the flip side of the donor's or testator's. If the donee or heir of real estate intends to inhabit the property, or the donee or heir of securities intends to hold them or live on their income instead of selling them, the basis is fairly irrelevant. But in many cases, a person who receives a gift or inheritance puts it on the market as soon as possible—and therefore faces capital gains tax as soon as the sale is consummated. Therefore, the lower the basis, the greater the tax liability.

How much does this matter in the elder care plan? Probably, the older person will be more concerned about his own tax position than the position of recipients of bounty, but this is one of the issues in the "who is the client?" question. A potential donor who is exceptionally generous may be willing to put the potential heir's tax position ahead of his own, but this is probably uncommon.

DISCLAIMERS AND POST-MORTEM PLANNING

Sometimes an inheritance is a "white elephant"—a valuable object that actually creates more disadvantages than it's worth. It would be an insult to return a white elephant to the person who gave it, but the Internal Revenue Code permits heirs to "disclaim"—refuse to accept an inheritance. The effect of a qualified disclaimer that satisfies the Code's rules is that, for tax purposes, the individual never received the inheritance; it is not treated as if the person got the inheritance but returned it to the estate. In effect, disclaimers can be used for postmortem estate planning, because the funds or property pass as if the disclaimant had died first.

A qualified disclaimer must:

- Be written, not oral
- Be made before the disclaimant has received any benefit from the inheritance

- Shift the property to someone else; the disclaimer doesn't count if the disclaimant ends up receiving the property in another role. As an exception, a surviving spouse can disclaim an interest that qualifies for the marital deduction yet receive the property in another way that does not qualify for the marital deduction.

- Be made within nine months of a lifetime gift, or nine months of the date of death for a bequest

These are the tax rules for disclaimers: for Medicaid purposes, a disclaimer is a transfer of assets and is likely to have negative consequences.

INCAPACITY PLANNING

Historically, the court system had very few tools for dealing with incapacity. After a hearing, a conservator could be named to take care of an "incompetent" person's property, or a guardian to take responsibility for the incompetent "ward's" well being. The problem was that a declaration of incompetency was not only psychologically shattering for the ward, but caused the ward to lose many civil rights. Thus, courts were reluctant to make the finding in borderline cases—leaving vulnerable people without help, and leaving their financial affairs in limbo.

Therefore, the modern guardianship procedure evolved. The modern theory is that it is not necessary to have black-and-white categories of "competent" and "incompetent"; but for some elderly or disabled people, some degree of "incapacity" exists. If the individual admits that incapacity is present, or if it is proved by a hearing, then the court will appoint a "guardian of the person" and/or "guardian of the property."

The court's guardianship order will spell out which powers are retained by the ward (person for whom a guardian is appointed), and which have been transferred to the guardian. The guardian will have only those powers specifically awarded by the court. Sometimes the court will find that a fullscale appointment is not necessary, but will appoint a limited purpose guardian for a single task, such as getting the elderly person admitted to a nursing home or continuing care retirement community, or setting up a trust.

PLANNING TIP: Testation (making a will or codicil) is usually considered so inherently personal that the guardian will not be allowed to do it, although a guardian of the property can handle day-to-day financial tasks and probably will be allowed to make transfers that save income and estate taxes. That means that the will is essentially "frozen" as soon as the senior citizen becomes a ward, so it should be drafted in general and flexible enough terms that it will not require constant retailoring to fit every year's new tax laws.

Most of the states allow advance designation of a guardian; any person who still has capacity can designate a trusted person to serve as guardian if one is ever needed. This allows the elderly person to pick the guardian he finds most acceptable; it also reduces the duration and expense of the guardianship proceeding.

PRACTICE TIP: The designated guardian (like the DPA agent, discussed below, or the trustee of a trust) must retain capacity even after the principal loses it, and must be expected to retain capacity throughout the ward's life. Therefore, selecting a spouse or sibling may be a poor idea if such person is at risk of the same illnesses and conditions that beset the principal.

DURABLE POWER OF ATTORNEY

The durable power of attorney (DPA) is a simple yet powerful tool, recognized in all 50 states, for incapacity planning. A power of attorney is a designation of someone else (whether a person, a business, a law firm, or a financial institution) as "agent," otherwise known as "attorney in fact," to carry out anything from one very specific task to complete management of the "principal's" financial affairs. A power of attorney is durable if its terms provide that it will remain in effect even after the principal becomes incapacitated. (An ordinary power of attorney ceases to be valid if and when the principal loses capacity.)

A power of attorney is "springing" if it does not take effect until a certain event occurs. In the elder planning context, this usually means a determination of incapacity confirmed by a doctor, or by two doctors. Springing powers of attorney are good to the extent that they allow hesitant senior citizens to sign a power of attorney that they would otherwise be uncomfortable with. They're bad, to the extent that it can be quite difficult for the agent to exercise a springing power of attorney, because financial institutions or contracting parties may be dubious that the event has actually occurred and the agent actually is legally entitled to act on behalf of the principal.

A simple workaround is for the older person to sign an ordinary DPA, but allow an attorney or other trusted person to hold onto it, not notifying the agent until the condition has occurred. However, this technique places the principal at the mercy of the good judgment (and memory!) of the person holding the DPA document in escrow.

The state laws about DPAs contain a list of statutory powers that automatically belong to the agent unless the principal actually refuses to grant them. In a few states, a DPA is only valid if it uses the official form. Most states do prescribe an official form, but let principals draft their own forms or customize the basic form. Note that, even if the state law automatically gives agents the power to handle tax matters, the IRS has its own Power of Attorney form, which should be filled out and signed at the same time as the basic DPA.

An important decision is whether or not the agent should be given the power to make gifts of the principal's property. This is a complex question. The ability to make gifts can safeguard the elderly person's Medicaid plan. However, if the agent has the power to make gifts (especially gifts to the agent), there is serious potential for abuse. If large enough gifts are made, the principal's estate plan will be destroyed, because there won't be enough left in the estate to carry out the plan (unless the gifts follow the same proportions as the dispositions in the will). Furthermore, some states actually forbid self-gifting by agents.

The basic tax rule is that gifts made by a DPA agent are removed from the principal's estate only if the agent was explicitly granted the gifting power under the terms of the document. Sometimes this rule can be averted if gifting is one of the basic powers of agents under state law; but it's better to make this point clear and save trouble in the future.

In many cases, the Durable Power of Attorney with a gifting power will also be a General Power of Appointment for tax purposes, because the agent will be able to appoint the principal's property for the benefit of himself, his estate, his creditors, or the creditors of his estate. So, if the agent dies before the principal, all of the property covered by the DPA will be included in the gross estate of the agent, based on the agent's holding a general power of appointment. The test is the amount over which the decedent had power, not the size of appointments or whether any appointments were ever made at all.

PRACTICE TIP: If this is a problem, then draft the DPA denying power to appoint to self, estate, or creditors. If gifting by the agent is an important part of the plan, perhaps the principal could purchase additional life insurance on the agent's life that will cover any estate tax liability that occurs if the agent dies before the principal.

In some states, the probate court will accept the argument that the presence of a durable power of attorney, plus trusts to administer an incapacitated person's funds, will make it unnecessary to appoint a guardian at all. However, in states that do not take this position, get advice from an experienced attorney about the interaction between the DPA and guardianship. In some states, the DPA retains all of its force; in others, the agent has to report to the guardian, and the guardian, not the agent, has primary responsibility for managing the incapacitated person's financial affairs. (For many smaller estates, there is no practical difference among these alternatives, because the same small pool of family members are tapped by the court to serve as guardian, and have already been named as agents and trustees.)

SUMMARY

Even if federal estate tax is not a consideration, it's important for the client to have an estate plan to take care of the client's family and dispose of property in accordance with the client's wishes. The larger the estate, the more significant tax planning becomes—and the more worthwhile it is to use multiple, complex, or expensive legal devices. A small estate can be handled with a simple will, enough life insurance to provide liquidity and "fill the gaps" in the provision for the surviving spouse—and an incapacity plan such as a Durable Power of Attorney and advance designation of a guardian.

As the estate becomes larger, the risk of a second estate problem becomes greater, and more protective devices are needed. Estate splitting is an easy way to reduce the problem. Creation of a credit shelter trust becomes worthwhile, whether it is left to the surviving spouse or is left to the children or other heirs, while the surviving spouse receives the balance of the estate. A QTIP trust can provide useful income for the survivor, but will be included in the survivor's estate. A split-interest charitable trust is another useful way to combine tax planning with generating additional current income. Properly handled, life insurance in trust can be an inexpensive and taxwise way to create major benefits for survivors.

Special situations call for special estate planning: disposing of interests in the family business while saving estate taxes, for instance. Or, the testator/trust creator may have an especially complicated dispositive scheme, which cannot be handled adequately with simple devices.

Until the year 2006, estate planners will face additional challenges, because the amount that can be sheltered by the unified credit will continue to change. It makes good sense to draft documents referring to the maximum amount that qualifies for the unified credit, rather than specifying a dollar amount.

Any good estate plan must respond to changes in the law; but when the client is a senior citizen, there is an additional risk that the client will decline in capacity, and it may become impossible to make necessary amendments to documents. The plan may also have to accommodate involvement by DPA agents and guardians, in addition to the original client and the client's spouse.

CHAPTER FOOTNOTES

1. States differ in their approach to the statutory share. Some of them allow the spouse to take a share only of probate assets; others allow a share of all the decedent's assets, including items such as insurance and living trusts. However, some of them also allow the provision for the surviving spouse to be less than an outright inheritance—putting funds into trust for the surviving spouse can satisfy the requirement.

2. If the spouse benefits both under a QTIP and under the bypass trust, the spouse should take money out of the QTIP trust first and preserve the bypass trust as much as possible, because the QTIP trust will be included in the spouse's estate; the bypass trust will not.

3. IRS Letter Ruling 9811008 deals with the situation in which the decedent's IRA is left to a trust and then is distributed to the surviving spouse. In general, the involvement of the trust would prevent the surviving spouse from rolling over the funds into the spouse's own IRA. But the letter ruling allows the rollover if the surviving spouse has the power to revoke the trust. Lynn Asinof's article, "New IRA Policies May Mean Big Savings," *Wall Street Journal,* March 3, 1999, p. C1, makes an important practical point. Some large financial services companies that administer IRAs allow persons who inherit an IRA to name a beneficiary, so that if the heir dies before the account is fully distributed, the payment schedule continues, merely substituting the beneficiary for the heir. But other companies take the position that the entire account balance must be paid out when the heir dies. The practical difference is that the designated beneficiary can save income and estate taxes by continuing the distribution schedule. There is no clear IRS direction on the subject, and the existing announcements and Private Letter Rulings can be interpreted to support either position.

4. This is a funded trust; an unfunded trust can also be created, and its terms set down, with the intention that funding will occur at a later time, e.g., when the grantor dies and insurance proceeds on the grantor's life become available.

5. If the survivor is given the power to withdraw principal from the trust, it is usually limited by what is called a "five or five" power, i.e., the maximum that can be withdrawn each year is the greater of $5,000 or 5% of the trust. This is done to assist the surviving spouse's gift tax planning, because IRC §2514 provides that if the power of withdrawal is more generous than "five or five," and the surviving spouse doesn't exercise the power in a particular year, the money that was not withdrawn from the trust is a taxable gift to the remaindermen of the trust.

6. Private Letter Ruling 9738010.

7. Technical Advice Memoranda 9645006.

8. This is generally true only of contributions to public charities, not private foundations; and there is a limitation calculated based on the taxpayer's "contribution base"; but the clients of most readers of this book will not be in a position to make contributions large enough to encounter the limitation.

9. CLTs are somewhat less common than charitable remainder trusts. There is no limit on the duration of the charity's income interest. If the trust earns more income than is needed to pay the annuity or unitrust amount (see below) to the charity, the excess income can be accumulated for the noncharitable remaindermen. The gift or bequest to the noncharitable beneficiary is the discounted present value of the remainder.

10. See Roy M. Adams, "Ask the Expert," *Trusts & Estates* (March, 1998), p. 71.

11. Technically, noncharitable trusts have to end no later than the time that the grantor's youngest living descendant named in the trust would reach age 21; in practical terms, until the grantor's youngest grandchild or greatgrandchild reaches adulthood.

12. For more information, see Douglas Blattmachr and Jonathan G. Blattmachr, "A New Direction in Estate Planning: North to Alaska," *Trusts & Estates* (September, 1997), p. 48; Jonathan Blattmachr, Richard Thwaites, and Howard M. Zaritsky, "New Alaska Trust Act Provides Many Estate Planning Opportunities," *Estate Planning* (October, 1997), p. 347; Donald F. Cady's "Alaska Trusts: Cool Idea or Merely A Snow Job?" *National Underwriter*, Life and Health/Financial Services Edition, January 4, 1999, p. 7.

13. See Thomas Abendroth and Charles Fox, "Avoid Common law Business Organizations," *Trusts & Estates* 3/98 p. 18.

14. See *Miller*, TC Memo 1996-3.

15. See Charles D. Fox IV and Theodora P. Karnegis, "The Impact of The 1998 IRS Restructuring Act" and Bernard Barnett et.al., "1998 Tax Legislation: The Child of TRA '97," both in the January 1999 issue of *Trusts & Estates*.

16. If the donor, e.g., a grandparent, serves as custodian, and dies while the donee is still a minor, the custodial account will be included in the donor's estate, possibly frustrating the estate planning purpose for establishing the account in the first place.

17. If one of the spouses is not a U.S. citizen, the nonmarital rules are applied.

Chapter 14

HOUSING AND CARE ALTERNATIVES

Access to appropriate, high-quality care is an essential part of the elder plan. Care is available in a confusing variety of settings, by a wide range of providers, and often at a wide range of prices and payment sources. Some of the alternatives involve substantial investments of money. Many care settings voluntarily provide, or are legally obligated to provide, voluminous financial disclosures. The planning team can provide tremendous benefit to elderly clients and their families by assessing and explaining these disclosure documents, and by offering an objective determination of the comparative financial, tax, Medicaid, and estate planning implications involved in making a selection.

The choice has immense implications. Some financial decisions are hard to reverse for several reasons: refunds are unavailable; the care provider has either engaged in deliberate fraud, or has failed financially despite good intentions; or, there simply are no suitable alternatives for the older person's changed needs.

Furthermore, the concept of "transfer trauma" is well-recognized in the social sciences. The mere act of moving from one residence or nursing home to another can be risky, or even fatal, for a frail elderly person — even if, objectively speaking, the quality of care is better in the second setting. The more confused the elder is, the more likely that transfer trauma will occur. Even for a strong, healthy elderly person, making multiple moves is not only inconvenient, it is also expensive.

As Chapter 13 indicates, eventually estates under $1 million will generally be exempt from estate taxation. However, the full $1 million exemption is not scheduled to phase in until 2006. (Some members of Congress advocate a faster schedule, so the exemption may be accelerated if they get enough votes to prevail.) Between now and then, some of your clients will have moderate estates that are at risk of estate taxation absent effective planning steps. Chapter 13 outlines the basic planning steps.

A slightly more exotic variation to be considered involves providing for present and future care needs by using funds (e.g., from investments, a lump-sum distribution from a pension plan, or the sale of the family home) to purchase entry into a Continuing Care Retirement Community (or "CCRC," see below) in which the resident does not receive an equity interest in the residential unit. In that case, future care is provided for irrespective of the client's medical condition (which might make it impossible to qualify for long-term care insurance, "LTCI"), and without the limitations of Medicaid planning. Furthermore, funds that could trigger estate taxation are removed from the estate. (Purchasing a unit that comes with an equity interest will not accomplish this because the estate will include the value of the unit, which may appreciate over time, thus making the problem worse rather than better.)

THE CONTINUUM OF CARE

Our society recognizes that "one size fits all" works better for T-shirts than for elder care. The concept of the continuum of care is best described as a series of services that can be combined in many ways to suit differing needs. Usually, a person enters the continuum of care with a small need for services, but over time the individual's need for services will increase and ultimately, it may be necessary to provide care in a more specialized, intensive medical setting.

The base of the continuum of care pyramid is care in the home and in the community. Services can be rendered at home by the few physicians who make house calls, professional nurses, lower-skilled home health aides who provide personal care, and by homemakers who provide non-medical services such as cooking and cleaning. In this context, personal care means vital services that do not require professional training (e.g., feeding a person who cannot eat independently, bathing a person with limited mobility, helping a person dress, pushing a person's wheelchair). Home delivery of meals is an important service that can make the difference between continued independent living and the need for institutionalization. (See Chapter 5 for a discussion of Medicare coverage of home care, and Chapter 6 for Medicaid home care.) Although it is possible to purchase a LTCI policy that pays benefits only for institutional care, most insureds choose a policy that combines institutional and home care benefits.

Services can be rendered outside the home, but within the community. For instance, senior centers provide companionship, and perhaps meals and social services. Adult day care centers usually serve a somewhat more impaired population. They may also provide screening and other health services, or specialized services for demented persons.

If remaining at home is no longer desirable or feasible, there are many kinds of specialized housing for the elderly. Some of them, such as retirement communities, are oriented toward leisure and recreation. Other facilities target the needs of individuals for whom a medical setting is inappropriate (and excessively expensive), but who cannot live entirely independently either. These settings provide some services, such as congregate meals, transportation, or assistance with taking prescribed medications, but do not offer nursing care or medical services.

The life-care community, or Continuing Care Retirement Community (CCRC), attempts to make the full continuum of care available. At first, new residents live in conventional housing units and have access to social and recreational activities. However, nursing care is also available on-site and, if necessary, residents can move into assisted living or nursing home units within the same complex (or nearby, subject to transfer agreements).

There are also several kinds of facilities that are operated and licensed as health care, rather than housing facilities, including Skilled Nursing Facilities (SNFs) qualifying for Medicare reimbursement (see Chapter 5), and facilities with a custodial orientation. Medicaid refers to its participating nursing homes as "nursing facilities." Medicaid formerly had separate rules for SNFs and Intermediate Care Facilities (ICFs), but now has a single set of rules. Depending on local law, there may also be lower-level facilities (e.g., Health-Related Facilities, or HRFs) that offer a less intensive level of medical services.

Some questions for analyzing any potential housing/care situation include:

- Does the facility consider itself residential, medical, or both?

- Is the facility required to have a state license? If so, what kind of license? What are the licensing requirements, and is the facility in good standing with regulators?

- Is the facility subject to financial disclosure requirements (see Chapter 5)? CCRCs, for instance, must provide prospectuses to potential entrants.

- Are there minimum requirements for entering the facility? An individual cannot simply reserve a bed at a nursing home, even if he or she wants to — instead, an individual has to suffer at least a minimum level of disability, as measured by a standard assessment process.

- Is there a maximum level of disability that the facility can handle (in practical terms), or is allowed to handle (in legal terms)? Typically, Assisted Living Facilities (ALFs) laws allow a facility to have only residents who are healthy enough to leave by themselves in a fire or other emergency.

- Is there a requirement for a deposit or other lump-sum payment prior to entry? If so, how much is it, what is its tax status, and under what circumstances are refunds available?

- Do community residents receive an equity interest in their unit?

- Does residence at the facility, or care provided by the facility, qualify for reimbursement from Medicare, Medicaid, and/or the potential resident's own LTCI policy?

Older persons' abilities — or, more accurately, disabilities — are often measured on the basis of ADLs (Activities of Daily Living) and IADLs (Instrumental Activities of Daily Living). ADLs are bedrock capabilities, such as being able to move from bed to chair, being able to remain continent, to use the toilet, and to dress or bath oneself. IADLs are socially significant activities with a lesser physical component (for instance, the ability to manage money, shop, or use a telephone).

Senior citizens can suffer problems with physical illness, cognitive deterioration, or both. Frustratingly, a person whose cognitive disability is so severe that he or she might endanger himself or others, may nevertheless be in good shape physically — perhaps strong enough to harm a nurse or aide if he becomes agitated. The problem is that an Alzheimer's patient (or other cognitively disabled person) may unpredictably do any of the following: wander and be unable to find the way home; leave water running until it causes a flood; ingest household chemicals, thinking they are food; cause a fire by leaving an empty pot on a stove burner; or create many other dangerous situations.

THE CONTINUUM OF PAYMENT

It is vital that senior clients have access to quality medical care and other services that they need, but access probably will not begin, and certainly will not continue, unless the means for payment are in place.

Under the current system, the basic source of payment for long-term care is out-of-pocket spending by elders and their families. However, there are many other potential payors, and one of the planning team's tasks is to sort out which payor is responsible for paying what.

As Chapter 5 shows, once the necessary deductibles and co-insurance payments have been satisfied, or if the senior client is a managed care beneficiary, Medicare will assume a major role in paying hospital and doctor bills. It will cover up to 100 days of post-hospital recuperation in a skilled nursing facility, but will not cover any custodial, long-term care. It will also provide part-time or intermittent home care to homebound beneficiaries, especially if they are recuperating after a hospitalization or a skilled nursing home stay. However, if an older person is covered by an Employer Group Health Plan (EGHP), in most instances the EGHP, and not Medicare, is supposed to be the primary payor (see Chapter 5).

Medicaid is supposed to be a payor of last resort, so if services can be covered under both Medicare and Medicaid, Medicare is supposed to pay first. The Balanced Budget Act of 1997 made health care providers very unhappy by allowing providers to be paid at the Medicaid rate (which is almost always lower than the Medicare rate) when providing care for "dual eligibles" (senior citizens eligible for both Medicare and Medicaid.)

So far, long-term care insurance (see Chapter 4) is not a major factor in paying for long-term care, but that should change as more and more policyholders age and require services. Naturally, LTCI policies provide benefits according to their own terms, so policy selection involves selecting the correct mix of benefits as well as choosing the most cost-effective policy from a quality insurer.

Many states have non-Medicaid programs that provide services to elderly and disabled persons, such as: senior centers; adult day care; home care; housekeeping and chore services; home-delivered meals; caregiver training; and respite care (which provides a part-time or temporary substitute caregiver to relieve some of the stress of caregiving). Many of these programs are funded under the federal

Older Americans Act (OAA), so a good place to find out about them is the nearest "single state agency" delegated to handle OAA matters. Similar programs are frequently offered by religious and charitable organizations. Although these programs are usually paid for out-of-pocket by the person receiving the services (or his or her family), it is typical for the fees to be set on a sliding scale, so that less affluent people pay less.

HOME CARE

There are two important basic questions in setting up a home care plan. First, does the senior citizen want to stay home? Second, if so (which is usually the case), how realistic is this desire? "Home" is a very emotive word, and most people have a strong desire, and even a willingness to make sacrifices, in order to remain in their home and in the community in which they are accustomed to living.

Depending on the older person's needs, wishes, family situation, financial situation, insurance coverage, and eligibility for insurance and government benefits, home care can be a small-scale, informal process or a full-scale deployment of resources from many directions. Home care has its own continuum, from a little bit of help from family and friends to the equivalent of nursing home care provided at home by skilled professionals with assistance from paraprofessionals.

Home care usually involves two components: (1) the health and personal care of the older person; and (2) the housekeeping and home maintenance tasks. The distinction is important because it determines which health care professional can perform these services, their eligibility for reimbursement, and their income tax status. For example, a professional nurse might make periodic visits to the elder to assess his health status and to perform skilled services (such as wound care and giving injections). A physical therapist might visit to help a stroke patient regain mobility.

These professional visits could be supplemented by less-skilled personal services, such as bathing the elder, giving him a shampoo, seeing that he takes prescribed medications, or feeding him if he is immobile. Under appropriate circumstances, a person who qualifies for Medicare home care can get some household services performed by a home health attendant, but household services are not covered unless they are needed in conjunction with skilled professional and personal services.

Home care, like penicillin, is a valuable remedy but not a panacea, and it is not without risks. Home care works well when it promotes the happiness of a person who does not want to leave a beloved home, but does not work when a person is trapped in a dilapidated, unsafe home in a dangerous neighborhood. It is difficult to supervise what goes on in home care. In the best case, a skillful, compassionate worker not only does hands-on care, but also recognizes when medical assistance is needed. In the worst case, a poorly trained worker fails to recognize emergencies (or even inadvertently creates them by making mistakes), shows up for work late (or inconsistently), neglects the elderly person, or even steals from or abuses the elderly person.

A frequent assertion is that home care is an economical alternative to institutionalization. This is true only if the person's home care needs are fairly light — imagine the cost of employing several full-time workers, or even the three shifts of workers needed for around-the-clock care of a demented or very physically debilitated person. Sometimes institutionalization actually saves money because of economies of scale, and because the cost of the institution replaces both health care costs and ordinary living costs such as rent and food. That does not make home care either good or bad, only a tool that works in some situations and not in others.

Employment Issues

What if there are no family members or friends available to provide care, but the person needing the care is not homebound (ruling out Medicare services), not eligible for Medicaid, and there are no available state-run or voluntary programs that meet the person's needs? In all probability, the older person will hire someone on a part-time or full-time basis as a companion or housekeeper. Although enforcement is sparse, employing an individual creates legal obligations. The employer must go through the Form I-9 process of ascertaining either that the employee is a citizen, or that he or she is a legal immigrant permitted to work in the United States.

Household employees are subject to the so-called "Nanny tax" rules, and are, therefore, subject to FICA (Social Security/Medicare) tax if they earn more than $1100 per year. The employer must either pay the entire FICA tax (15.3% of wages), or pay one-half of the FICA tax and withhold the other half from the worker's wages. However, instead of the complex procedures for reporting and remitting tax that regular employers are subject to, household employers can simply report and remit the FICA tax with their own tax return (Schedule H).

(Federal unemployment tax (FUTA) is also due if the employee's cash wages are greater than $1000 in any calendar quarter. The FUTA tax equals 8/10 of 1% of the first $7,000 of the household employee's wages.) Household employers are not legally obligated to withhold federal income taxes on employee wages. A household employer should withhold federal income tax only if the employee requests withholding, and the employer agrees to do it. See IRS Publication 926 for details on taxes on household employment.

Who is the "employer" of the home health worker or housekeeper? If the senior citizen or family member hired the worker directly, then clearly the parent or child is the employer. However, if the worker was provided by a home health agency, the question becomes more complex. If the agency provides the worker and controls what the worker does and how the worker does it, then the home health worker is an employee of the home health agency, and the agency is responsible for employment-related taxes. But if, despite the agency's involvement, the family controls what the worker does and how it is done, then the family member is the official employer.

PRACTICE TIP: If any of your clients employ home health workers, clarify this point. "Gee, I thought the agency was taking care of it" is not a valid defense, and people who fail to remit FICA taxes are personally liable for the failure. The penalty can be as much as 100% of the unpaid taxes.

Some state Medicaid agencies have an option known as "vendorization," under which a person who applies for Medicaid home care, and who already has a successful working relationship with a home care worker, can get the worker qualified for Medicaid reimbursement.

Another option that is usually more convenient, but also more expensive, is to hire a Home Health Agency (HHA) to coordinate the care plan and to provide care. The HHA will screen workers (it is a legal requirement that potential workers' names be checked against a database of convicted criminals and elder abusers), assign them, supervise them, and handle all of the tax paperwork. Furthermore, the agency has many workers, so a substitute can be assigned if the client and worker do not get along well, or if a particular worker is ill or on vacation.

It is usually the case (but not always) that Medicaid and insurance reimbursement will be unavailable for paid services rendered by relatives. Check with an experienced elder law attorney to see if there are regulations that allow the hiring of a relative.

COMMUNITY ALTERNATIVES

A wide range of services and care settings exist at the lower end of the continuum of care, coping with elderly people who are at risk if they live entirely alone, but who do not require a full-scale medical setting. This is a hard sector to quantify or even describe because there are many alternatives, and not all of them are subject to state licensure or any kind of regulation. Possibilities include:

- *Home-sharing* — where a more able-bodied person moves in and provides companionship and perhaps some assistance with chores.
- *Adult foster care* — where an impaired adult becomes a paying "boarder" in a household, which may also have a small number of other foster residents; the "hosts" may be reimbursed by state programs in some circumstances.[1]
- *Group homes* — homes for several physically or mentally disabled persons, under the supervision of one or more paid staff members.
- *Adult homes, domicilliary homes, personal care homes, rest homes* — names for various kinds of residences (which may or may not require state licensure or qualification for reimbursement) providing some degree of supervision and services to persons who are basically capable of self-care with some help.

Often, these facilities operate with little or no state supervision; thus, they offer little protection for residents. There have been some reported scandals (e.g., financial improprieties, or physical abuse of vulnerable residents). Many residents of these facilities get SSI (federal and state Supplemental Security Income) and/or other forms of disability benefits. A federal law called the Keys Amendment (an amendment to the Social Security Act) requires the states to create and enforce standards for housing operations where a significant number of SSI recipients live. (The standards are supposed to deal with admissions, residents' rights, sanitation, safety, etc.)

Even elderly tenants in conventional apartments may have some special entitlements — check to see if they are entitled to rent rebates, homestead tax rebates, protection against excessive rent increases and eviction, or entitlement to remain as tenants without purchasing their apartments if the building becomes a co-op or condominium.

ASSISTED LIVING FACILITIES

There are many elders who would be at risk if they lived entirely alone, without supportive services or assistance with basic activities such as mobility and continence — yet they do not need, or want, to pay for full-scale nursing care either (even if they could be admitted to a facility). Furthermore, the more pleasant and home-like a setting is (and the less restrictive and "institutional" it is), the more attractive it will be to potential residents. That is the rationale for the development of Assisted Living Facilities (ALFs). These are predominantly developed by religious organizations, or in the private sector (especially by hotel chains). The assisted living philosophy calls for promotion of autonomy, and catering (where possible) to residents' preferences.

The definition of an ALF is not very precise. Many of these facilities are considered private housing developments, not subject to any form of licensure or regulation; thus, it is hard to be certain of how many ALFs exist nationwide. The Assisted Living Federation of America ("ALFA," formerly known as the Assisted Living Facilities Association of America) estimates that about one million elders live in the approximately 40,000 ALFs currently in operation.[2] A 1999 GAO report states that estimates of the number of ALF beds range all the way from 800,000 to 1.5 million. The report, "Assisted Living: Quality of Care and Consumer Protection Issues in Four States," looks at ALFs in the states of California, Florida, Ohio, and Oregon, and raises questions about whether residents and potential residents get enough disclosure about ALF facilities and operations. The report also points out that in those states, about one-quarter of the facilities had been cited for violations by state regulators. So a planner can help his or her clients greatly by learning about the actual behind-the-scenes conditions in local ALFs, and sharing this information with them.

The American Association of Homes and Services for the Aging defines assisted living as providing and/or arranging for meals, personal and supportive services, health care, and 24-hour supervision to residents in a group facility. The Assisted Living Federation of America's formulation "is a special combination of housing, personalized supportive services and health care designed to respond to the individual needs of those who need help with activities of daily living but do not need the skilled medical care provided in a nursing home."

ALFA commissioned a study done by Coopers and Lybrand in 1996. Results from 268 ALFs with a total of 15,000 units showed that:

- the average cost of a month of ALF residence was $2,150;
- the average resident was an unmarried female, age 84;
- the average resident was dependent in three ADLs;
- about one-half of the resident population suffered from Alzheimer's Disease or other cognitive impairment; and
- over one-third of the residents used walkers or wheelchairs to move around.

Most ALF residents pay privately (out-of-pocket) for their stay at the facility. However, according to the American Public Welfare Association, it is possible to get Medicaid coverage of an ALF stay in 22 states. In 12 of those states, the application should be made under the state's "home and community-based waiver," an arrangement between the state and the Health Care Financing Administration (HCFA) under which HCFA will allow the state to by-pass some requirements that would otherwise apply. In the other 10 states, the program might be called "domiciliary care," "supported living," or "adult congregate living facility." An experienced elder law attorney should be able to direct the client toward the correct program.

Although the first generations of LTCI policies sold do not cover assisted living, viewing it as a form of housing (i.e., a personal expense) rather than as a form of medical treatment, some later policies cover assisted living under the heading of "innovative benefits." An increasing number of insurers have realized that it makes more sense to pay a smaller amount for ALF costs, promoting the happiness of the insured person, than to make expensive institutionalization the only route to insurance reimbursement.

ALFs are subject to some federal regulation, but states are primarily responsible for regulating and monitoring ALFs. States vary in their treatment of ALFs. Some states consider ALFs to be board and care facilities. Twenty-two states have laws specific to ALFs,[3] dealing with issues such as who can live in an ALF, the design and maintenance of a facility, and the services provided there.

The prospective resident will sign a contract prior to moving to an ALF. There is no government-prescribed or industry-standard ALF contract, so careful review by the planning team is especially important. An optimum contract would cover items such as:

- what services the facility offers;
- the extent and degree of available services;
- which services are covered under the basic fee;
- the optional services available, and the extra charges for those services;
- the number of staff, and the qualifications for the staff;
- staff coverage at night and on weekends;
- the facilities available for coping with medical emergencies and for transferring residents to hospitals; and
- refund provisions.

However, in practice, contracts often fail to cover important issues, and may even require the potential resident to relieve the facility of liability (e.g., if a person decides to remain in the facility despite experiencing deterioration in his or her physical condition).

There are at least two quality control initiatives for the assisted living sector, the American Health Care Association's Quality Initiative for Assisted Living, and the Assisted Living Quality Coalition (created by AARP, the Assisted Living Facilities Association, the American Association of Homes and Services for the Aging, and the Alzheimer's Association).

In August, 1996, the Assisted Living Quality Coalition published a paper titled "Assisted Living Quality Initiative: Building a Structure That Promotes Quality." The coalition's recommendations include:

- choosing a facility that accepts and adheres to guidelines issued by the National Assisted Living Quality Organization (an independent industry association);
- insurers and other third-party payors should support quality by providing reimbursement for private rooms for all ALF residents who want them;

- building codes should be reformed so that ALFs can conform to the codes and provide safety in emergencies without "breaking the bank";
- residents, their families, and advocates should be included on each facility's internal quality assessment team; and
- facilities should create a database of quality indicators (such as improvement, or at least non-deterioration, in the functional status of residents), so that facilities can be compared and a facility's performance over time can be assessed.

CONTINUING CARE RETIREMENT COMMUNITIES

The terms "life care community" and "Continuing Care Retirement Community" (CCRC) are broadly similar, although some state statutes use one term rather than the other; there may also be technical differences in the way the two terms are applied. Nevertheless, the basic theory is that a developer constructs a community containing residential units, community and recreational facilities, and varying levels of medical care, up to skilled nursing. Most people who move to the community are fairly healthy when they arrive, and so they will move to residential units and take advantage of the recreational opportunities. Over time, they may need home care that will be administered within their units, or they may have to move to the facility's nursing unit.

CCRCs use a team approach in identifying residents' needs and keeping them healthy and functional as long as possible (e.g., by monitoring arthritis, high blood pressure, and other chronic conditions). According to the GAO, this approach is effective in maintaining residents' health, but it is not necessarily effective in reducing overall health costs.[4]

According to the GAO, approximately 350,000 people lived in about 1,200 CCRCs as of the beginning of 1997. (The American Seniors Housing Association, a trade association for CCRCs, has a much higher estimate — about 2,700 facilities nationwide.) The average CCRC had about 300 residents, most of them living independently in housing units. The GAO visited 11 CCRCs, finding that entry fees ranged from $34,000 (studio apartment) to $439,600 (two-bedroom home). In addition to the entry fee, single people and couples had to pay monthly charges of $1,383 and $4,267, respectively.

Thirty-six states have some degree of CCRC regulation; unfortunately, that leaves 14 states that do not. (It is interesting to note that regulation is usually handled by a state's insurance department, not its department of public health. The focus of enforcement is on the kind of disclosure usually found in a securities prospectus, information that is usually not provided in a typical doctor-patient relationship.)

Furthermore, state regulation may be porous. There may be no requirement that facility operators keep entry fees in escrow (so that they will be available if refunds are called for), and reserves for operating expenses are not always mandated. In the best case scenario, residents either never need a nursing home bed, or they find one available when they need it. In one worst case scenario, the facility underestimated the number of nursing home level beds that would be available, or filled beds with non-residents to earn extra money — leaving residents unable to access the necessary level of care. Nursing home beds in CCRCs will probably not be Medicaid-participating, so if residents need to pay extra fees for nursing care, but run out of money, they probably will not be able to get Medicaid reimbursement.

Some facility operators are unscrupulous and deliberately exploit residents. However, it is far more likely that financial problems, including facility bankruptcy, will be caused by the facility operator's inexperience or inability to estimate future costs. Residents may be forced to pay additional fees, or to leave facilities that are being closed down in conjunction with a bankruptcy.[5]

Factors to consider in assessing a brochure or contract include:

- the sponsor's track record;
- the financial history of the project, and projections for the future;
- whether the actuarial assumptions about residents' longevity and care needs are reasonable;
- what happens to residents who need a nursing-home level of care when all the nursing home beds are full;
- the conditions for canceling the contract and getting a refund (e.g., whether the refund may be deferred until someone else buys the unit);

- when, and how often, housekeeping and laundry services are provided; and
- the extent to which the sponsor can raise fees, or cut back on services, if it runs into financial trouble.

Determine whether your state publishes an official state consumer guide to CCRCs. These guides can be an excellent resource for potential residents and their families (and a convenient source of information about where to reach regulators to file a complaint).

NURSING HOMES

Too many caregivers think they have only two (or perhaps three) alternatives to consider: (1) do nothing; (2) maybe "have Mom move in with us"; or (3) "put Mom in a nursing home." Nursing home placement is often seen by elders, and perceived by caregivers, as an act of hostility and abandonment. Certainly, inappropriate institutionalization is bad for everyone — bad for elders who feel imprisoned, bad for the institutions that care for residents who really do not belong there, and bad for Medicaid, insurance companies, and out-of-pocket payors who pay for a higher level of care than is required.

Senior citizens and caregivers who have access to a qualified planning team should have a greater degree of insight into the continuum of care, and should be able to understand the resources available in the senior citizens' community.

However, not all institutionalization is inappropriate. Sometimes the senior citizen has such intensive health care needs that a medical setting is required. Furthermore, especially in rural areas, it might be theoretically possible to put together a plan of home care and community services, but the plan might not work as a practical matter because there are not enough agencies and workers in the area, or because the distances to be covered are too great. Another common reason for moving to a nursing home is a change in the availability of care from family members. The death of a caregiver spouse (particularly the wife) may make it impossible for the survivor to remain at home any longer. A child or in-law who formerly provided care may move away, get a new job or a more demanding job, have to care for a spouse, or assume increased child care responsibilities — once again, making it necessary for the elder to be placed in a nursing home. In these circumstances, it must be understood that a nursing home is the best choice for care, and the focus will then be to pick the best available facility.

Placing a parent in a nursing home is, in some respects, like enrolling a child in his or her first-choice of colleges — an individual needs a rational plan for paying for it all, but money is not the only factor. Whereas college admission revolves around factors such as GPAs, SAT scores, and extracurricular activities, nursing home admission depends on "assessment" — a standardized test used to determine the elder's degree of physical and cognitive disability, and the areas in which assistance will be required. As a general rule, unless the assessment score is higher than the cut-off level (i.e., unless the applicant is seriously ill), nursing home admission cannot occur.

The Nursing Home Market

The federal Department of Health and Human Services (HHS) does periodic nursing home surveys at ten-year intervals.[6] The most recent survey was done in 1995 (it takes several years to interpret the survey results). Between 1985 and 1995, although the elderly population increased significantly (18%), and America "aged" (i.e., a higher proportion of its citizens were middle-aged, elderly, or very old), the increase in the number of nursing home residents was small (a mere 4%), so that the total nursing home population reached 1.5 million in 1995.

The number of nursing homes actually shrank by 13%, to 16,700, although the average home in 1995 was larger than its 1985 counterpart, so there were 9% more beds overall. The 1995 bed capacity was close to 1.8 million beds. Occupancy rates went down between 1985 and 1995 (i.e., it became easier to find a nursing home bed because the number of nursing home beds increased faster than the number of nursing home residents). In one sense, it is wasteful; however, in another sense, it is good to have those nursing home beds in reserve as the Baby Boom generation ages.

These seemingly paradoxical results are due to improvements in medicine, and to the continuum of care. The longer disability can be staved off, and the more options for home care and specialized housing that exist, the less need there will be for nursing home beds.

As of 1995, close to 90% of nursing home residents were senior citizens (the others were younger people disabled by accidents or disease). Over one-third of the residents were over the age of 85, and over two-thirds were female. The overall occupancy rate nationwide was 87.4%, although voluntary and government homes had higher occupancy rates than proprietary ones, and there were meaningful regional differences — the lowest occupancy rate was in the West, at 83.2%, and the highest rate was in the Northeast, at 91.5%.

An important change between 1985 and 1995 was the way facilities were owned and operated. Currently, approximately two-thirds of nursing homes are proprietary (i.e., operated as profit-making businesses, not as charitable organizations). In 1985, 41% of proprietary homes were part of a nursing home chain; by 1995, 55% were chain-affiliated.

According to the NCHS' Advance Data No. 280, the average nursing home had 106 beds. There was no real difference in average size based on whether they were proprietary, voluntary (not-for-profit) or government-owned. Most of the nursing homes (69.7%) were certified for participation in both Medicare and Medicaid, and 20.1% were Medicaid-certified but did not offer Medicare SNF-level care. In other words, 89.8% of nursing homes were enrolled in the Medicaid program, which is logical because Medicaid pays for over 70% of all nursing home days nationwide; therefore, losing access to Medicaid funds would be a poor business decision for most facilities. About 6% of facilities were Medicare SNFs but not Medicaid-certified, and 4.2% were not certified at all. This does not necessarily mean that the uncertified facilities were poor quality facilities; on the contrary, they may have had a good enough reputation to attract private-pay patients and, thus, avoid the massive paperwork involved in obtaining and maintaining certification.

Advance Data No. 289 provides a picture of nursing home residents over age 65: 17.5% of the residents entered the home between the ages of 65 and 74; 42.3% were between the ages of 75 and 84, and 40.2% entered at age 85, or older. In other words, over 80% of the admissions occurred after age 75 rather than in the "young-old" group. However, the patterns were somewhat different for the male residents than for their female counterparts — 27.3% of the male residents, versus only 14.2% of the female residents entered between the ages of 65 and 74, 41.8% of the males and 42.5% of the females entered between the ages of 75 and 84, and 30.9% of the males and 43.3% of the females entered at age 85, or older. These differences are probably attributable both to women's generally better health and longevity, as well as to women's greater skills in housekeeping and self-care.

Overall, only 16.5% of nursing home residents were married. The gender difference here is especially striking — 37% of the male residents were married, versus only 9.8% of the female residents.

About three-quarters of the female residents, but only about one-third of the male residents, were widowed. (The rest were divorced, or had never married.)

Before being placed in the nursing home, about one-third of the residents had lived in private homes in the community; 40.6% had been placed in a nursing home after being discharged from a hospital, 4.9% had come from a board and care or residential facility, 2.2% had come from a retirement home, and 11.6% had come from another nursing home, most likely a Medicare SNF.

Nearly all nursing home residents (over 96%) were ADL-dependent (i.e., they needed assistance to perform at least one fundamental, basic activity of daily living). Almost all residents needed assistance when bathing or showering. Approximately 90% of the residents needed help dressing, although only one-quarter needed help transferring from the bed to the chair, or back again. Two-thirds of the residents were dependent in three or four ADLs.

In business terms, as of mid-1998, 20% of all nursing home beds in the United States were controlled by the 10 largest public companies in this business sector, although the merger and acquisition trend was marked, and further concentration was expected. For instance, Mariner Post-Acute Network, Inc., created by several mergers, had over 400 facilities in 32 states. Even before the last in the chain of mergers, the company had 51,576 beds, second only to Beverly Enterprises' 63,376 beds, followed by Sun Healthcare Group's 47,103 beds, and Vencor's 45,656 beds.[7]

The federal Agency for Health Care Policy and Research performed a massive study of nursing home conditions in 1996, known as the Medical Expenditure Panel Survey (MEPS). MEPS shows that, on January 1, 1996, approximately 1.6 million people were nursing home residents, divided among some 16,800 facilities. About 19% of nursing homes had special-needs nursing units. Approximately 2,100 homes had Alzheimer's Disease units, taking care of an average of 34 patients each. About one-half of the residents were demented to some extent, and 83% were dependent in three or more ADLs.[8]

Factors in Choosing a Nursing Home

An individual who has already qualified for Medicaid and who needs to enter a nursing home is given no choice in picking a nursing home. That person must enter the first Medicaid-certified nursing home within a certain geographic radius of the home or hospital that has an available Medicaid bed. (Nursing homes are allowed to, and generally do, have separate waiting lists for private-pay and Medicaid patients.)

In contrast, a private-pay patient can select any nursing home that he or she wishes. However, since high-quality nursing care is always in demand, the best facilities may have a long waiting list, and it may be impossible to enter the preferred home at the time that institutionalization is required. To a certain extent, it is possible to plan and reserve a bed in advance, but it is impossible to predict when a stroke, heart attack, or hip fracture will occur, or when it will become evident that a person is cognitively impaired, and not just mildly forgetful.

If a subsequent Medicaid application is contemplated, it makes sense to choose a facility that participates in Medicaid. The federal laws regulating nursing homes make it unlawful to evict a resident merely because the payment method changes from private-pay to Medicaid. Federal legislation signed in March, 1999 also protects Medicaid residents from being evicted after a nursing home terminates its participation in the Medicaid system. "Private-pay" contracts are also unlawful — the facility is not allowed to require new residents to agree *not* to apply for Medicaid, or *not* to apply for a certain period of time. A person who satisfies the Medicaid requirements has a legal right to get those benefits and, therefore, the right to apply for those benefits, even if the facility's financial interest is better served by the patient paying privately for a longer period of time.

Nursing homes are not allowed to impose a contractual requirement that the residents' relatives make donations to the facility, or use their own funds to guarantee that the resident's bills will be paid. (However, if the resident's son or daughter has access to the resident's funds in a joint checking account, or has been named as trustee, attorney-in-fact, or guardian, then it is entirely appropriate for the son or daughter to use the resident's money to pay for the care.)

PRACTICE TIP: HCFA maintains a current, on-line database of all Medicare- and Medicaid-certified nursing homes in the United States, and any enforcement actions against them, as well as their assessment surveys. The address is *www.medicare.gov/nursing/home.asp.*

Nursing Home Bill of Rights

Since 1987, federal law has provided protection for residents of nursing homes that participate in Medicare and/or Medicaid (most nursing homes do). Nursing homes have a legal obligation to protect and promote residents' rights, including:

- participation in medical decision-making, including free choice of physician;
- freedom from physical, mental, and financial abuse; facilities are not allowed to use physical or chemical restraints for their own convenience, only when they are actually medically necessary to protect the resident;
- the right to join in resident and family groups, and to express grievances without suffering discrimination;
- access to state and federal survey reports about the facility;
- advance notice of the cost of the facility's services;
- the right to be taken care of under a written plan of care supervised by a physician; and
- freedom from arbitrary transfer or discharge. Residents *can* be discharged if they are dangerous to other residents, if the facility cannot safely meet their needs, or if there is *no* source of payment for the resident's care. However, a facility that participates in Medicaid violates federal law by discharging or transferring a resident simply because the resident has switched from paying privately, or using LTCI to pay for care, to having his or her care paid for by Medicaid.

Reviewing the Nursing Home Contract

The contract should spell out which services are included in the basic price, and which services are optional "extras" provided at additional cost. (Nursing home residents and their relatives are often shocked to discover that although they pay substantial amounts of money for nursing care, some very simple items and services are not provided.) The contract should reflect compliance with applicable state and federal laws, and should *not* include any invalid provisions. For instance, it is unlawful to require residents' relatives to guarantee payment, or to require residents to refrain from applying for Medicaid.

Problem Facilities

Ironically, medical improvements and increased knowledge of, and access to, home care has only made it harder to operate nursing homes. The problems of caring for a few dozen sweet little old ladies with minor medical problems are infinitesimal compared to managing a large facility, over half of whose residents are severely demented and most of whom have complex medical problems that would have been fatal only a few decades earlier.

At the other end of the spectrum, nursing home residents are a very vulnerable, and often isolated population. Most residents never have any visitors at all, much less constant visits from highly involved relatives and friends who could spot deficiencies in the facility and complain vigorously. Because the majority of nursing-home days are paid for by Medicaid, those rates are critical to facilities' financial operations. Operators who believe that they are being underpaid by Medicaid may be tempted to cut corners. (Remember, most nursing homes are profit-making operations, and most for-profit nursing homes are part of a chain, so administrators are under constant pressure not only to enhance stockholder value, but to keep up with other units in the chain.)

In mid- and late 1998, the federal government targeted nursing home problems, finding that only one-third of nursing homes were in full compliance with all applicable regulations, yet very few nursing homes had been penalized for failure to comply. (A GAO study showed that one-third of California nursing homes studied had serious deficiencies that could imperil residents, not simply technical or record-keeping violations.) The situation will probably not have changed significantly by publication date. Consequently, the planner should be vigilant about checking inspection records for nursing homes his or her clients might enter.[9] (Advocates note that an important area of noncompliance is failure to make the mandated posting of survey information in a public area of the nursing home. Thus, the planner should demand a copy of the report or, advise his or her clients not to enter any nursing home that denies vital information to residents, potential residents and their families.)

COPING WITH PROBLEMS

There are a wide range of problems connected with housing situations. They can be caused by a mentally incapacitated person's fears or misperceptions (e.g., a person who has misplaced an object accuses the home care worker of stealing it, or a diabetic nursing home resident whose candy bars have been confiscated says the home is "starving" him or her), or by flagrant abuse of vulnerable residents, or anything in between. Sometimes, through no fault of the provider, the housing situation simply is no longer suitable for the older person's changed needs and the remedy is to find a more suitable setting (bearing in mind the potential for "transfer trauma").

All states maintain ombudsman programs for resolving complaints and disputes. Some of the programs are limited to nursing facilities, but others have a broader scope. Resort to these programs is free, but since they are bureaucracies, speedy response is not always possible.

Furthermore, all states have protective service programs which investigate situations in which vulnerable people are at risk. If necessary, the protective service programs can provide services, or have a guardian appointed for someone who is either incapable of self-care or who is being abused. Again, these programs are free and are publicly supported.

In the private sector, Geriatric Care Managers (GCMs) can do a great job of investigating and solving problems since they are objective professionals with a large database of information about local resources. They can make sure that a home health worker is replaced if there is a personality conflict, or they can recommend a better agency if there are problems with the agency itself. They can also advise senior citizens and their families about service availability (e.g., caregiver training, respite for caregivers, home-delivered meals, Alzheimer's day care), making recommendations, and assisting with the application process.

CHAPTER FOOTNOTES

1. George James' article, "Home and Not Alone: A Foster Care Program for Grown-Ups," *New York Times*, November 29, 1998, includes a resource listing for New Jersey foster care programs. The article notes that foster care is an economical alternative — adult foster care costs $40 per day versus a Medicaid nursing home daily rate of $92. The article estimates that 100,000 elders live in foster care placements nationwide. About half the states had active foster care programs, and eight more had limited programs.

2. GAO/HEHS-97-93, "Long-Term Care: Consumer Protection and Quality-of-Care Issues in Assisted Living," May 15, 1997. This report includes a lengthy bibliography for those who want to learn more about ALFs. The 1999 report is found in GAO/HEHS-99-27. See Laurie McGinley, "Assisted-Living Centers Criticized in Study," *Wall Street Journal*, April 16, 1999, p. A20. The Senate Committee on Aging held

a hearing on April 26, 1999, entitled "Shopping for Assisted Living: What Consumers Need to Make the Best Buy." Testimony was taken from children of ALF residents and from scholars and regulators. See *www.senate.gov/aging/hr31.htm.*

3. According to GAO/HEHS-97-93, the states are Alabama, Alaska, Connecticut, Florida, Hawaii, Iowa, Kansas, Kentucky, Louisiana, Maine, Maryland, Massachusetts, New Jersey, North Carolina, Oregon, Rhode Island, South Dakota, Tennessee, Utah, Virginia, Wisconsin, and Wyoming.

4. GAO/HEHS-97-36, "Health Care Services: How Continuing Care Retirement Communities Manage Services for the Elderly," January 23, 1997.

5. Michael Moss' article, "For Retirees, Moving Into 'Continuing Care' Offers No Guarantees," *Wall Street Journal*, October 8, 1998, p. A1, offers some sobering warnings.

6. The information in this section comes from the United States Department of Health and Human Services, Center for Disease Control, National Center for Health Statistics' (NCHS) Website, *www.cdc.gov/nchswww*, especially the news releases, fact sheets, and publications and product information sections.

7. Michael Moss, "Leon Black Bets Big on the Elderly," *Wall Street Journal*, July 24, 1998, p. B1.

8. "New MEPS Data Show Changing Nursing Home Market," *AHCPR Research Activities* (July, 1998), p. 4.

9. See GAO/T-HEHS-98-219, "California Nursing Homes: Federal and State Oversight Inadequate to Protect Residents in Homes with Serious Care Violations," July 28, 1998, discussed in Royce T. Hall's article, "GAO Says Serious Problems Afflict One-Third of California Nursing Homes," *Wall Street Journal*, July 27, 1998, p. B7; Robert Pear, "Government Easy on Errant Nursing Homes, Investigators Say," *New York Times*, July 29, 1998, p. A11. Also see Robert Pear, "Clinton Announces Drive to Cut Abuse at Nursing Homes," *New York Times*, July 22, 1998, p. A1; Monte Williams, "Nursing Homes Routinely Hide Reports of Flaws, Green Charges," *New York Times*, July 9, 1998, p. B3; and GAO/T-HEHS-97-114, "Nursing Homes: Too Early to Assess New Efforts to Control Fraud and Abuse," April 16, 1997. The problems continued in 1999. See GAO/HEHS-99-46, "Nursing Homes: Additional Steps Needed to Strengthen Enforcement of Federal Quality Standards," March 18, 1999; GAO/HEHS-99-89, "Nursing Homes: Stronger Complaint and Enforcement Practices Needed to Better Assure Adequate Care," March 22, 1999. HCFA officials appealed to state regulators to pay more attention to financially troubled nursing home chains, and to have a contingency plan in place if the chains went under. See Laurie McGinley, "Federal Officials Urge States to Boost Oversight of Some Nursing-Home Chains," *Wall Street Journal*, April 23, 1999, p. B6.

Chapter 15

CASE STUDIES AND THE COORDINATED PLAN

Elder care problems come in many varieties because of clients' individual preferences and their differing needs. Consequently, my intention here is not to tell you *the* answer because there are *many* valid responses to each problem. Rather, these hypothetical case studies are designed to provide some insight into the issues a planner might face in dealing with clients like the ones described below.

For instance, the client may be willing to "disinvest," or may insist on conserving capital, even at the risk of a great sacrifice in comfort. The client may consider leaving a large estate to his heirs absolutely critical, or not important at all. He may consider the mere act of applying for Medicaid to be humiliating or unethical; conversely, he may be willing to invest considerable time, trouble, and professional fees into constructing a Medicaid plan.

The range of elder planning problems is vast. For instance, the client could be a healthy, vigorous, affluent professional, executive, or business owner who wants to make sure that the complex structure of trusts in his or her estate plan will insulate a multi-million dollar fortune against the depredations of federal estate tax. Alternatively, the client could be a pitifully poor 89 year old who is suffering from multiple health problems and is the victim of elder abuse. The tools and strategies to be applied depend on: the amount of assets involved; the client's present and predictable future health problems; the availability of assistance from children and friends; the availability of local government, private sector, and volunteer services; and the personal preferences of the client and family.

One important problem many elderly people face is lack of liquidity — that is, even if they are theoretically far from destitute, quite frequently their only major asset is their home. Typically, they intend to continue living in the home until they die, then leave it to the surviving spouse, and upon the death of the surviving spouse, pass it on to one or more of their children. Therefore, it may be difficult to "unlock" the value of this asset.

HYPOTHETICAL PLANS

These brief scenarios raise some of the problems that might be brought to a financial planner by a client. In some of these situations, the tax and estate planning considerations are paramount, while in others, they are of secondary (if any) importance. Understandably, a healthy client will put less emphasis on planning measures for future ill health than a client already suffering from physical and/or cognitive problems will place on dealing with the existing problems and obtaining the necessary care.

1. Lewis and Milla Bolkowski

Lewis Bolkowski, age 67, knows that it is time to turn over the reins of his car dealership, although he is not quite ready to quit working. His son, Dennis, and the dealership manager, Carlton Jackson, have agreed to pay $250,000 to Lewis in five $50,000 installment payments, and to give Lewis a five-year consulting agreement under which he is paid $40,000 per year. Lewis' compensation is a legitimate business expense because Lewis will continue to work as an executive of the company with significant responsibilities. (If he dies or becomes incapacitated in the interim, the balance of the $250,000 will have to be paid, but the consulting payments will end.) Milla Bolkowski, age 63, earns $50,000 per year as purchasing administrator for a manufacturing company, and plans to keep working until her health problems (arthritis and heart disease) make it impractical to continue.

The Bolkowskis own a $350,000 home and have a portfolio in the $750,000-$1,000,000 range. Although their insurance agent has quoted them a price of about $10,000 per year for long-term care insurance (LTCI) policies for both of them, they believe that the premium is, in fact, a good bargain because Medicaid is not a possibility for them. Furthermore, the Bolkowskis know that in five years (or sooner, if Milla has to stop working at her current annual salary of $50,000, and start receiving her pension of $27,000 per year), their income will decrease significantly. Consequently, they plan to "live beneath their income" and to continue their investment program. They know that they can expect over ten years (perhaps even over twenty years) of longevity, so they want to continue to invest in growth stocks. However, they are also seriously considering shifting some funds into a deferred annuity that will provide income when the consulting and buy-out payments end.

Whether estate taxes will be due depends on what level the estate tax exclusion has reached (unless they both live until 2007). Clearly, however, they are affluent enough to require professional estate planning. It would probably make sense to set up credit shelter trusts and perhaps a QTIP trust. (In any event, their estate planning attorney will advise them about this decision.) Perhaps one of the trusts should be set up to manage assets in case of incapacity. Naturally, each should have a durable power of attorney. However, keep in mind that it probably makes more sense for Lewis to designate Milla as his attorney-in-fact than vice versa because Lewis is older than Milla, and is at a greater risk of losing capacity sooner than Milla will.

Because these individuals are still working, it probably makes sense for them to remain in their present home. However, a viable alternative is for them to find a luxury retirement community and move there. Even if the community provides only housing and leisure services, if they have adequate LTCI they can have their health needs taken care of through insurance benefits, rather than by living in a health-oriented setting.

2. Jane Pergolesi

Jane Pergolesi, age 71, was sorrowful but not surprised when her husband, Alex, at age 76, succumbed to the cancer he had been battling for years. Jane inherited a large, somewhat run-down house worth about $200,000, a joint savings account of $65,000, and received the proceeds from her husband's $100,000 insurance policy.

Prior to his death, Alex received $2,000 per month in pension payments. Since this pension was payable in joint-and-50% survivor annuity form, Jane will now receive only $1,000 a month. (Although Jane held paid jobs sporadically, she does not have a pension of her own.) When Alex was alive, he received $700 a month in Social Security benefits and Jane received $350 a month as his spouse; now she will receive a widow's pension of $700 a month. In other words, she has a monthly income of $1,700, plus earnings on the savings account (possibly $300 a month). Thus, while Jane is far from affluent, she is not destitute either. Clearly, estate planning is not much of a problem for her, but she may have some problems in paying for health care.

Jane decides to take the life insurance proceeds in the form of a settlement option, yielding another $6,000 per year in income ($500 per month) bringing her income up to $2,500 a month. Her main asset is the house. It so happens that her son, Dan, is unemployed. Dan suggests that he, his wife, and their three children move in with Jane. Dan is confident that he can fix up the house and increase its value. Of course, he expects that Jane will leave the house to him, or transfer it to him during her lifetime.

Jane agrees to the move since she does not want to live alone right now. Her health is reasonably good and she is mentally acute. She thinks it might be fun to have her lively young relatives around — and it is comforting to know that her son and daughter-in-law would be able to summon help if she ever needed it, or they could take care of her at home if her ability to function declined. However, she is not positive that this arrangement will work out, so she is not ready to enter into any formal agreements. If it does work out, she will consider signing a formal care contract, and if Dan stays around long enough to be a "caregiver child" (see Chapter 6), Jane will consider transferring ownership of the house to him, perhaps subject to her own life estate.

In case the living arrangement does not work out, Jane is gathering information about reverse mortgages (see Chapter 7) as an extra source of income that will not impair her Medicaid eligibility. She is also considering the purchase of an actuarially sound, immediate annuity with part of her savings — once again, with the goal of receiving extra income without having to make a transfer for Medicaid purposes.

Since Jane does not want to trust her entire financial future to only one of her children, as part of her incapacity plan she grants a durable power of attorney to her daughter, Dottie Lynn Asher, and makes an advance designation of Ms. Asher as her guardian, should she ever need one.

3. Elizabeth and Timothy Hodge

Elizabeth Hodge, age 72, suffers from mental problems that might be due to early-stage Alzheimer's disease, as well as several moderately severe physical problems. Timothy Hodge, also age 72, is cognitively intact, but has leukemia, which is fairly well under control. Timothy's vision and hearing are also limited.

The Hodges own a condominium unit that is worth about $200,000. Elizabeth receives a pension of $1,500 per month, Timothy's pension payments are $3,000 per month, and their Social Security benefits total $1,500 per month. Thus, they have $6,000 per month to work with, plus income from $100,000 in savings and investments.

Elizabeth owns a LTCI policy with benefits of $100 per day for care provided in an institution, and $50 per day for home care. Timothy does not have LTCI and certainly would be a poor candidate to purchase it at this time, given his age and physical condition. An important first step is to rule out non-Alzheimer's causes of Mrs. Hodge's problems — for instance, she might benefit from antidepressants or treatment of high blood pressure. However, if Alzheimer's is diagnosed, the question becomes whether she can be cared for appropriately and safely at home. She probably fits the Medicare definition of "homebound," so she could qualify for some home health assistance from Medicare. In addition, state agencies or charitable organizations may provide services for those with Alzheimer's, such as adult day care.

A geriatric care manager (GCM) should be consulted about how to structure the home health plan, balancing professional services with non-skilled services, such as housekeeping and personal care. The GCM can also advise the Hodges about which local home health agencies are best. Unfortunately, Elizabeth's home care will probably cost more than $50 per day, so there will be a need to make co-payments. The home health worker can also help Timothy by taking care of tasks that would tax his visual or communicative abilities.

However, an "assessment" of Elizabeth's condition may result in a high enough "score" to justify institutionalization. Again, it is quite likely that the $100 daily benefit will not be adequate for actual needs. Medicare will probably do a fairly good job of caring for Timothy's leukemia (including providing hospice services if his condition becomes terminal).

4. Donald and Myra Jennings

Donald Jennings is 71 years old; his second wife, Myra, is 54. Donald is retired, receives a pension of $38,000 per year, and also receives $12,000 per year in Social Security benefits. Myra is the assistant headmistress of a private school, earning $75,000 per year. She will have access to a pension ($40,000 per year) in another seven years, if she chooses to retire, based on her long period of employment with the same school.

No children were born to Donald and Myra, but Donald has three children by his first marriage, and Donald adopted Myra's son by her first marriage. The couple has five grandchildren.

Their portfolio, including IRA accounts, is worth $1 million and generates $60,000 of income (because they have chosen to use a high-growth strategy and have reinvested much of the income from the portfolio). Their income may be increased, if needed, by taking the income, currently, instead of reinvesting it. (After all, they are already paying income tax on it). They can also sell a portion of the portfolio, or shift the allocation of assets to obtain more income.

Since their income is $185,000 per year, they are an atypical couple in that they are able to pay for extensive long-term care out of their current income. (Note, however, that their income will diminish after Myra retires.) This also means that they probably will not want to jump through the hoops required to establish a Medicaid plan for an affluent couple.

Depending on Donald's health status, it may be worthwhile for him to buy LTCI (keeping in mind that Donald and Myra have plenty of cash to pay premiums). However, it is crucial that Myra obtain such coverage. The sad statistical fact is that Myra will probably be a wealthy widow. If Donald dies at age 79, and Myra dies at age 83, Myra will have survived Donald by 21 years — with two decades worth of income and potential health care needs to be provided for.

Given the couple's profile, estate planning assumes an important role in their long-range planning. There is a risk that, without planning, Donald will have a taxable estate (not taking into account the marital deduction), and it is almost certain that Myra will encounter a taxable "second estate" problem based on the build-up of income on her inheritance. Therefore, at least basic estate planning steps are vital.

One option is for Myra and Donald to each place some assets into trust. If they want to keep their Medicaid planning options only, they should favor the "income-only" trust form (which forbids invasion of principal). This type of trust, in conjunction with a durable power of attorney, can also provide major protection in case of incapacity. Alternatively, each should have a credit shelter ("bypass") trust. Given Myra's status as second wife, it might also make sense to make some provision for her in the form of a QTIP trust, in which she receives income for life, but after her death the principal reverts to the children of Donald's first marriage. Purchase of a second-to-die life insurance policy might also be prudent under this plan.

Donald and Myra should also consider a gifting program. Each year, Donald, with Myra's consent (or vice versa) can make "split-gifts," giving $20,000 to each donee without incurring gift tax. (The amount will be adjusted for inflation.) Potential donees include the children and grandchildren. They may also wish to give to their favorite charities, perhaps in the form of a charitable remainder trust that would generate some extra lifetime income for them. Until the $1 million unified credit is fully phased in, the Jennings may prefer to use a charitable remainder *unitrust*, rather than a charitable remainder *annuity* trust, since the unitrust allows them to place additional funds into the trust (to keep pace with the increasing unified credit). Charitable remainder annuity trusts do not allow additional deposits after they are funded.

Although it probably would not be suitable now, moving to a *non-equity* continuing care retirement community could be a good choice in the future. If a suitable facility can be located, such a move might be worthwhile because these facilities combine a comfortable (or even luxurious) housing unit with a promise of nursing care on-site, if and when required. The non-equity feature allows removal of funds from the taxable estate, whereas the value of an equity interest would remain within the estate.

5. Steve and Jill Florian

The Florians are house-rich in comparison to their somewhat limited income. Steve Florian, age 70, is a retiree with a pension of $16,000 per year and Social Security benefits of $8,000 per year. He has had two mild heart attacks, and has moderately severe arthritis. Jill Florian, age 66, is also retired, but her pension is only $5,000 per year. She is diabetic and has had a cataract operation. Her own Social Security benefit would be lower than her spouse's benefit of $4,000 per year, so she draws the spouse's benefit instead. That gives the Florians a basic sum of $33,000 to work with (plus $4,000 in investment income; see below). The availability of long-term care insurance is something worth exploring, but given their ages, health, and income, they might find it hard to secure affordable coverage.

Steve and Jill's major asset is their home, which they have owned for many years and have lovingly improved. The Florian's residence is presently worth about $450,000; their basis is only $100,000. (Of course, if they choose to sell the home, the $350,000 capital gain would be excluded from taxation due to the $500,000 exclusion for married couples filing joint returns.) Their IRAs, savings accounts, and investments are fairly limited ($60,000), yielding $4,000 per year in additional income. They should consider liquidating their entire portfolio in return for an immediate annuity that provides an easily manageable income stream.

The Florians will probably be able to create a Medicaid plan with little difficulty because their home, which has special status for Medicaid purposes, is their major asset. If they are not primarily interested in leaving the house to their children, they can simply retain ownership of the home (and perhaps use some of their excess resources to fix it up). If either of them enters a nursing home and applies for Medicaid, the other can remain in the home since the Medicaid lien cannot be enforced as long as the survivor continues to live there. (However, if Steve, or Jill, moves out and sells the home, the Medicaid lien can then be applied to the proceeds of the sale.)

Assuming that the Florians live in a "medically needy state," and not a "cap" state, whichever spouse applies for Medicaid will probably have a spend-down obligation, even after transferring the "community spouse's income allowance" to the healthy spouse.

For Medicaid purposes, a good move would be for Steve and Jill to place their savings into an income-only trust. Trusts below $50,000 are usually too small to be worth the trouble and costs of administration, but a $60,000 trust, though small, is feasible. Another option is a charity's "pooled fund." If neither of them ever applies for Medicaid, they can still benefit from the income, and the trust principal can be left to the surviving spouse.

It is unlikely (but possible) that federal estate tax problems will arise, since the first spouse to die will probably have an estate below the federally taxable level (although continued appreciation in the value of the home and the savings may push the second estate over the limit). Either Steve or Jill will probably want to leave most of his or her estate to the surviving spouse, so the marital deduction will shelter the estate of the first to die. If they are very concerned about estate tax, they may want to make some lifetime gifts to reduce the estate below the taxable figure. (The estate tax exemption gradually phases in, reaching $1 million in 2006.) For this couple, the probability of having to make a Medicaid application is greater than ending up with a taxable estate. Consequently, care should be taken to avoid making gifts that might fall into the "look-back" period and, thus, create a penalty period of Medicaid ineligibility.

In this plan, estate planning is sacrificed to Medicaid eligibility. If Steve and/or Jill do receive Medicaid benefits, both the income-only trust and the homestead (after the death of both spouses) will be vulnerable to estate recovery (see Chapter 6).

6: Georgia Hailey

Georgia Hailey was widowed at age 66. For a few years afterward, Mrs. Hailey's daughter, Patricia Dawkins, visited her occasionally and telephoned once or twice a week. When Mrs. Hailey was 71, Patricia noticed that the once immaculate home was becoming run down, and her mother sometimes seemed confused or sounded vague over the phone. Patricia nagged until her mother consulted her internist, who diagnosed moderate hypertension and prescribed medication that was helpful, but also caused some unpleasant side effects. Patricia encouraged her mother to hire a neighboring high school student to do chores and heavy cleaning, and Mrs. Hailey agreed.

At about this time, Patricia decided that she needed to keep an eye on her mother, so she started driving her mother to church or to run errands. When Mrs. Hailey was 72, Patricia observed that her mother's vision had deteriorated somewhat, and that her hands trembled. The new internist in Mrs. Hailey's HMO eventually referred her to an ophthalmologist, who recommended cataract surgery, and a neurologist, who diagnosed a mild case of Parkinson's Disease. Medicare covered most of the costs of the surgery, and the cost of the neurologist (but not the prescribed medications).

The cataract surgery was performed on an outpatient basis. Since Mrs. Hailey did not satisfy the definition of "homebound," she was not eligible for Medicare home care. At this point, Patricia hired a Geriatric Care Manager. (Patricia's brother, Peter, who lives 500 miles away, contributed most of the GCM's fee.) The GCM recommended a local home health agency, which sent a worker to Mrs. Hailey's home twice a week for four-hour intervals to see that Mrs. Hailey was functioning well, to help her bathe, and to clean the house. Patricia continued her Sunday visits, and took over responsibility for shopping, some of the cooking, and helping her mother pay bills.

At present, Mrs. Hailey is doing fairly well at home. Patricia cannot increase her hands-on caregiving because of her obligations to her job and to her husband and children. Peter Hailey has agreed to contribute $200 per month toward the cost of his mother's medications and home care, but cannot afford to contribute much more. Patricia and the GCM, Nina Roskova, have researched local housing options, but have not found any high-quality, affordable congregate housing or assisted living facilities. Everyone hopes that the home care plan will continue to be satisfactory.

There could eventually be a problem if it is no longer safe for Mrs. Hailey to remain at home by herself, but her condition is not bad enough to qualify her for nursing home admission. Patricia's husband and teenage children do not want Mrs. Hailey to move in with them. Patricia hates to admit it, but she really does not want this either. Peter Hailey lives far away, in a one-bedroom condominium. He is single and owns a small business that consumes his time and income, so he is an unlikely candidate to be a hands-on caregiver.

ISSUE SPOTTING: ANALYZING ACTUAL CASES

This is a checklist of some factors to consider when determining the needs and desires of your clients, and when discussing strategies with the other members of the planning team:

Marshalling Assets

- Based on the client's own reports, what is the value of:
    - the family home
    - the investment portfolio
    - the insurance portfolio
    - the IRA/Keogh/401(k) accounts?
- Is there any reason to doubt the client's veracity or accuracy? If so, what do you estimate the true values to be?
- Are there any assets of which the client is unaware?
- If the client is still employed, what is his/her income? Spouse's income?
- If retired, what is his/her Social Security benefit? Spouse's benefit?
- How much income does the client currently receive from his/her investment portfolio?

- Is the client entitled to income from any other sources (e.g., pensions from former employers other than the most recent employer, veterans' benefits, disability benefits)?

- Does the client own personal property of significant value (e.g., artwork, silverware, antiques)? Has the property been professionally appraised?

Insurance

- How much life insurance does the client have?

- For term insurance, when does the term expire? Is the insurance renewable? What would it cost to continue or convert the coverage?

- For whole life insurance, how much is the death benefit? The cash value? What accelerated death benefit provisions does the policy have?

- Is the client insurable, rated-up, or uninsurable for additional coverage?

- Is the type of coverage suitable, and the amount of coverage adequate? What are the alternatives if additional coverage is needed, but is unavailable or unaffordable?

- Does the client have Medigap insurance? If so, is it the appropriate form? Is the coverage cost-effective, or would switching to another insurer or another policy form be helpful?

- Does the client have LTCI? If so, what benefits are provided? Is the policy qualified? What are its tax implications? Is a change in coverage warranted?

- If the client does not have LTCI, does he/she want it? Is he/she insurable? What do you advise, and what does the client want with respect to daily benefits, duration of coverage, services covered, etc.? What would such a policy cost with/without inflation protection and nonforfeiture protection?

- If the client wants LTCI but does not think it is affordable, are there options for finding premium dollars (e.g., receiving contributions from the children, selling part of the investment portfolio, tapping the home equity)?

- Should LTCI be purchased to provide funds for private payment during a Medicaid penalty period?

Investments

- Are the client's assets allocated appropriately for his/her age, income tax bracket, investment and estate planning objectives?

- What additional investments should be made in the future?

- Does the portfolio have enough growth elements to deal with the projected life expectancies of the client and his/her spouse?

- Is the portfolio adequately documented so that a fiduciary could readily begin managing the investments, if necessary?

- Does the portfolio offer opportunities for profit-taking?

- What are the tax consequences of selling investments now?

- Will the client be eligible for the reduced rate for certain capital gains (after 2005)? How will this affect investment plans?

Capacity Issues

- Does the client possess full mental capacity, or has there been some cognitive decline?

- Are there medical options for improving alertness and memory?

- Does the client have a durable power of attorney? If so, does the agent know that he/she has been named as agent? Is he/she willing to serve in that capacity?

- Does the agent have gifting (and self-gifting) powers? Should these powers be added or removed?

- Has the client designated a guardian, to be appointed if necessary?

- If there is no existing guardian designation, is a guardianship proceeding appropriate? If so, who should file the petition, who should be named as the guardian (for the person and/or property of the senior citizen), and what powers should the guardian be given?

- How would appointment of a guardian affect the operation of the financial plan?

- In planning for gifts, transfers, and bequests, have capacity issues of the recipient(s) been considered?

Housing Issues

- Is the client's home safe and appropriate for his/her needs for the foreseeable future?

- Has the home been "elder-proofed" (e.g., have additional lights been added, loose rugs secured or removed, doorways widened for use with a wheelchair or walker, alarm and security system installed or expanded)?

- Does it make sense for the client to live with his/her son or daughter, or for his/her son or daughter to move into the client's home?

- Is there space for home-sharing, or for a live-in companion or home health worker?

- How far away is the client willing to move?

- What is the availability, within this radius, of specialized apartments for the elderly? Retirement communities? Assisted-living facilities? Continuing care retirement communities? Nursing homes?

- Which of these facilities have the best reputation for quality? Which ones are the most attractive? If they are subject to inspection requirements, have the inspection reports uncovered problems?

- How does the client feel about moving to specialized housing, or to a medical facility?

- If the client is opposed to moving, and wants to remain at home, is this a realistic desire in terms of safety and affordability of home care?

- What are the costs (e.g., entry fee, ongoing payments, payments for supplementary services) of the various housing options that are not only suitable for the client's needs, but also attractive to the client?

- Does the client receive an equity interest in the housing unit?

- Is the housing facility eligible for insurance, Medicare, or Medicaid reimbursement? Is any part of the cost tax-deductible?

- What refund provisions are available if the client is dissatisfied and wants to move out?

Health Care Planning

- Does the client know the reputation, services, and pros and cons of the local medical practices, hospitals, and home health agencies?

- Does the client have a Geriatric Care Manager (GCM)?

- Does the client have an emergency response alarm system at home?

- Does the client get Medicare benefits through the conventional system, or through managed care? Would a change be better for the client?

- Does the client have any advance directives (e.g., living will; durable power of attorney for health care (health care proxy); instructions concerning "do-not-resuscitate" orders and artificial nutrition/hydration; anatomical gift forms)? If so, are the forms complete, current, and in conformity with state law? Are the patient's doctors aware of these instructions and willing to comply with them? Does the designated proxy decision-maker know that he or she is the proxy, does he or she understand the senior citizen's wishes, and is he or she willing to carry them out (even in the face of opposition)?

Estate Planning

- How likely is it that the client will have a federally taxable estate (or that the client's spouse will have a federally taxable second estate)?
- How is the estate plan handling the phase-in of the increases in the unified credit?
- Is the client already using trusts for incapacity planning? If so, how do these trusts fit into the estate plan?
- Is it worth creating one or more revocable living trusts for probate avoidance purposes, or for professional asset management purposes?
- Should income-only trusts be created for Medicaid planning purposes?
- Should title to the family home be placed into trust?
- Does each spouse have a credit shelter trust? Should the spouse or someone else be the beneficiary of the credit shelter trust?
- Is a QTIP trust a logical addition to the estate plan?
- Is the client's will complete, current, and flexible enough to operate if the client is incapacitated at a time when tax laws are being amended?
- Does the client wish to make major donations to charity, and if so, should they be made during lifetime (outright gifts or in trust) or by testamentary bequests?
- If you believe that your client will receive Medicaid benefits, how do you think Medicaid estate recovery will affect the estate plan?

Income Tax Planning

- Are the client's Social Security benefits taxable?
- Is the client a dependent of a caregiver child?
- Is the caregiver child entitled to an income tax deduction?
- Is the client entitled to a long-term care insurance premium deduction?
- Has the client received benefits under a long-term care insurance policy? Are the benefits taxable?
- Is the client entitled to the larger standard deduction for taxpayers age 65 (or older), and/or the credit for the elderly?
- Has the client incurred enough medical expenses, unreimbursed by Medicare or Medicaid, to be able to deduct those expenses?

Medicaid Planning

- What kind, and amount, of home health care can be covered under your state's Medicaid plan?
- Is your state a "cap" or a "medically needy" state?
- In a "cap" state, can any measures be taken to restrict your client's income?
- Can your client set up a trust for the excess income to preserve Medicaid eligibility?
- What asset transfers have your client and his/her spouse made within the past five years (with respect to irrevocable trusts) or three years (otherwise)?
- Do you predict that your client, or the client's spouse, will need nursing home care within the foreseeable future? If so, when?
- What are your client's non-exempt assets?

- Should ownership of the homestead be changed (e.g., to prevent estate recovery)?
- Should the client use otherwise-available funds to fix up the homestead?
- If your client made an immediate, non-exempt transfer of all non-exempt assets, how long would the penalty period be?
- If your client is married, how much could he/she transfer to his/her spouse as a "Community Spouse Resource Allowance" (CSRA)? How much could he/she transfer each month as a "Community Spouse Income Allowance" (CSIA)?
- If you live in a "medically needy" state, how much would your client have to "spend-down" each month for nursing home care (or for home care that follows the nursing home financial eligibility rules)?
- Should your client start making "half-a-loaf" transfers now?
- Should your client place assets into an income-only trust?
- Can your client use LTCI to cover the payment obligation during the penalty period?

THE ELDER-FRIENDLY PRACTICE

Experienced elder planners have developed some techniques for making it easier to communicate with senior citizens, and for optimizing their office arrangements for working with the elderly, as listed below:

- Use more written communications for older persons whose hearing is impaired, and more oral communications (for instance, a cassette recording of you reading a document) for those individuals with visual limitations.
- Make large-print versions of all documents available.
- If clients need a little extra time to think things over, schedule another appointment, and make sure they have written documentation of all the issues.

- If possible, locate your office near public transportation (since not all senior citizens still drive), or near a senior center (where specialized transportation may be available).

- Older people often find it easier to get up from a hard chair than a deep, cushiony one.

- Try to locate your office in a handicap-accessible building, or add your own ramps and widen doorways so cane and wheelchair users can easily get through them.

- If you can manage them, home and hospital visits can be real practice-builders

- The phenomenon of "sundowning" is well known in elder care: many people who start out the day fairly cogent may become more and more confused as the day goes on. So the earlier in the day you can schedule your elder planning appointments, the easier it may be for your clients to grasp what you are saying.

- Sometimes a temporary or long-range change in medication can clear up mental confusion, so work with the patient's doctor if an especially important transaction must be carried out.

SUMMARY

Not every issue will arise in every case. Some of your clients will need help with only one or two simple issues, and you will be able to answer their questions and solve their problem fairly quickly. Other clients will present far more complex problems such that even maximum deployment of products and services will resolve only part of the problem. You will be able to manage some clients' situations by yourself, while other clients will call for the skills of a full team. Some situations can be happily resolved in a short period of time, others can be unhappily resolved in a somewhat longer period of time (e.g., the death of the client and the administration and closing of his/her estate), and other situations may require years of continued attention to changing needs.

Personal preferences are also significant — even if you have two cases with virtually identical fact situations, you may discover that your clients, after receiving appropriate advice, choose completely different strategies. In some plans, staying at home is the client's top priority, and tremendous money and effort will be devoted to that objective, whereas other plans will revolve around an immediate move to a new housing or medical facility. Some caregivers are willing to devote endless hours to caring for a parent or in-law, including performing the most personal of tasks; certain caregivers will even go so far as to learn sophisticated nursing skills. There are other cases in which no caregiver is available or willing to provide hands-on or financial assistance.

Elder planning involves more than dollars and cents. You will be deeply involved in the lives of families, as well as single or widowed people who may have few other meaningful contacts with the community. Elder planning can be much more psychologically demanding than business planning where "only" money is involved, but it can also be extremely satisfying to know that you are making a real difference in the lives of senior citizens and their families.

INDEX

A

B

C

D

E

Use this handy postage-paid form to order additional copies of *Financial Planning For The Older Client,* or its companion *Financial Planning For The Baby Boomer Client.*
Or call 1-800-543-0874 or FAX this form to 1-800-874-1916.

Single copy	$29.95	25 copies, ea.	25.50	250 copies, ea.	21.00
5 copies, ea	28.45	50 copies, ea.	23.90	500 copies, ea.	19.45
10 copies, ea	26.95	100 copies, ea.	22.50	1,000 copies, ea.	18.45

PAYMENT INFORMATION

*Add shipping & handling charges to all orders as indicated. If your order exceeds total amount listed in chart, call 1-800-543-0874 for shipping & handling charge. Any order of 10 or more or $250.00 and over will be billed for shipping by actual weight, plus a handling fee. Unconditional 30 day guarantee.

Shipping & Handling (Additional)

Order Total	Shipping & Handling
$10.00 - $19.99	$5.00
20.00 - 39.99	6.00
40.00 - 59.99	7.00
60.00 - 79.99	9.00
80.00 - 109.99	10.00
110.00 - 149.99	12.00
150.00 - 199.99	13.00
200.00 - 249.99	15.50

SALES TAX (Additional)

Sales tax is required for residents of the following states: CA, DC, FL, GA, IL, NJ, NY, OH, PA.

2-BB

NATIONAL UNDERWRITER®
The Last Word For Over 100 Years

The National Underwriter Co.
Orders Dept #2-BB
P.O. Box 14448
Cincinnati, OH 45250-9786

Please send:

______copies of *Financial Planning For The Older Client,* 4th edition (#297) $29.95

______copies of *Financial Planning For The Baby Boomer Client* (#512) $29.95

______copies of both *Financial Planning For The Baby Boomer Client* and *Financial Planning For The Older Client,* 4th edition for $53.90. **Save 10%**

______copies of **CE exam & grading service *Financial Planning For The Older Client,* 4th edition (#29761) $25.00

______copies of **CE exam & grading service *Financial Planning For The Baby Boomer Client* (#51261) $25.00

❑ Check enclosed* ❑ Charge my VISA/MC/AmEx (circle one) ❑ Bill me

*Card #*______________________________ *Exp. Date*______________

*Signature*____

*Name*______________________________ *Title*______________

*Company*____

*Street Address*____

*City*______________________ *State* __________ *Zip+4*__________

Business Phone (_______)____________________ *Email*______________

**Make check payable to The National Underwriter Company. Please include the appropriate shipping & handling charges and any applicable sales tax. **Approved in most states. Call 1-800--543-0874 for availability. Offer expires 12/31/2000.*

NATIONAL UNDERWRITER®
The Last Word For Over 100 Years

2-BB

The National Underwriter Co.
P.O. Box 14448
Cincinnati, OH 45250-9786

PROOF OF PURCHASE FOR CONTINUING EDUCATION
***Financial Planning For The Older Client,* 4th edition**
by Dana Shilling, J.D.

YOU MUST RETURN THIS PROOF OF PURCHASE WITH YOUR COMPLETED EXAM.

NO POSTAGE
NECESSARY
IF MAILED
IN THE
UNITED STATES

BUSINESS REPLY MAIL

FIRST CLASS MAIL PERMIT NO. 68 CINCINNATI, OH

POSTAGE WILL BE PAID BY ADDRESSEE

The National Underwriter Co.
Orders Dept. #2-BB
P.O. Box 14448
Cincinnati, OH 45250-9786